P9-BIE-850

# THE RULE OF LAW

EDITED BY
Robert Paul Wolff

A TOUCHSTONE BOOK
Published by
SIMON AND SCHUSTER

A Touchstone Book
Published by Simon and Schuster
Rockefeller Center, 630 Fifth Avenue
New York, New York 10020

SBN 671-20890-X Casebound
SBN 671-20891-8 Paperback
Library of Congress Catalog Card Number: 72-139669
Designed by Irving Perkins
Manufactured in the United States of America
2 3 4 5 6 7 8 9 10

# CONTENTS

# INTRODUCTION

## Robert Paul Wolff

In the spring of 1968, during the now-famous uprising at Columbia University, the leaders of the strike and building occupation distributed a handbill on the campus in the form of an open letter from S.D.S. leader Mark Rudd to President Grayson Kirk. The letter began: "Dear Grayson:"

No flood of gutter obscenities, no scatological graffiti painted on a marble wall, no act of symbolic or physical confrontation, captured the spirit of the moment quite so well as that bit of youthful impertinence. In subsequent months, as the affair stumbled clumsily to its indecisive conclusion, the challenge to authority symbolized by Rudd's gesture virtually eclipsed the substantive issues of university governance, community relations, and national policy on which the students had originally focused their protest. In the end, it was the demand for "amnesty" which obstructed a genuine reconciliation of the university community. The trustees, administration, and some senior faculty insisted on punishment of the student activists with an obsessive intensity entirely out of proportion to any useful consequences—even from their own point of view—that might be hoped for.

In the years since, defiance of established authority on and off the campus has grown to a point where Columbia '68 is a nostalgic memory of simpler times. To be sure, students at Columbia were beaten, but they were not gassed or shot. A few faculty members also got in the way of police clubs, but no attempt was made to jail them, as has now happened in Buffalo, New York. What began at Berkeley and Columbia as a protest against specific policies by identifiable institutions and administrators has become a full-scale assault on legal and political authority itself.

Political authority, unlike parental, religious, military, or bureaucratic authority, expresses itself in the form of legislation and judicial decision. Consequently, the attacks on political authority have more and more come to be focused on the institutions of the law. To put the point simply and bluntly, many Americans no longer take "Because it's the law" as a good reason for complying with a governmental directive. Defiance of the law has spread across the political spectrum, from open rejection of court desegregation orders, through massive violation of the legal injunctions against strikes by government employees, to systematic, principled resistance to the draft.

It is common, particularly in European intellectual circles, to label every minor ripple in the great river of history as a "crisis of culture and civilization," perhaps because a little excitement is thereby injected into the otherwise tranquil realm of ideas. I do not think I am succumbing to that temptation when I suggest that something very like a crisis is developing in this nation's traditional habits of authority and obedience. Patterns of deference and status, of command and compliance, seem to me to be breaking up, with consequences which cannot yet be confidently projected. In large segments of American society, it has become acceptable—indeed praiseworthy—to have done time in jail in the service of one's social and political beliefs.

Needless to say, most Americans are still repelled by those who defy the law. There is, to many men, something frightening and uncontrollable about an individual who insists upon taking his own reasoned judgment as the final authority for his actions. A society of such autonomous individuals would, in the strict sense of the term, be *anarchy,* or the absence of any ruling authority. Not surprisingly, most people equate that state of affairs with riot, pillage, and an orgy of licentious self-indulgence!

On the assumption that this dramatic diagnosis contained some significant element of truth, it seemed worthwhile to try to provoke some new thinking about the history, nature, institutions, and rationale of the law. Diane Neustadter of Simon and Schuster explored with me the idea of a collective book on the subject, and we decided that the best tactic was to solicit essays from a number of scholars distinguished by the originality of their minds and the provocative force of their previous writings. In order to guarantee the most exciting results, we placed virtually no restraints on their choice of topic or approach, asking only that they try to think in new ways about the law. We sought scholars from a diversity of disciplines, not excluding the law itself. The result is this book.

As editor of the volume, it was my job to organize the essays into a coherent order so as to exhibit their relationships, interdependencies, and logical progression. As I had hoped, the nine essays fell nicely into a natural sequence, proof that a genuine dialogue can be achieved among thoughtful minds without the artificiality of committee meetings, memoranda, and weekend conferences!

The nine essays divide into three sections and a conclusion. We open the volume with three strong—sometimes bitter—attacks on the institution, ideology, and rationale of the law from the political left. Howard Zinn's essay "The Conspiracy of Law" sets the tone of the section with an exploration of the ways in which legal institutions are systematically unjust, preserving patterns of inequality irrespective of the motives or intentions of those who administer the laws. It is part of Zinn's purpose to move beyond the simplistic search for villains that vitiates so much contemporary radical social criticism, directing our attention to the structural inadequacies of our legal system and to the political interests served by it.

Edgar Friedenberg in his essay on "The Side Effects of the Legal Process" extends Zinn's analysis by showing how law achieves *some* sorts of order at the expense of *other* sorts. Our choice, he argues, is not between legally sustained order on the one hand and chaotic disorder on the other, but between different sorts of order. Like Zinn, Friedenberg emphasizes the fact—so often obscured in American political commentary—that each choice serves the interests of some groups in the society and obstructs the interests of others.

My discussion of "Violence and the Law" shifts to a more abstract level of theoretical analysis in an attempt to throw doubt upon some of the most widespread and unexamined assumptions in our political debate. Drawing on other writings in which I have defended the principle of philosophical anarchism, I argue that the distinction between violent and non-violent modes of political action depends upon the prior distinction between legitimate and illegitimate forms of political authority. Since the latter distinction is incoherent, so also is the former. Talk about violence or non-violence in politics, I conclude, is ideological rhetoric designed to advance the concrete interests of particular social groups.

The second section, which we may label diagnostic rather than partisan in its character, consists of three attempts to analyze the elements of the current internal dissension. Anthony Wallace's striking discussion of revitalization movements, in his essay "Violence, Morality, and Revitalization," defines two opposed moral orientations with their concomitant attitudes toward law and justice. In a sense, Wallace has written an acute diagnosis of Zinn, Friedenberg, and myself, for all three of us very closely fit his portrait of the teleological moralist.

Daniel Boorstin's historical study of "The Perils of Indwelling Law" draws a strikingly similar pair of attitudes toward law out of the past two hundred years of the American experience. Boorstin rather pessimistically portrays contemporary Americans as inclining once again to the rigidities of what he calls a belief in "legal immanence" as opposed to "legal instrumentalism." Wallace and Boorstin together serve as a somber reminder of the dangers inherent in the radicalism of the first section.

The section concludes with Stanley Diamond's unconventional claim that law is neither necessary nor sufficient for social order, and that the emergence of law as a major institution in a society is a symptom of the breakdown of social order. Diamond uses both historical and cross-cultural evidence to buttress this view of the law, which completely contradicts the conventional wisdom concerning the relation of law to social order. In elaborating this conception of the law Diamond makes a radical departure from all of the standard interpretation of legal institutions. What is more, although his essay is happily free from the Marxist jargon to which we have become accustomed, the portrait of law as a reflection of underlying socio-economic conflict is a deployment of one of Marx's most important insights. Professor Diamond's views are sure to draw heavy fire from many quarters.

After the radical attack and the social scientific diagnosis, the jurisprudential reconsideration. In a sense, the two essays of section three are the most conventional of the lot, for one would expect Lon Fuller and Ronald Dworkin to turn up in a book devoted to a discussion of the law. In relation to the standard approaches of their discipline, however, these two legal scholars have broken significantly new ground. Lon Fuller undertakes a rehabilitation of customary law which turns into a full-scale moral-social-institutional analysis of the origins and foundation of legal obligation. In his essay "Human Interaction and the Law" Fuller employs what might be called a social anthropological mode of analysis to reveal the interactional roots of the law. One might fruitfully read Fuller as an attack on the Austinian view that governments rule—and must rule—by a combination of threats and blandishments.

Ronald Dworkin, writing in a deceptively modest and tentative style, strikes another blow at legal positivism in his essay "Philosophy and the Critique of Law." Arguing along lines which are remarkably similar to those adopted by Fuller, Dworkin articulates a theory of law which allows for continuing argument and counterargument over legal decisions and social policies within the framework of the legal system. Dworkin seeks to avoid the tendency of both radical critics and their conservative adversaries to conclude too hastily that their differences are ultimate, and hence not resoluble by reasoned debate.

The book concludes in appropriate fashion with a look at the wider world beyond the law and the domestic American experience. Richard Barnet sounds the death knell of the existing order in "The Twilight of the Nation-State: A Crisis of Legitimacy." Weaving together a number of themes which appear in the first section, Barnet translates the discussion to the international level. He sees a growing demand among many peoples for a moral standard of human welfare to which the rulers of the world can be held accountable. What I described in the opening paragraph of these introductory remarks as a "crisis" is for Barnet a hope and an opportunity.

I do not suppose anyone will find it surprising that so many of the contributors to this volume quite independently arrive at the conclusion that law in the United States is in bad shape both in theory and in practice. Pessimism has become commonplace, if not yet quite fashionable, in our society. It remains to be seen whether passionate criticism, insightful diagnosis, and thoughtful reconsideration can advance some beneficial change.

# PART

# I

# THE CONSPIRACY OF LAW

Howard Zinn

There is, of course, some irony in speaking of the law itself as a conspiracy, when the law so often hounds others as conspirators. But beyond that, there is sense in using a term that suggests a collective will, lending a systematic character to events. What is different about the conspiracy of law from that of men is that men are not initiators but executors; there is no overall planning by men, but men carry out acts which lead to certain consistent results.

The human intent in the long-term social development is missing, but there is human purpose on the individual level; the scheme of the social structure is internalized as a variety of individual motivations which, as they are acted out, realize certain consequences with remarkable regularity. We are familiar with such motives. Marx, Weber, Michels, Harry Stack Sullivan taught us something about them: the desire for profit in business, for power in politics, for efficiency in bureaucracies, for approval by "significant others." Working in and around all these other motives is the social need for legitimacy, which reduces many of the complex requirements of modern society to a simple rule which, if followed, will maintain all results as before: Obey the law.

I use the term "conspiracy" therefore to retain the idea of systematic results. The word "systematic" avoids the extreme claim of inevitability, which has brought forth a fury of rejoinders (especially against Marx); it suggests, rather, strong tendencies and overall consistency. I use it also to retain the human element in our modern complicated system, even if this is diffused and differentiated, to insist on individual human responsibility. Otherwise, looked on as unmalleable monsters, such systems reduce us to impotency. We carry out the "will" of the structure by what we do. And it will take our action to thwart that will.

Radical critics of society (as well as the chief administrators of that society) have sometimes adopted "conspiracy theories" in which various groups of men have been accused of plotting against the rest of us. Radicals are led to this by their accurate perception of the repetitiveness of certain phenomena in modern society—war, racial hatred, political persecution, poverty, alienation—and by a false conclusion that this must be the work of a plot. The effect of this conclusion is to lose potential allies, who are properly dubious that there is evidence for a plot; it also misleads friends, because it turns them toward superficial actions aimed at particular plotters rather than at larger structural defects. (If anyone is innocent of exaggerating evil it surely must be the black South Africans, but I once heard a black man from Johannesburg say, "I don't want to exaggerate our situation, because it will mislead *me*.")

Since I am not defining "conspiracy" in the customary way, by whether or not it breaks laws, I must find an end for this conspiracy which is beyond the realm of law, and so I will find it in the violation of ethical goals. As a rough guide, I will use men and women's equal rights to life, liberty, and the pursuit of happiness, and speak of law conspiring against these rights.

This is still a crude test, but it is better than "the rule of law," which has no ethical content that I can see. What would seem to be an inherent ethic of stability turns out to be quite undependable, as we find the rule of law in practice creating certain kinds of stability at the expense of other kinds: national at the expense of international, civil at the expense of personal; or as we find that a "peace" enforced by the rule of law is purchased at the price of future disorder.

In our general overestimation of the benefits of that modernization (industrialization, urbanization, science, humanism, education, parliamentary government) which followed the feudal era in the West, we have magnified the advantages of "the rule of law" supplanting "the rule of men." Our histories show varying degrees of reverence for the Magna Carta, which stipulated what are men's rights against the king; for the American Constitution, which made specific (and supposedly limited) the powers of government as against the people; and for the Napoleonic Code, which introduced uniformity into the French legal system. Writing to the new king of Westphalia in 1807, Napoleon enclosed "the constitution of your kingdom" to replace "arbitrary Prussian rule" with "a wise and liberal administration," and urged him: "be a constitutional king." The comment of historians Robert Palmer and Joel Colton on Napoleon (*A History of the Modern World*) bears out my point: "Man on horseback though he was, he believed firmly in the rule of law."

The modern era, presumably replacing the arbitrary rule of men with the objective, impartial rule of law, has not brought any fundamental change in the facts of unequal wealth and unequal power. What was done before—exploiting men and women, sending the young to war, putting troublesome people into dungeons—is still done, except that this no longer appears as the arbitrary action of the feudal lord or the king; it is now invested with the authority of neutral, impersonal law. Indeed, because of this impersonality, it becomes possible to do far more injustice to people, with a stronger sanction of legitimacy. The rule of law can be more onerous than the divine right of the king, because it was known that the king was really a man, and even in the Middle Ages it was accepted that the king could not violate natural law. (See Otto Gierke, *Political Theories of the Middle Age,* Notes 127–134.) A code of law is more easily deified than a flesh and blood monarch; in the modern era, the positive law takes on the character of natural law.

Under the rule of men, the enemy was identifiable, and so peasant rebellions hunted out the lords, slaves killed plantation owners, and radicals assassinated monarchs. In the era of the corporation and the representative assembly, the enemy is elusive and unidentifiable; even to radicals the attempted assassination of the industrialist Frick by the anarchist Berkman seemed an aberration. In *The Grapes of Wrath,* the dispossessed farmer aims his gun confusedly at the tractor driver who is knocking down his house, learns that behind him is the banker in Oklahoma City and behind him a banker in New York, and cries out, "Then who can I shoot?"

The "rule of law" in modern society is no less authoritarian than the rule of men in premodern society; it enforces the maldistribution of wealth and power as of old, but it does this in such complicated and indirect ways as to leave the observer bewildered; he who traces back from cause to cause dies of old age inside the maze. What was direct rule is now indirect rule. What was personal rule is now impersonal. What was visible is now mysterious. What was obvious exploitation when the peasant gave half his produce to the lord is now the product of a complex market society enforced by a library of statutes. A mine operator in Appalachia (in a recent film made by Vista volunteers) is asked by a young man why the coal companies pay so little taxes and keep so much of the loot from the coal fields, while local people starve. He replies, "I pay exactly what the law asks me to pay."

The direct rule of monarchs was replaced by the indirect rule of representative assemblies, functioning no longer by whim and fiat but by constitutions and statutes, codified and written down. Rousseau saw clearly the limitations of representation, saying, "Power can be transmitted, but not will." And: "The English people think that they are free, but in this belief they are profoundly wrong. . . . Once the election has been completed, they revert to a condition of slavery: they are nothing." The idea of representation, he says, "comes to us from the feudal system, that iniquitous and absurd form of Government in which the human species was degraded and the name of man held in dishonour."

The conspiracy of law occurs in the age of literacy and makes the most of the power of the printed word. Thus, the potential for hypocrisy, which is man's gift to the universe through symbolic communication, is enormously expanded. In slavery, the feudal order, the colonial system, deception and patronization are the minor modes of control; force is the major one. In the modern world of liberal capitalism (and also, we should note, of state socialism), force is held in reserve while, as Frantz Fanon puts it (*The Wretched of the Earth*), "a multitude of moral teachers, counselors, and bewilderers separate the exploited from those in power." In this multitude, the books of law are among the most formidable of bewilderers.

History, which comes of age in modern times and reaches the status of a profession, is used selectively, politically. In our histories, we make much of the great transition to "modern" times, thus obscuring the continuity of injustice from the premodern to the modern era, from the rule of men to the rule of law. And when it suits us, we become completely ahistorical—for instance, when we talk as if liberal democracy really did have an immaculate conception out of some noble compact among men, rather than out of the bloody struggles of ambitious and profiteering revolutionaries. David Hume tries to straighten us out: "Almost all the governments which exist at present, or of which there remains any record in story, have been founded originally, either on usurpation or conquest, or both, without any pretense of a fair consent or voluntary subjection of the people" (*Of the Original Contract*). Hume also neatly disposes of Socrates' talk of our "obligation" to obey the laws of the state in which we reside as based on some mythical original "contract" by saying, "Thus, he [Plato] builds a Tory consequence of passive obedience on a Whig foundation of the original contract."

The decade of the 1960's, as we know, has been marked by widespread disorders. This, even in the absence of other evidence, might make us suspect the nation's claim to be the leader of "the free world" and make us wonder if its staggering production (50 per cent of the world's output) were being used in a rational way. We need not listen to the radical critics, only to government reports and other sources devoid of subversive intent, to reinforce our suspicions: the Kerner Commission tells us race prejudice is pervasive and virulent; the *Statistical Abstract* tells us that 40 million Americans have trouble just getting adequate food and shelter; the New York *Times* tells us that the oil companies, through government quotas, extract $5 billion a year in excess profits from the American consumer; the national television networks tell us of the massacre of women and children at Sonmy, and also tell us enough of the war to suggest that Sonmy is not an aberration but one stark instance of that colossal atrocity which is American military action in Vietnam.

We have been through periods of national self-criticism before. But this one is different. Previous protests were limited, addressed to what were seen as unhealthy growths in an otherwise admirable society, and quickly remedied. Thus, abolitionists calmed down when slavery was made illegal, despite the persistence of semi-slavery and racism. Populists, and radicals of the 1930's, were cooled by Wilsonian and Rooseveltian reform legislation, and by the easing of hard times. The anti-imperialist movements died out when the glaring wrong of the Spanish-American War faded. The current disaffection of the ghettos comes not in a depression but in a period of "prosperity"; urban riots take place not in reaction to a wave of lynchings but shortly after a battery of "civil rights laws" has been passed by Congress; the protest against the Vietnam War has turned against national military policies in general; lack of faith in the political system grew while liberals (Kennedy and Johnson) were in the White House; disillusionment with the judicial system becomes most manifest during the era of the "Warren Court" and its expansion of procedural rights.

In short, the target of discontent is not an abnormal event: a depression, lynchings, a particularly brutal war, the Sacco-Vanzetti case. The target is the normal operation of American society. The problem of poverty is no longer one of hard times but of good times. The problem of race is not in the South but in the whole country. The problem of war is not a specific adventure but the entire foreign policy. The problem of politics is not conservative Republicans but liberal Democrats. It is no longer the slums that smell bad but the whole atmosphere of the country. It is the norms, not the aberrations of American culture, which have come under scrutiny, criticism, attack. That is why the current movement of protest is so important, why it will not fade away, why it will either grow or be crushed in a frenzy of fear by those in power.

When it is the *normal* functioning of society which produces poverty, racism, imperial conquest, injustice, oligarchy—and when this society functions normally through an elaborate framework of law—this suggests that what is wrong is not aberrational, not a departure from law and convention, but is rather bound up with that system of law, indeed, operates through it.

History argues against the notion of aberrational wrong; it shows the persistence over centuries of the social ills that bother us today. The maldistribution of wealth in America goes back to the colonial era; Bacon's Rebellion, indentured servitude, and the labor struggles of the nineteenth century all testify to a class structure which spans our entire natural history. Mistreatment, to the point of murder, of blacks and Indians stretches from seventeenth-century Virginia and the Pequot Wars, through slavery and the extermination of the Plains Indians, down to the murder of black men in the Algiers Motel in Detroit. From the Sedition Act of 1798 to the Rap Brown statute of 1968, we have passed laws to jail protesters in times of tension. And the war in Vietnam is only the most recent of a long series of acts of aggressive expansion by this country, from a tiny strip of land along the Atlantic to the point where our hydrogen missiles and our soldiers encircle the globe.

All this happened not in violation of law, but through it and in its unblinking presence. It is not a straight-line progression of identifiable evil; if it were, we would have caught on long ago. The persistence of the system's traits is hidden by ups and downs, backs and forths, a bewildering succession of bad times and "good" times, conservative leaders and "liberal" leaders, war and "peace." We are left somewhat breathless, and in the end persuaded of the basic kindness of the system (we who have time to think, talk, write about it have indeed been treated rather kindly). Only now have we suddenly awakened, startled by a new thought—that it is not just the "bad" times and "bad" leaders, and "bad" wars, that what is wrong is built into the whole bloody system, at its best as well as at its worst.

We have always been naïve about what seemed like games of chance; we had eras of depression and eras of prosperity, times of war and times of peace, times of witch hunts and times of justice, times of lynchings and times of civil rights laws. "And so it goes," in Kurt Vonnegut's phrase. It is like roulette; sometimes you win and sometimes you lose; you win, you lose, you lose, you win. Indeed, no one can predict in any one instance whether the little ball will fall into the red or the black, and no one is really responsible. Yet, in the end, in roulette, you almost always lose. What keeps you from suspecting a conspiracy is that "almost" (*sometimes* somebody wins) and the fact that no one spin of the wheel has been contrived—it is just the historic totality that has a predictable direction.

Thus with the social structure. There are enough times of reform, enough times of peace, enough reactions against McCarthyism, to make up that "almost." And each event itself seems to come from a crazy concatenation of individual decisions, group conflicts, personality quirks, trials and errors, with no overall purpose or plan. It is just the *results* that, on inspection, show a pattern.

If the pattern is indeed as I describe it, there are important implications for our attitude toward law, and our willingness or unwillingness to disobey the law. Much of the caution against civil disobedience in the United States is based on the essential goodness of our society, whatever might be the admitted wrong of a particular law or partial condition. For instance, in the symposium *Law and Philosophy,* John Rawls says he assumes at the start, "at least in a society such as ours, a moral obligation to obey the law," with the premise that "the legal order is one of a constitutional democracy." In the same symposium, Monroe Beardsley urges caution against disobedience because of "every individual's general stake in the whole legal structure . . ." In a paper delivered last year at the American Political Science Association meetings, Joseph Dunner writes:

> I submit that while there is frequently not only a moral right but even a moral obligation to practice civil disobedience under conditions of political despotism, the advocacy and practice of civil disobedience in a democracy, far from "expressing the highest respect for law" might easily be one of the means used by totalitarians for the deliberate destruction of the democratic process and the establishment of their despotic rule.

This is the general presumption of most American writers on the subject of civil disobedience: that the United States, as a "constitutional democracy," is a special case. In this country, presumably, the law works mostly for good; therefore, respect for the law is of such a value as to create a strong case against diminishing that respect by acts of civil disobedience.

The evidence on how good a society is seems crucial to any argument on civil disobedience. It was on this basic ground of *fact* that Hume challenged Socrates, for Socrates' decision to submit to Athenian law was based on the supposition that when Athenians remained in the community it was a sign that they enjoyed its benefits; otherwise they could have left at any time. Hume argues: "Can we seriously say that a poor peasant or artisan has a free choice to leave his country, when he knows no foreign language or manners, and lives, from day to day, by the small wages which he acquires?"

For us too, our perception of the facts is crucial. Is it not time that we reconsidered the easy judgment, passed on in an atmosphere of self-congratulation from one American generation to the next, that we indeed have "democracy," that there is such a polarity between our system and other systems as to require a different attitude to law and disobedience? I am arguing here that the evidence on the functional realities of our system—as opposed to democratic theory and political rhetoric—does not justify such an overriding respect for the laws. Rather, most of these laws have supported, through vagaries and deviations, a persistent pattern of injustice through our history.

How do the laws, and the accompanying culture of "the rule of law," maintain that pattern of injustice? I would list a number of ways:

1. The idea of a *system* of law, to which we are asked to give general and undiscriminating support, disguises the differences among various categories of law. We are made aware of our constitutional rights, in the Bill of Rights and other provisions, from the earliest grades in school, with such fanfare and attention as to persuade us that these are the most important parts of our law; when we think of "respect for law" we are likely to think of these benign provisions of law which speak of rights and liberties. But we are told very little—so little as to escape our consciousness quickly—about the vast body of legislation which arranges the wealth of the nation: the tax laws, the appropriations bills (on the local level as well as the national level), and the enormous structure of law which is designed to maintain the property system as is—and therefore the distribution of wealth as is. One has only to look at the curricula of law schools, and see students staggering through courses titled *Property, Contracts, Corporation Law, Torts,* to understand how much of our legal system is devoted to the maintenance of the economic system as it now functions, with its incredible waste, with its vast inequities.

Consider the public relations job that has been done on the birth of the Bill of Rights in 1791, and how little attention has been paid to Alexander Hamilton's economic program, promulgated around the same time. The Bill of Rights was hardly more than a showpiece for a very long time, but Hamilton's program of tariffs, the assumption of debts, and the national bank were the start of a long history of federal legislation creating a welfare system for the rich. (See Charles Beard's essay of 1932, "The Myth of Rugged Individualism," for an account of the many ways in which the government in the nineteenth and twentieth centuries passed laws to aid big business.) From Hamilton's "Report on Manufactures" to the current oil depletion allowance, this bias of national legislation toward the interests of the wealthy has been maintained.

It is not just the volume of legislation which is important, but the force of it. The existence of a law, or a constitutional provision, on the books tells us little about its effect. Is the law immediately operative (like a tariff) or does it require long litigation and expense and initiative (like the First Amendment) before it is of use to anyone? Is it given prompt attention (like the assumption of debts) or is it ignored (like the provision that "Congress shall make no law . . . abridging the freedom of speech, or of the press.")?

We have a striking illustration from those early days of the Republic. The First Amendment was so little observed that hardly seven years after it went into effect Congress passed a law, the Sedition Act of 1798, which indeed did abridge the freedom of speech, and with such vigor as to send ten persons to jail for their utterances. One could hardly claim that the First Amendment was being enforced. On the other hand, the Excise Tax on whiskey (needed to pay off rich bondholders on the Assumption scheme) was so efficiently enforced that when small farmers in western Pennsylvania rebelled against the tax in 1794, Secretary of the Treasury Hamilton led the troops himself in putting them down. The government enforces those laws it wants to enforce; that fact is part of the American legal tradition.

Ironically (in view of the customary assumption that the legal system guards us against anarchy), it is the laws, either by what they provide as they are passed or by what they permit when they are not passed, which contribute to the anarchy of the economic order. They either permit or subsidize the unfettered spoliation of natural resources; they permit, indeed pay for, the production of dangerous things—poisons, guns, bombs. The allocation of the nation's colossal wealth to the production of either weapons or junk takes place not contrary to law but through a vast network of contractual arrangements.

2. The idea of a *system* of law disguises another distinction in categories of laws: between laws which protect us against bodily harm and laws which protect property from theft. When we are cautioned against chipping away at the structure of law, what is usually uppermost in our minds is that the law protects us from the constant danger of assault, rape, and murder. But most law-enforcing is designed to protect property, not human beings. Most crimes, by far, are crimes against property, not against persons. (In 1966, there were 120,000 offenses against persons and 1,670,000 offenses against property.)

We are constantly reminded of the priorities of law enforcement—property over human beings—by the repetition of certain events: the policeman shooting someone who has committed a petty theft (a man who steals a million dollars in a price-fixing swindle is never personally harmed, but a kid who runs off with five dollars is in danger of summary execution); police cars killing or injuring people in mad chases after robbers (a recent report to the American Medical Association said five hundred people die each year as a result of police auto chases).

The quality of justice depends on who is the person assaulted, and what is the nature of the property crime. On the same day in February 1970, the Boston *Globe* reported the results of two trials. In the case of policemen who admitted killing two black men in the Algiers Motel in Detroit, and were charged with conspiring to deprive persons of their civil rights, the verdict was acquittal. In Texas, a man who stole seventy-five dollars from a dry cleaning store was given a sentence of a thousand years.

Most of our legal system is designed to maintain the existing distribution of wealth in the society, a distribution which is based not on need but on power and resourcefulness. Most criminal penalties are used not to protect the life and limb of the ordinary citizen but rather to punish those who take the profit culture so seriously that they act it out beyond the rules of the game. Property crimes are a special form of private enterprise.

3. Seeing the legal system as a monolith disguises the fact that laws aimed at radicals, while pretending to protect the society at large, really try to preserve the existing political and economic arrangements. The Espionage Act of 1917 (even its title deceives us into thinking its aim is protecting the community) sought to prevent people from communicating certain ideas to soldiers or would-be soldiers which might discourage their carrying on a war. The Act begs the question of whether carrying on the war is a blessing to the society at large or a danger to it.

The Smith Act provision against teaching the violent overthrow of the government assumes the government is not evil enough to deserve being overthrown. The Selective Service Act assumes the draft protects us all when indeed it may take our sons to die for someone else's privileges. This is a small class of laws, but its psychological impact on the right of protest ("Watch your step, or else . . .") can hardly be overestimated. It stands ready for use any time dissidence threatens to become too widespread. The recent Chicago "conspiracy" trial is an example.

4. The three distinctions I have made so far are intended to illustrate how the general exhortation to preserve the legal system as if it were a benign whole glides over the fact that different kinds of laws serve different purposes. More justifiable laws (for free speech, against rape or murder) stand in the front ranks as a noble façade concealing a huge body of law which maintains the present property and power arrangements of the society. Buried in the mass is a much smaller body of law which stands guard against those who would rebel in an organized way against these arrangements.

Underlying these distinctions is a more fundamental one: between rules of conduct, which are necessary for human beings in any social order to live with one another in harmony and justice, and those rules which come out of some specific social order, the product of a particular historical culture. H. L. A. Hart speaks of "primary rules of obligation" (*The Concept of Law*), which include restrictions on the free use of violence and "various positive duties to perform services or make contributions to the common life." These rules are not enforced by the coercive techniques of modern society but rather by "that general attitude of the group toward its own standard modes of behavior."

Bakunin distinguished between "natural laws," created by the facts of human nature, and "juridical laws," like the law of inheritance. What separates Hart from Bakunin is his acceptance of the need for "secondary rules" in more complex societies. I would claim that Hart accepts too easily the need for these secondary rules, but the distinction he makes is important because it enables us to examine more closely than he did himself the possibility of a society, even a modern one, that would be guided by primary rules. The distinction takes us out of our present social arrangements and back to an examination of what laws are necessary and just on the basis of human nature. We can look backward to primitive societies (as Hart does) but also forward, in a utopian (eu-topian) imagining about the future. The ideology of any culture tries to obliterate the distinction between what is humanly necessary and what merely perpetuates that culture.

5. We make a fetish of "obedience to law" (put more delicately by philosophers as the concept of "obligation") without making it clear to all citizens of whom this obedience is demanded that government officials have an enormous range of choice in deciding who may and who may not violate the law. One person's failure to honor the obligation is ignored, another's is summarily punished.

The most flagrant illustration of this is in racial matters. When I speak of selective enforcement of laws on racial equality, I am not speaking of the South but of the national government. Before the Civil War, the legal prohibition against the importation of slaves was ignored by the national executive, but the Fugitive Slave Law was enforced by armed soldiers (as in the rendition of Anthony Burns in Boston). From 1871 on, with a battery of statutes giving the national government the power to prosecute those denying constitutional rights to the black man, every President, liberal and conservative, from Hayes through Theodore Roosevelt, Woodrow Wilson, Franklin Roosevelt, John F. Kennedy, and Lyndon Johnson, refused to use that power on behalf of the black man. As one example, under Attorney-General Robert Kennedy, a series of violations of the constitutional rights of blacks in Albany, Georgia, in 1961–62 led to only one federal prosecution—against black and white members of the civil rights movement in Albany who had picketed a local merchant.

Unequal law enforcement in racial matters is most obvious, but it is also true in economic questions, where corporations violating the law may be ignored or gently rebuked; note the light sentences given in the General Electric price-fixing case, where millions were taken from the consumer. We find it also where rank and status are involved, as in the military. In 1966, an American Army captain in Saigon, found guilty of fraudulently doing off with imported silk, military planes and Treasury checks, was allowed to retire with a pension; in 1968, various enlisted men who sat in a circle and sang "We Shall Overcome" to protest conditions in an Army stockade in San Francisco were sentenced to years in prison at hard labor, on charges of "mutiny." Selective enforcement of the law is not a departure from law. It is *legal*.

6. Also concealed from the public, as it is bidden sternly to honor the law, is the record of law enforcement agencies in breaking the law themselves. This includes wiretapping by the FBI (admitted by FBI agents in court proceedings at various times) and countless cases of assault and battery, up to murder, by local police.

7. A restricted definition of "corruption" in our culture leads to cries of outrage against politicians and businessmen who break the law for their private aggrandizement. What is thus hidden from the public is the larger corruption of the law itself, as it operates to distribute wealth and power. Thus, our history

books draw our attention to the Teapot Dome scandals and other legal shenanigans of the Harding Administration, while ignoring the far more serious (not only because of its scale but because of its permanence) reallocation of wealth that took place legally, through the tax laws proposed by Secretary of the Treasury Andrew Mellon and passed by Congress in the Coolidge Administration.

Similarly, the headlines parade Adam Clayton Powell's payroll padding, and bury the legal appropriation of the citizens' money by contracts to General Dynamics and Lockheed, by huge subsidies to poor farmers like James Eastland and Herman Talmadge. Thus, one Supreme Court nominee is pushed aside because of acts of dubious legality, while another breezes through the Judiciary Committee because he is legally proper, though morally more opprobrious than the first. We forget that the problem is the structure of the roulette wheel, not the occasional appearance of a dishonest croupier. The responsibility for what we see around us belongs to the legal system itself, not to the deviations from it.

8. The rule of law, whatever its effects, is restricted by our national boundaries. International law, being far weaker, permits even greater selectivity in adherence to it. Contracts, and compensation for expropriated property, are likely to be given strict attention, while prohibitions against the use of force to settle international disputes will be ignored, as in Vietnam. While at home it can be claimed that we get a modicum of order along with injustice, in the international arena we observe neither order nor justice.

9. Attached to the law in our culture is the notion of solidity as against transience, of the stable against the erratic. Hegel, in the preface to his *Philosophy of Right,* asks that we recognize the rationality in the state, as that in nature, rather than leaving us all "to the mercy of chance and caprice, to be Godforsaken." But this attractive quality of "rationality" conceals the motive of thwarting change, the demand of "law and order" against reform and revolution. Thus, Hegel denounces his colleague J. F.

Fries for a speech on the state in which Professor Fries said, "In the people ruled by a genuine communal spirit, life for the discharge of all public business would come from below, from the people itself." Fries was punished by the German government for participating in the Wartburg Festival of 1817, and Hegel's translator, T. M. Knox, comments, "This was a liberal demonstration in favor of German unity and Stein's reforms. Hegel supported both of these but he held that enthusiastic demonstrations were no substitute for thinking and could only lead to immorality and anarchy."

The claim of permanence and rationality has some truth, but its other side is the natural tendency of law (at its best) to represent past conditions, past needs. As Professor Richard Wasserstrom has put it (in his talk "Lawyers and Revolution," given to the National Lawyers Guild in July 1968), "the law is conservative in the same way in which language is conservative. It seeks to assimilate everything that happens to that which has happened." In an age where change has become exponential, this natural disability of law is especially marked. Granted, there is a value in acting on rules and principles derived from long-term experience as opposed to acting only on the ephemera of the moment. But that experience must not become an absolute; rather, it should be weighed constantly against the fresh perceptions of existential reality.

For such a mediation between past and present, Nietzsche is a better guide than Hegel, about whom he seems to be speaking when he talks (*The Use and Abuse of History*) of "the historically educated fanatic of the world process" who "has nothing to do but to live on as he has lived, love what he has loved, hate what he has hated, and read the newspapers he has always read. The only sin is for him to live otherwise than he has lived."

10. The law neither has to be violated nor does it need to *do* anything drastic in order to maintain existing inequities in wealth and power. It needs only to renew itself in the same basic patterns, to enlarge the scale but retain the same theme, to permit reforms, but within limits. At the time of legal codification

(as in the United States Constitution, for instance), the basic pattern of modern life was set: the irrationality of a productive system driven by business profit; the concentration of political power in deputies, of judicial power in magistrates; the control of communication by schools, churches, and men of wealth. From that point on the system of law needed only elaboration, and it was resilient enough to absorb gradual reform. It performed as Madison predicted it would, to cool, through its political system of representation, any possible passion for tumultuous change, and to control any "rage" on the part of the propertyless. With the basic patterns set, it could afford a certain magnanimity in its pronouncements of equality before the law. Anatole France's comment is still apt: "The law in its majesty draws no distinction, but forbids rich and poor alike from begging in the streets or sleeping in the public parks."

11. So far, I have been talking of the passage of laws by legislatures and the enforcement of laws by the executive. By the time the law appears in the courtroom, to be applied by judges, juries, lawyers, and marshals, it has already been subject to enough of the social strictures mentioned above so as to make injustice probable even before the judge has taken his seat on the bench. But inside the judicial process, all of the built-in ordinary *legal* mechanisms act to reinforce what society has ordained.

The sociology of the judge needs to be considered. The awesome black robes conceal men who come to their posts through the most sordid corridors of local politics, or by political appointment. If cronyism appears on the Supreme Court (Truman and Vinson, Kennedy and Whizzer White, Lyndon Johnson and Abe Fortas), then how much more often must it be true on the local level, where most judicial decisions are made?

The judge is monarch of the courtroom: he decides the composition of the jury; he decides what evidence is admitted or excluded; what witnesses may be heard or not heard; what the jury may listen to or not listen to; what bounds lawyers must observe; even what lawyer the defendant may have; what limits the jury must stay within in making its decision. He can dismiss a case, or so charge the jury as to make conviction certain. His background is middle- or upper-class parents, law schools, private clubs. His mind is in the past. His environment is limited: a splendid city apartment, a home in the country, the courtroom itself. The world of anguish, of social protest, is a threatening dark form on his window shade. In the play *The Chalk Garden* the old judge, off duty, muses about the man on the bench: "The line on the judge's face is written by law, not life."

Most law is decided on the local level, and while there are occasional exceptions, far more typical is the evidence of narrowness, class and race prejudice, and a hatred of social rebels. Judge Elijah Adlow, senior judge of the Boston municipal court, told a leader of a tenants' movement (who had helped a destitute family move—illegally—into a vacant apartment and was charged with assault after he had been beaten by police), that he would have to go to jail "unless you change your philosophy." But behind the glamorous injustice of the occasional Adlow or Julius Hoffman there is a parade of obscure judges making obscure decisions for obscure defendants, putting them away and out of sight.

The sociology of lawyers—the socialization of law school, the practice in obsequiousness before judges, and deals with prosecutors—is too long a story to tell in detail. The sociology of juries includes a process of unnatural selection which turns up, again and again, white middle-class citizens of orthodox views, common prejudices, and obedient disposition, mostly middle-aged or old.

The economics of justice in America—the systematic prejudice against the poor at every stage—the arrest, the setting of bail, the trial, the choice of counsel, the sentence, the opportunity to appeal, the chance of parole—is too well known to need documentation. (A newspaper item of last week: Dozens of inmates in one New York jail had spent from six months to two years behind bars, waiting for their trials, because they could not afford bail—all this while they are presumed to be innocent, and while whatever innocence they had is long gone.)

As one moves up from municipal courts to state supreme courts and federal courts, the basic sociological and economic facts of justice change very little, but this is concealed by a certain regal mustiness of the atmosphere which puts a coat of respectability on a fundamentally inhuman process. What Herbert Read described in British justice differs only in detail (see his essay "Chains of Freedom," in *Anarchy and Order*) from the American judicial system:

> The independence of the judiciary is symbolized in various ways. By means of wigs and gowns, the participants are dehumanized to an astonishing degree. If by chance, in the course of pleading, a hot and flustered barrister lifts his wig to mop his brow, an entirely different individual is revealed. It is as if a tortoise had suddenly dispensed with its shell. The whole business is carapaceous; a shell of custom and formality against which life, plastic and throbbing, beats in an effort to reach the light.

12. The main decisions have been made outside the courtroom, by the society and the culture that brought this combination of persons to this place at this time. But this is made explicit by the deliberate attempt of courts to limit the scope of argument and decision, thus ensuring that court decisions will have minimum effect on the direction of society. On the appeals level, including the Supreme Court, this means deciding cases on technical or narrow grounds wherever possible, postponing fundamental questions as long as possible. It has been most difficult, for instance, in cases of draft resistance, to get the Supreme Court to rule on a question far more important to society than the disposition of one resister: Is the war in Vietnam illegal?

This attitude is expressed by one of the judges in Lon Fuller's mythical case of "The Speluncean Explorers," when he refuses to deal with the moral complexities of a community decision to sacrifice one person so that others might live: "The sole question before us for decision is whether these defendants did, within the meaning of NCSA Sec. 12A, willfully take the life of Roger Whetmore."

Not so mythical are the actual cases of political protesters hauled into court on ordinary criminal charges and prevented by the judge from airing the political grounds of their actions. (Theodore Mommsen put it well: "Impartiality in political trials is about on the level with Immaculate Conception: one may wish for it, but one cannot produce it." Quoted in Otto Kirchheimer, *Political Justice*.) It should make us all pause to know that within the space of a few months similar pronouncements were made in a court in Moscow and a court in Milwaukee. The Moscow judge refused to let a group arrested for distributing leaflets in Red Square against the Russian invasion of Czechoslovakia discuss anything political; the only issue, he said, was: Did they or did they not break the law in question?

The Milwaukee judge similarly refused to let the priests who had burned draft records explain their motivation. The only question, he said, was: "Did the defendants commit arson, burglary, and theft?" When one witness began to discuss the idea of civil disobedience, the judge interrupted him with what must be a classic judicial statement: "You can't discuss that. That's getting to the heart of the matter."

That is also getting to the end of my argument, which is always, of course, the beginning of another. A general "obligation to obey the law" is a poor guide in a time when revolutionary changes are needed and we are racing against ominous lines on the social cardiograph. We need to separate whatever there is in law that serves human ends from everything else that rides along with it, on the backs of so many people. We need to get away from pleasant abstractions and look at the functional reality of the legal structure which guides our society: its sociology, its economics, its human consequences.

Philosophical speculation tells us that civil disobedience may be necessary under certain conditions of injustice. Historical evidence—the facts of the lives of people around us—tells us that those conditions exist and that they are maintained by the present structure of law. To know this is only the beginning. I have tried here, by inculcating a proper disrespect for "the rule of law," only to put us at the starting point, in a mood to run. The same modern civilization which has given us unjust laws has given us great ideals. We need to learn how to violate these laws in such a way as to realize those ideals.

Each of us, depending on where we are in the social structure, must draw his own existential conclusion on what to do. In Tolstoy's "The Death of Ivan Ilyich," the proper, perfect, successful magistrate Ilyich agonizes on his deathbed about his sudden awareness that his life has been wasted, useless, wrong:

> "Maybe I did not live as I ought to have done," it suddenly occurred to him. "But how could that be, when I did everything properly?" he replied.
>
> "If I could only understand what it is all for! But that too is impossible. An explanation would be possible if it could be said that I have not lived as I ought to. But it is impossible to say that"—and he remembered all the legality, correctitude and propriety of his life.

# THE SIDE EFFECTS OF THE LEGAL PROCESS

Edgar Z. Friedenberg

On the subject of law and society conventional wisdom is even more banal than usual. It is, however, probably less misleading, since it is less widely believed. Both the phrases "justice under law" and "law and order" retain their familiar ceremonial ring; but the latter has become the slogan of racism in the United States while the imagery suggested by the former has become unpleasantly sexual. It is not customary for Law to yield Justice; if Law is to perform its social function, Justice must yield to Law.

The central function of any legal system is the maintenance of the stability and continuity of the society of which it is a part. The relationship of law to order is therefore highly ambiguous, for reasons I shall subsequently discuss. So, for essentially converse reasons, is the relationship of law to liberty. But the relationship of law to justice is not even ambiguous; it is essentially negative. This seems inevitable, which is, I believe, what Thomas Jefferson meant by saying that every nation needed to have a revolution from time to time.

For, in order to maintain the stability and continuity of any society, the law must encode and legitimate its existing status arrangements, defend their institutional sources, and insure the prerogatives on which succession rests. The legal system, in short, is inherently highly conservative. It is not, of course, impossible to use it to buck the system; it is not, in fact, even uncommon; but it requires a special oblique approach—like tacking a sailboat—and cannot be expected to make much headway. Often, it makes none at all; the litigant might as well be trying to breach the remarkable chronosynclastic infundibulum Kurt Vonnegut, Jr., describes in *The Sirens of Titan*. And sometimes he is destroyed in the attempt.

Legal systems provide explicit safeguards against their abuse in the interests of justice. The absolute immunity of legislators to actions for slander based on statements made on the floor of Congress and the provision that the Government of the United States can only be sued with its own consent are examples. Other comparable obstacles have evolved from case law; victims of police brutality, for example, are usually barred from collecting damages from the municipality or shrievalty that hires the police, even when they can prove that such brutality occurred and that they sustained damages from it, unless they can further prove that the governing body itself explicitly authorized brutal police action. There is, however, no comparable obstacle to recovering damages from a town or county for torts unrelated to the exercise of authority—injuries sustained in an automobile accident caused by negligence in street repair, for example. Persons who have been mistreated by police can also expect to find their access to possible redress effectively barred by "cover charges" of resisting arrest, "obstructing administration," or assault immediately filed against them without evidence or much probability of successful prosecution because the courts customarily refuse to hear complaints against the police until the charges against their victims have been disposed of, on the grounds that the police could not testify in support of their own complaint if this might subsequently jeopardize their position as defendant. By the time charges brought by the police have been tried, however, the statutory period for filing complaints against them at an administrative hearing has usually expired.[1]

But the devices by which the law frustrates the ends of justice need not be and usually are not explicit provisions of the legal system, nor are they peculiar to modern life. "The law's delay, the insolence of office" were familiar to Hamlet. But the law's delay is, after all, largely a matter of social policy; a society that wanted less delay would have more courts and larger legal staffs. Judges are not as expensive as antiballistic missiles.

Administrative delay effectively tips the scales of justice in favor of the state in criminal cases and the wealthier and, especially, the corporate litigant in civil cases. The poor must settle sooner; they cannot risk the possibility of extended court costs; they have no staffs and files prepared to hold litigation in abeyance for a period of years. By setting bail higher than they can raise, poor defendants may be punished without trial, a common practice with those charged with highly unpopular or quasi-political offenses like draft evasion or for those, like young offenders or blacks, whom many judges regard as "uppity" if they behave as if they had any legal rights at all.

The fact that the quality of legal service available to the poor is inferior to that available to the wealthy would hardly be worth mentioning except that it may be useful to point out that more is involved here than the simple question of having a less qualified attorney and fewer services from him. Except in actions covered by insurance and cases taken on a contingency basis the civil courts are unavailable to poor plaintiffs. If charged in the criminal courts, their defense is likely to be hampered at least as much by the late entry of their defense attorney into the proceedings, and the peculiarities in the way his role is institutionalized, as by his casualness or incompetence.

Most convicted criminals are, of course, poor; more privileged members of society tend to avoid prison. The best way of avoiding prison, however, is to avoid the criminal courts. Rather astonishingly, there is not much difference between the proportion of wealthy and of poor defendants convicted if the comparison is limited to those actually brought to trial. The process of fighting prosecution is remarkably similar to that of fighting a serious infection; prophylaxis is much more effective than cure, and the actions which provide an effective defense early on become less and less efficacious if delayed. A potential defendant who voluntarily seeks advice as soon as he finds himself under suspicion may avoid errors in responding to police interrogation that would seriously jeopardize his defense; pretrial motions may result in the exclusion of evidence improperly obtained, witnesses may be examined who will be unavailable by the time a trial is held. But only persons who seek and can pay for legal assistance can take advantage of these aspects of adversary procedure; the poor and ignorant are hauled into court as they are hauled into the emergency rooms of hospitals, with their prospects aleady hopelessly damaged by neglect.

The legal services they then receive are, moreover, usually of a totally different character from those available to a sophisticated defendant with the foresight to retain a competent attorney early. A public defender and, to a lesser degree, the kind of lawyer most often appointed by the court to defend the indigent, is in actual effect a member of the district attorney's organization so far as his career interests are concerned.[2] He is extremely unlikely to give his client the best defense the law allows even if he is competent to do so; he is not paid enough to provide the resources to do it, is likely to regard his client with some condescension or contempt, and, in any case, to believe him guilty—an attitude which is unlikely to affect the actions of a voluntary attorney if he agrees to accept a defense brief at all. Consequently, the role of the assigned attorney has largely evolved into that of a broker who attempts to arrange a compromise for his client in the form of a plea of guilty to certain of the charges against him, or to a lesser charge, in return for having the more serious charges dropped.

The law, as it affects lower-status members of society, then, is essentially designed to facilitate what higher-status clients would regard as a miscarriage of justice. In so doing, however, the law clearly contributes more to social stability and continuity, in the fundamental sense that it protects and preserves existing status arrangements from disruption. Weaker members of society are not forbidden access to it—which would destroy the integrative power of the myth of "equal justice under law"—but they find it far more unwieldly in their defense than in the hands of their attackers. "Due process" has, however, another more limited value even to the poor. To a degree, at least, it protects them from *arbitrary* action: they cannot easily be treated very differently from their neighbors; they are unlikely to disappear without a trace; convicts may usually expect to be released from prison after the maximum time provided by their sentence if not earlier. Considering total human history, these gains are not to be despised; nor can they be taken for granted. Their known inability to take full advantage of the facilities available to higher-status persons for legal defense makes stigmatized individuals—whether they be poor, black, disfranchised like the young, or sexually deviant—far more liable to arbitrary and often brutal police action than "straight" people are. The nearly universal use of the "indeterminate sentence," which was introduced to provide flexibility in allowing earlier discharge of those thought rehabilitated, has tended rather to make the treatment of prisoners more arbitrary; the average length of time served by prisoners convicted of major categories of offenses has increased rather than decreased with the use of the indeterminate sentence. Even so, as Hollingshead and Redlich[3] long ago observed, lower-class individuals tend to be much more fearful—and realistically so—of the consequences of being sent to a mental hospital than to a prison, largely on the grounds that, with the level of diagnostic and psychiatric services available in huge overcrowded mental hospitals, any such remand may turn into a life sentence. For the poor, "due process" of law may not provide much protection, but it may be better than what would happen to them without it. Their acceptance of these minimal protections in lieu of open and probably unsuccessful revolt again contributes to stability and continuity in society. In a sense, the poor, black, young, or otherwise vulnerable maintain what little status and security society allows them by "copping a plea" and accepting poorer treatment than might be due them in return for limited assurance that the worst shall not befall.

If law be ill-designed to secure justice, how well does it maintain order? This is a question we are all competent to answer, if we can find an adequate basis for comparison in our minds. The law provides the kind of order we have, which, as Max Beerbohm observed in a different connection, is the sort of thing you like if you like that sort of thing. It provides the kind of order associated with particular institutional forms and prevents the establishment of other kinds of order. Indeed, the central institutions of any society are in a sense nothing *but* manifestations of the kind of order its legal system establishes. Private property, the family, the armed services, the schools, would all take a very different form and in some cases sag into nothingness if not supported by the corset of existing legislation.

It is more usual to regard major social institutions, including the law itself, as having evolved to meet the needs of society, as the organs of the bodies of successful species evolve to maintain the species' viability. But societies are less like organisms than they are like arenas in which conflicting interests compete, and the law as a social institution occupies the enviable position of being not merely one of the competing interests but the referee among their conflicts. It maintains order, but it also disrupts those social processes by which a new order might develop. It defends the home against trespass, but it prevents people from forming a home if they are already married to others, or are of the same sex, or wish to develop a commune whose members share conjugal rights and child-rearing responsibilities—though none of these arrangements is inherently disorderly except for the strains imposed upon it by its illegitimacy. In the metaphor of society as organism, the law must often be regarded as a cancer, as in the invasion of campus communities by narcotics agents and of private communication by ubiquitous wiretapping.

Whether law is regarded as more effective in promoting order or disorder depends very largely on the perspective one brings to events. What is certain is that, in the conventional view, law and order are so closely associated that the disorders provoked by law enforcement become imperceptible, even when they lead to massacre. The police often slay; but they are seldom socially defined as murderers. Students who block entrances to buildings or occupy a vacant lot and attempt to build a park in it are defined as not merely disorderly but violent; the law enforcement officials who gas and club them into submission are perceived as restorers of order, as, indeed, they are of the *status quo ante* which was orderly by definition.

If by violence one means injurious attacks on persons or destruction of valuable inanimate objects—whether or not these are property—then nearly all the violence done in the world is done by legitimate authority, or at least by the agents of legitimate authority engaged in official business: police, armed forces, intelligence agencies, public executioners, freeway builders. Yet, their actions are not deemed to be violence; and the resulting chaos is not regarded as disorder. This immunity of legitimate authority to the charge of disorderly conduct of which it is often patently guilty casts doubt on the validity of one of the oldest issues that is thought to divide liberals and conservatives fundamentally: the conflict between justice and order. Both Shakespeare and Goethe, for example, were powerful advocates of legitimacy and obedience even to a cruel and incompetent authority on the grounds that the chaos of revolution would surely prove more oppressive than the burden of a secure despotism; in a slightly different way Socrates, in choosing the hemlock instead of flight into exile, took a similar position. And the choice might, indeed, be defensible if the issue were real. But in modern society, at least, it appears to be largely phony. Can there be greater disorder, internal or external, than that created by the modern industrial state in the pursuit of its lawful interests? Have the Vietnamese reason to be grateful that we have spared them the horrors of a civil war? Could anarchy result in more filth, pollution, and degradation than normal social development has imposed on our cities and countryside? If Spiro T. Agnew has become the face of Western civilization, would not the regularity of its features be improved by taking a Cleaver to it?

Much of what is called a "revolutionary mood prevailing on the planet today" may be attributable less to the severity of oppression than to the fact that no corresponding order is gained by submitting to its constraints. If my generation found a bitter irony in the attempts of Fascist sympathizers to justify the Mussolini regime by boasting that he made the trains run on time, what can the present generation make of Governor Rockefeller, helpless and impotent when confronted by the Long Island Railroad and yet the representative and symbol of myriad regulatory bureaucracies that encumber and strangle life in New York State? Freedom and order are supposed to be related as yang and yin; each imposes on the other, but each makes the other possible; there is a genuine dialectic between them. It is possible for a defender of liberty to sacrifice some freedom for the sake of the order that secures liberty; but the legitimate constraints imposed by the modern industrial state seem more and more clearly inimical to both freedom and order and, indeed, to life itself. Law and order may seem the very cornerstone of liberty to a people as riven as those of Belfast, but the slogan rings a little hollow in Chicago or Saigon, or even in the splendidly hospitable city of Bucharest.

What legitimacy clearly grants is not order but power—or rather, access to force, which, as any Vietnam veteran could attest, is not quite the same thing. Modern technology has made legitimacy irresistible—and also asymmetrical. Only the legitimate authorities could have bombed Hiroshima or Dresden, or placed two men on the moon and, having established their fortitude and programmability, brought them from its austere tranquility to the more complex threats presented by Los Angeles and Houston. Best of all, the speed and massiveness with which power can now be asserted permit legitimacy to ignore its own limits; the legitimacy of the Presidency has, for example, effectively nullified the constitutional reservation of the power to make war to the Senate. How Richard III would have envied the *simplicity* with which Richard Nixon can commit himself and his nation to an enterprise, even though the outcomes of their enterprises may not be as dissimilar as their beginnings.

The assertion that law preserves order is logically similar to the statement that the medieval Church preserved and transmitted the culture of antiquity. It is both true and false, and altogether too simple. It preserved some of it, deliberately destroyed some, and allowed far more than could be either preserved or destroyed to perish because it could find no value or significance in it and was intent on other purposes. Would we even possess the works of Aristophanes, for example, if his wit and ribaldry had been as fundamentally subversive as that of Dylan or Lenny Bruce? Or does Aristophanes' immortality depend on his having expressed, albeit with rather more talent, social attitudes that Al Capp or Bob Hope would have found congenial? In any case, what we have is what it did preserve, altered by its manner of preserving it and the conditions it imposed. And more influential even than the process of natural selection that thus affects the evolution of culture is the fact that our image of order, like our image of antiquity, is determined by what, in fact, has been allowed to survive. A different system of jurisprudence, reflecting the needs of a less anxious and power-hungry people or a society less dependent on property as the root source of status and continuity, might have left us today with a quite different idea of what an orderly society might be—and a far more humane one.

The relationship of law to liberty is even more paradoxical than that between law and order. Law is essentially a system of constraint and, as such, is hostile to freedom. But it is also a system of guarantees, explicitly so in the United States, where the first ten amendments to the Constitution are the Bill of Rights, and the principal of judicial review of the constitutionality of statute law, though not in itself provided by the Constitution, has become fairly firmly established as legal process. Judicial review is not, however, as firmly established as it is probably thought to be: The insistence of the Supreme Court to rule on the few cases, among those brought before it, which it agrees to hear on any but the narrowest grounds possible, and its refusal to rule on legal questions of apparent simplicity that directly challenge massive concentrations of power, like the legality of undeclared wars, make it clear that the Court is well aware that it may lose its lease on life if it obstructs massive social forces. A Supreme Court of the U.S.A. also meets, after all, in Pretoria; and it used to have much the same power to resist tyranny as its sister institution in Washington. It doesn't now.

Nevertheless, under our legal system, the courts have remained so far relatively more sympathetic to liberty than the legislative or executive branches; in fact, the defense of civil liberty against continuous intrusion by the legislature and erosion by the executive has become a major social function of the courts. This does not mean that they discharge it willingly or consistently. The role of the appellate courts in dispensing liberty is comparable to that of pharmacies in dispensing narcotics; only they can lawfully do so, and they do so niggardly and suspiciously, ever ready to defend themselves against charges of license or indulgence. American courts have handed down many noble decisions, but no Justice—not even Mr. Justice Douglas—can be said to have become a pusher for freedom.

Moreover, the conception of liberty the courts recognize and defend has very ambiguous consequences. The liberties guaranteed by the Bill of Rights—and other guarantees like freedom of contract, of interstate movement, or what is loosely called "states' rights"—have been rendered largely inoperative by social change and technological advance. What conceivable meaning has the concept of "states' rights" at a time when every hundredth child conceived in New York over a period of years may be aborted by radioactive contamination introduced into the air by a federal agency conducting weapons testing in Nevada? Still worse, these freedoms may be not only obsolete in form, they may be traps. Not only may lawful means of protest and expression be ineffective in a mass society, they may be lawful precisely *because* they are ineffective; their acceptance and use guarantee that the force of social protest will dissipate itself harmlessly. The Bill of Rights has traditionally been criticized as elitist, as, of course, it is; it explicitly exempts certain essentially bourgeois modes of political discourse and action from popular review. But the contemporary effect of these provisions is not so much to strengthen the bourgeoisie as to render it irrelevant by legitimating only a political style that is manifestly archaic and irrelevant. Power, then, passes to the creatively illegitimate and, especially, to the new men on the make within the social system: the technicians who, as long as they do not become troublemakers within their own bureaucratic structure, are held virtually harmless from external social action. Nothing the American legal system authorizes in the way of legitimate protest is likely to have much effect on the urban schools, or the Selective Service System, or the pollution and spoliation of natural resources.

Among the traps implicit in excessive faith in the traditional liberties and responsibilities of citizenship, none seems to me more blatantly illogical than the conception of civil disobedience most strongly urged in recent years, probably, by former Justice Abe Fortas. The essence of this conception is that civil disobedience is simultaneously an affirmation of fealty to the state and of resistance to laws deemed unjust, and the former protects the body politic from fundamental damage by the latter. Civil disobedience is a form of toxin-antitoxin in which the citizen's willingness to accept lawful punishment for his resistance adds to the gravamen of his charges against the state and attests to his fundamental intent to preserve rather than to attack it. Socrates, too, believed this—which greatly eased the task of the Athenian oligarchs who destroyed him. Plato, I would infer, did not. A better rule to remember, both for self-preservation and for political effectiveness, is "If you have something serious to fight the state about, don't play games with it."

The notion that civil disobedience is both a moral and a politically effective way of asserting defiance of unjust law while simultaneously pledging allegiance to the principle of law and the sovereignty of the state depends on assumptions about the nature of society that are no longer valid, and can hardly have been so in any social group too large or complex for its members to observe, judge, or be personally moved by one another's conduct. To be effective, civil disobedience requires a society bound by certain moral norms, whose conflict with the law can be dramatized by an act of defiance. It requires that the act of civil disobedience be reported sufficiently widely and fairly, and with sufficient emphasis in comparison to other events, to elicit a response from most of those who might be concerned. It requires a citizenry that can remember longer than the interval between pseudo events, and that feels itself a participant in public affairs rather than a spectator watching a contest of—as a Buffalo television station, reporting the beating and arrest by United States marshals of a group of draft resisters who had taken sanctuary in a church here, put it—"the Feds versus the Dodgers." It requires a society in which events can still be distinguished from pseudo events. Saint Joan herself, today, would be thought to have gone to the stake in a final effort to improve her image; and the British would be very careful indeed not to burn her during prime evening time.

Whether the law is broken in order to assert a superior moral principle or for more pragmatic reasons, the response of the state is to seek to punish and isolate the miscreant and to render him powerless if possible. The more fundamental the social issue raised by his unlawful conduct the more repressive his adversary is likely to become. Generally speaking, it is not in his interests or those of the cause he seeks to advance to submit to its sanctions; indeed, if he has not the power or intent to defend himself against the state, he can hardly advance the cause of liberty by challenging it. His services will be lost to his movement, and his submission, though an example to his colleagues, is unlikely to encourage them or win new adherents.

But even those who challenge the state—either by willful disobedience of laws they perceive as unjust or immoral, or by actions they believe to be lawful but recognize may subject them to prosecution—with every intent to defend themselves and confident of ultimate victory in the courts, may nevertheless misunderstand fundamentally the way in which the process of legal restraint operates upon individual action—and hence incur a far greater drain on their resources than they had anticipated. For, conviction of a crime, though the ultimate sanction the law may impose upon the individual, is not the most important from the point of view of social control; nor is it necessarily the most severe. Due process is cumbersome and expensive; arrest and prosecution are very effective forms of harassment and constraint and may be undertaken by authorities who are quite well aware that they have no case for conviction. Even the legal safeguards specifically guaranteed the defendant may serve to encumber him, and there is little doubt they are deliberately so employed.

Wholesale "busts" of protest demonstrators on charges of trespassing, unlawful assembly, interfering with an arrest, refusal to obey the reasonable request of a police officer, obstructing governmental administration, or any of a number of similar offenses too vague to be precisely defined but too trivial to be subject to the full process of judicial review on constitutional grounds, have the immediate effect of using up the funds available to usually impoverished protest groups in desperate efforts to raise bail. The more trivial and dubious the charges, and hence the bigger the "bust," the more effective it is in depleting the resources of its victims, not only because of the sheer numbers involved but because crowding court dockets delays trials and makes the need for bail all the more urgent. Since the only way such demands can be met is by widespread use of bail bonds, for which the fee is at least 10 per cent of the bail fixed, and this, of course, is not returnable, the "bust" is a perfectly certain way of alienating the funds of any dissenting group sufficiently unpopular to induce judges to set a high bail—and transferring them to the pockets of bail bondsmen, a group notably sympathetic to the pretensions of the authorities, without any legal process or finding of malfeasance at all. Such busts and harassment may be repeated until the resources of the group are exhausted and its members dispersed—all without winning a single case in court, or even bringing one to trial.

Pending criminal charges also act as an obstacle to the physical movements of those charged; but this device is effective only against leaders who require a wider field of operations than the judicial district provides, and such individuals may be sufficiently well known that the threat of publicity protects them from unusual judicial constraint. Even H. Rap Brown was finally permitted to travel from New York, where he was awaiting trial for possession of a gun, to Washington in order to attend a conference. The most serious pre-trial impediment is simply the cost in time, money, attention, and anxiety, of the legal process itself, and the uncertainty of its outcome, especially for an impoverished defendant with an unpopular cause.

The presumption of innocence, upon which our adversary system depends, is thus largely an irrelevance; for highly significant and destructive sanctions are imposed by the mere act of formal accusation. A somewhat similar set of considerations applies to the appellate process available to those convicted of serious offenses as a further protection presumably afforded the innocent. Far fewer persons are, of course, affected by the appellate process than by the rigors of awaiting trials. For minor offenses in most jurisdictions, the number of levels of appeal to which a convicted defendant is entitled is sharply limited; in some jurisdictions to a single level of appeal by right, though higher courts may grant certiorari in misdemeanor convictions if they choose.

In any case, those who avail themselves of the appellate process in attempting to modify or reverse a criminal conviction find that the appellate courts exercise a rather peculiar social function. However they may decide the case of an individual appellant, for the society as a whole the appellate structure serves as a "cooling-out" device for conflicts between different social classes, and between local interests and more cosmopolitan ones. As Jerome Skolnick[4] has made very clear, the quality of justice in the lower courts is so appalling that they can hardly be regarded as instruments of justice in the conventional sense at all. If courts of original jurisdiction attempted to provide actual due process to all those brought before them, they would collapse under the pressure of their dockets; as it is, defendants may wait months for a trial lasting a matter of minutes. Lower-court judges are usually elected for short terms, are subject to all the pressures and prejudices of the districts in which they serve, and are often political hacks of very low prestige and legal ability. The relative ignorance of lower-court judges, who know far less law and are less inclined to be bound by it than the abler attorneys who appear before them, is a major and apparently insoluble problem in American jurisprudence.

But like most persistent social problems, the miserable and arbitrary quality of lower-court procedures turns out to have a positive social function. Most persons brought before these courts are members of lower-status and discriminated social groups, inadequately represented by counsel, who can do very little to assert their putative legal rights. They know this very well; it is central to the folklore of the life of the poor and has been at least since the time *The Beggar's Opera* was written. Bad justice is *itself* the sanction by which they are controlled. What keeps them in line is precisely the knowledge that, whatever the little card the police have to give them with their rights on it says, they had better stay out of trouble. If they possessed the means to assert those rights, they could not be controlled; the police and the judiciary are simply inadequate both in number and in skill to make cases against them that would stand up in a properly conducted court.

In this way, what appears to be a serious inadequacy in the public provision for legal process turns out to be one more way in which the law contributes to the maintenance of the existing status system and hence to the stability and continuity of society. But the procedural inadequacy and parochialism of the lower courts perform this function, though in a somewhat different manner, in their dealings with higher-status defendants and those with the means to avail themselves of adequate counsel and the appellate process.

The most valuable service of competent legal counsel, as I have indicated earlier, is to prevent the accused from being brought to trial at all, especially on charges that the community regards as heinous or even controversial. Failing this, however, the higher-status adequately represented defendant may still anticipate that something like the following series of events will ensue: (1) He will be convicted in the court of original jurisdiction, and the hostilities of the community will thereby be assuaged and the validity of its folkways and prejudices reaffirmed. (2) The lower court will, however, be sufficiently incompetent technically that a firm basis for appeal will have been established. (3) The superior courts, though still firmly bound by convention as well as law, will have legally competent presiding judges with more secure tenure of office, who are less swayed by local interests and parochial hostilities than their colleagues in the lower courts. (4) The determination of the lower courts may therefore be reversed, or at least found seriously defective, and a new trial ordered which the prosecution may not bother to hold. (5) If the case is retried, the climate of opinion my have shifted in favor of the defendant. (6) The entire process is so costly in time and treasure that the defendant, even if finally vindicated, will have been fully occupied with his defense for a period of years and will think twice about continuing to be a troublemaker, even if technically innocent of any violation of law.

This, too, is a cooling-out process, in which the routines and interests of society are substantially protected from those whom it has deemed its adversaries. Even the appellant who is finally successful will have suffered formidable social sanctions. How successful he will finally be depends on his original status and resources, and the depth and permanence of the hostility he has aroused, as well as on the merits of his case. Caryl Chessman failed, though convicted in a trial that was demonstrably a tissue of judicial error, and though the offense for which he was finally put to death—kidnaping with intent to do bodily harm—bore no conceivable relationship to the sexual offenses imputed to him by public opinion, for which he was never tried and which would not, in any case, have been capital. One gathers that, after eleven years, the people of California were simply not about to permit the cancellation of an event in which they had invested so much and which they had so eagerly anticipated. Dr. Spock, whose status is high and whose public character is impeccable, and who stood accused of an offense on which public opinion was sharply divided—with higher-status elements tending to be more sympathetic—has been more fortunate. His case, in fact, is really a classic example of the effective functioning of the appellate process under conditions most favorable to it—and of the enormous costs and burdens borne by the defendant even then.

Taken all in all, it is just not possible to say whether the law is an instrument for the preservation of liberty, or a foul abyss in which the unrighteous, or those thought to be by their neighbors, struggle and are entrapped. It is both; and by being both, serves the ends of the society that maintains it. It cannot really transcend the moral limitations of that society, however; and in a society in which those moral limits are grave—and in what society are they not?—though the right of every citizen to his day in court must be zealously defended, the wise citizen must surely hope that this day will never come.

## NOTES

1. Paul G. Chevigny. *Police Power*. New York, Pantheon Books, 1969, Chapter 8, "Force, Arrest, and Cover Charges."
2. David Sudnow. "Normal Crimes: Sociological Features of the Penal Code in a Public Defender's Office," *Social Problems, 12*, 3, Winter 1965, pp. 255–276.
3. August B. Hollingshead and Frederick C. Redlich. *Social Class and Mental Illness*. New York, Wiley, 1958, p. 175.
4. Jerome H. Skolnick. *The Politics of Protest*. New York, Simon and Schuster, 1969, pp. 313–324.

# VIOLENCE AND THE LAW

Robert Paul Wolff

Everything I shall say in this essay has been said before, and much of it seems to me to be obvious as well as unoriginal. I offer two excuses for laying used goods before you. In the first place, I think that what I have to say about violence is true. Now, there are many ways to speak falsehood and only one way to speak truth. It follows, as Kierkegaard pointed out, that the truth is likely to become boring. On a subject as ancient and much discussed as ours here, we may probably assume that a novel—and, hence, interesting—view of violence is likely to be false.

But truth is not my sole excuse, for the subject before us suffers from the same difficulty that Kant discerned in the area of metaphysics. After refuting the various claims that had been made to transcendent rational knowledge of things-in-themselves, Kant remarked that the refutations had no lasting psychological effect on true believers. The human mind, he concluded, possessed a natural disposition to metaphysical speculation, which philosophy must perpetually keep in check. Somewhat analogously, men everywhere are prone to certain beliefs about the legitimacy of political authority, even though their beliefs are as groundless as metaphysical speculations. The most sophisticated of men persist in supposing that some valid distinction can be made between legitimate and illegitimate commands, on the basis of which they can draw a line, for example, between mere violence and the legitimate use of force. This lingering superstition is shared by those dissenters who call police actions or ghetto living conditions "violent"; for they are merely advancing competing legitimacy claims.

I shall set forth and defend *three* propositions about violence:

*First:* The concept of violence is inherently confused, as is the correlative concept of non-violence; these and related concepts depend for their meaning in political discussions on the fundamental notion of legitimate authority, which is also inherently incoherent.

*Second:* It follows that a number of familiar questions are also confusions to which no coherent answers could ever be given, such as: when it is permissible to resort to violence in politics; whether the black movement and the student movement should be non-violent; and whether anything good in politics is ever accomplished by violence.

*Finally:* The dispute over violence and non-violence in contemporary American politics is ideological rhetoric designed either to halt change and justify the existing distribution of power and privilege or to slow change and justify some features of the existing distribution of power and privilege or else to hasten change and justify a total redistribution of power and privilege.

Let us begin with the first proposition, which is essential to my entire discussion.

## I

The fundamental concepts of political philosophy are the concepts of power and authority.[1] Power in general is the ability to make and enforce decisions. Political power is the ability to make and enforce decisions about matters of major social importance. Thus the ability to dispose of my private income as I choose is a form of power, whereas the ability to make and enforce a decision about the disposition of some sizable portion of the tax receipts of the federal government is a form of *political* power. (So too is the ability to direct the decisions of a large private corporation, for the exercise of political power is not confined to the sphere of government.) A complete analysis of the concept of political power would involve a classification both of the means employed in the enforcing of decisions and of the scope and variety of questions about which decisions can be made.[2] It would also require an examination of the kinds of opposition against which the decision could be enforced. There is a very considerable difference between the ability a parliamentary majority has to enforce its decisions against the will of the minority and the ability of a rebel military clique to enforce its decisions against the parliament as a whole.

Authority, by contrast with power, is not an ability but a right. It is the right to command and, correlatively, the right to be obeyed. Claims to authority are made in virtually every area of social life, and, in a remarkably high proportion of cases, the claims are accepted and acquiesced in by those over whom they are made. Parents claim the right to be obeyed by their children; husbands until quite recently claimed the right to be obeyed by their wives; popes claim the right to be obeyed by the laity and clergy; and of course, most notably, virtually all existing governments claim the right to be obeyed by their subjects.

A claim to authority must be sharply differentiated both from a threat or enticement and from a piece of advice. When the state commands, it usually threatens punishment for disobedience, and it may even on occasion offer a reward for compliance, but the command cannot be reduced to the mere threat or reward. What characteristically distinguishes a state from an occupying army or private party is its insistence, either explicit or implicit, on its *right* to be obeyed. By the same token, an authoritative command is not a mere recommendation. Authority says, "Do this!" not, "Let me suggest this for your consideration."

Claims to authority have been defended on a variety of grounds, most prominent among which are the appeal to God, to tradition, to expertise, to the laws of history, and to the consent of those commanded. We tend to forget that John Locke thought it worthwhile to devote the first of his *Two Treatises on Civil Government* to the claim that Europe's monarchs held their authority by right of primogenitural descent from Adam. It is common today to give lip service to the theory that authority derives from the consent of the governed, but most of us habitually accord *some* weight to any authority claim issuing from a group of men who regularly control the behavior of a population in a territory, particularly if the group tricks itself out with flags, uniforms, courts of law, and printed regulations.

Not all claims to authority are justified. Indeed, I shall suggest shortly that few if any are. Nevertheless, men regularly accept the authority claims asserted against them, and so we must distinguish a descriptive from a normative sense of the term. Let us use the term "de facto authority" to refer to *the ability to get one's authority claims accepted by those against whom they are asserted.* "De jure authority," then, will refer to *the right to command and to be obeyed.* Obviously, the concept of de jure authority is primary, and the concept of de facto authority is derivative.

Thus understood, de facto authority is a form of power, for it is a means by which its possessor can enforce his decisions. Indeed, as Max Weber—from whom much of this analysis is taken—has pointed out, de facto authority is the *principal* means on which states rely to carry out their decisions. Threats and inducements play an exceedingly important role in the enforcement of political decisions, to be sure, but a state that must depend upon them entirely will very soon suffer a crippling reduction in its effectiveness, which is to say, in its political power. Modern states especially require for the successful prosecution of their programs an extremely high level of coordination of the behavior of large numbers of individuals. The myth of legitimacy is the only efficient means available to the state for achieving that coordination.

*Force* is the ability to work some change in the world by the expenditure of physical effort. A man may root up a tree, move a stalled car, drive a nail, or restrain another man *by force.* Force, in and of itself, is morally neutral. Physically speaking, there may be very little difference between the physical effort of a doctor who resets a dislocated shoulder and that of the ruffian who dislocated it. Sometimes, of course, force is used to work some change in the body of another man—to punch him, shoot him, take out his appendix, hold his arms, or cut his hair. But there is in principle no significant distinction between these uses of force and those uses which involve changing some other part of the world about which he cares. A man who slips into a parking place for which I am heading inflicts an injury on me roughly as great as if he had jostled me in a crowd or stepped on my toe. If he destroys a work of art on which I have lavished my most intense creative efforts, he may harm me more than a physical assault would.

Force is a means to power, but it is not, of course, a guarantee of power. If I wish to elicit hard work from my employees, I can threaten them with the lash or tempt them with bonuses—both of which are employments of force—but if my workers prefer not to comply, my threats and inducements may be fruitless. It is a commonplace both of domestic and of international politics that the mere possession of a monopoly of force is no guarantee of political power. Those who fail to grasp this truth are repeatedly frustrated by the baffling inability of the strong to impose their will upon the weak.

There are, so far as I can see, three means or instruments by which power is exercised—three ways, that is to say, in which men enforce or carry out their social decisions. The first is *force,* the ability to rearrange the world in ways that other men find appealing or distasteful. In modern society, money is, of course, the principal measure, exchange medium, and symbol of force. The second instrument of power is *de facto authority*—the ability to elicit obedience, as opposed to mere compliance, from others. De facto authority frequently accrues to those with a preponderance of force, for men are fatally prone to suppose that he who can compel compliance deserves obedience. But de facto authority does not reduce to the possession of a preponderance of force, for men habitually obey commands they know could not effectively be enforced. The third instrument of power is *social opinion,* or what might be called the "symbolic" use of force. When a runner competes in a race, he may want the first-prize money or the commercial endorsements that will come to the winner, or he may even just like blue ribbons—but he may also want the acclaim of the fans. Now, that acclaim is expressed by certain uses of force—by clapping of hands and cheering, which are physical acts. But its value to the runner is symbolic; he cherishes it as an expression of approval, not merely as a pleasing sound. To say that man is a social creature is not merely to say that he hangs out in groups, nor even to say that he engages in collective and cooperative enterprises for self-interested purposes; it is most importantly to say that he values symbolic interactions with other men and is influenced by them as well as by the ordinary exercise of force and by claims of authority. This point is important for our discussion, for, as we shall see, many persons who shrink from the use of force as an instrument of political power have no compunctions about the use of social opinion or what I have called the "symbolic" use of force. Anyone who has observed a progressive classroom run by a teacher with scruples of this sort will know that a day "in coventry" can be a far crueler punishment for an unruly ten-year-old than a sharp rap on the knuckles with a ruler.

We come, finally, to the concept of violence. Strictly speaking, *violence is the illegitimate or unauthorized use of force to effect decisions against the will or desire of others.* Thus, murder is an act of violence, but capital punishment *by a legitimate state* is not; theft or extortion is violent, but the collection of taxes *by a legitimate state* is not. Clearly, on this interpretation the concept of violence is normative as well as descriptive, for it involves an implicit appeal to the principle of de jure legitimate authority. There is an associated sense of the term which is purely descriptive, relying on the descriptive notion of de facto authority. Violence in this latter sense is the use of force in ways that are proscribed or unauthorized by those who are generally accepted as the legitimate authorities in the territory. Descriptively speaking, the attack on Hitler's life during the Second World War was an act of violence, but one might perfectly well deny that it was violent in the strict sense, on the grounds that Hitler's regime was illegitimate. On similar grounds, it is frequently said that police behavior toward workers or ghetto dwellers or demonstrators is violent even when it is clearly within the law, for the authority issuing the law is illegitimate.

It is common, but I think wrongheaded, to restrict the term "violence" to uses of force that involve bodily interference or the direct infliction of physical injury. Carrying a dean out of his office is said to be violent, but not seizing his office when he is absent and locking him out. Physically tearing a man's wallet from his pocket is "violent," but swindling him out of the same amount of money is not. There is a natural enough basis for this distinction. Most of us value our lives and physical well-being above other goods that we enjoy, and we tend therefore to view attacks or threats on our person as different in kind from other sorts of harm we might suffer. Nevertheless, the distinction is not sufficiently sharp to be of any analytical use, and, as we shall see later, it usually serves the ideological purpose of ruling out, as immoral or politically illegitimate, the only instrument of power that is available to certain social classes.

In its strict or normative sense, then, the concept of political violence depends upon the concept of de jure, or legitimate, authority. If there is no such thing as legitimate political authority, then it is impossible to distinguish between legitimate and illegitimate uses of force. Now, of course, under any circumstances, we can distinguish between right and wrong—justified and unjustified—uses of force. Such a distinction belongs to moral philosophy in general, and our choice of the criteria by which we draw the distinction will depend on our theory of value and obligation. But the distinctive political concept of violence can be given a coherent meaning *only* by appeal to a doctrine of legitimate political authority.

On the basis of a lengthy reflection upon the concept of de jure legitimate authority, I have come to the conclusion that philosophical anarchism is true. That is to say, I believe that there is not, and there could not be, a state that has a right to command and whose subjects have a binding obligation to obey. I have defended this view in detail elsewhere, and I can only indicate here the grounds of my conviction.[3] Briefly, I think it can be shown that every man has a fundamental duty to be autonomous, in Kant's sense of the term. Each of us must make himself the author of his actions and take responsibility for them by refusing to act save on the basis of reasons he can see for himself to be good. Autonomy, thus understood, is in direct opposition to obedience, which is submission to the will of another, irrespective of reasons. Following Kant's usage, political obedience is heteronomy of the will.

Now, political theory offers us one great argument designed to make the autonomy of the individual compatible with submission to the putative authority of the state. In a democracy, it is claimed, the citizen is both law-giver and law-obeyer. Since he shares in the authorship of the laws, he submits to his own will in obeying them, and hence is autonomous, not heteronomous.

If this argument were valid, it would provide a genuine ground for a distinction between violent and non-violent political actions. Violence would be a use of force proscribed by the laws or executive authority of a genuinely democratic state. The only possible justification of illegal or extralegal political acts would be a demonstration of the illegitimacy of the state, and this in turn would involve showing that the commands of the state were not expressions of the will of the people.

But the classic defense of democracy is *not* valid. For a variety of reasons, neither majority rule nor any other method of making decisions in the absence of unanimity can be shown to preserve the autonomy of the individual citizens. In a democracy, as in any state, obedience is heteronomy. The autonomous man is of necessity an anarchist. Consequently, there is no valid political criterion for the justified use of force. Legality is, by itself, no justification. Now, of course, there are all manner of utilitarian arguments for submitting to the state and its agents, even if the state's claim to legitimacy is unfounded. The laws may command actions that are in fact morally obligatory or whose effects promise to be beneficial. Widespread submission to law may bring about a high level of order, regularity, and predictability in social relationships which is valuable independently of the particular character of the acts commanded. But in and of themselves, the acts of police and the commands of legislatures have no peculiar legitimacy or sanction. Men everywhere and always impute authority to establish governments and they are always wrong to do so.

## II

The foregoing remarks are quite banal, to be sure. Very few serious students of politics will maintain either the democratic theory of legitimate authority or any alternatives to it. Nevertheless, like posttheological, demythologized Protestants who persist in raising prayers to a God they no longer believe in, modern men go on exhibiting a superstitious belief in the authority of the state. Consider, for example, a question now much debated: When is it permissible to resort to violence in politics? If "violence" is taken to mean an *unjustified* use of force, then the answer to the question is obviously *never*. If the use of force were permissible, it would not, by definition, be violence, and if it were violent, it would not, by definition, be permissible. If "violence" is taken in the strict sense to mean "an illegitimate or unauthorized use of force," then every political act, whether by private parties or by agents of the state, is violent, for there is no such thing as legitimate authority. If "violence" is construed in the restricted sense as "bodily interference or the direct infliction of physical harm," then the obvious but correct rule is to resort to violence when less harmful or costly means fail, providing always that the balance of good and evil produced is superior to that promised by any available alternative.

These answers are all trivial, but that is precisely my point. Once the concept of violence is seen to rest on the unfounded distinction between legitimate and illegitimate political authority, the question of the appropriateness of violence simply dissolves. It is mere superstition to describe a policeman's beating of a helpless suspect as "an excessive use of force" while characterizing an attack by a crowd on the policeman as "a resort to violence." The implication of such a distinction is that the policeman, as the duly appointed representative of a legitimate government, has a right to use physical force, although no right to use "excessive" force, whereas the crowd of private citizens has no right at all to use even moderate physical force. But there are no legitimate governments, hence no special rights attaching to soldiers, policemen, magistrates, or other law enforcement agents, hence no coherent distinction between violence and the legitimate use of force.

Consider, as a particular example, the occupation of buildings and the student strike at Columbia University during April and May of 1968. The consequences of those acts have not yet played themselves out, but I think certain general conclusions can be drawn. First, the total harm done by the students and their supporters was very small in comparison with the good results that were achieved. A month of classwork was lost, along with many tempers and a good deal of sleep. Someone—it is still not clear who—burned the research notes of a history professor, an act which, I am happy to say, produced a universal revulsion shared even by the S.D.S. In the following year, a number of classes were momentarily disrupted by S.D.S. activists in an unsuccessful attempt to repeat the triumph of the previous spring.

Against this, what benefits flowed from the protest? A reactionary and thoroughly unresponsive administration was forced to resign; an all-university senate of students, professors, and administrators was created, the first such body at Columbia. A callous and antisocial policy of university expansion into the surrounding neighborhood was reversed; some at least of the university's ties with the military were loosened or severed; and an entire community of students and professors were forced to confront moral and political issues which till then they had managed to ignore.

Could these benefits have been won at less cost? Considering the small cost of the uprising, the question seems to me a bit finicky; nevertheless, the answer is clearly no. The history of administrative intransigence and faculty apathy at Columbia makes it quite clear that nothing short of a dramatic act such as the seizure of buildings could have deposed the university administration and produced a prudent and restrained use of force.

Assuming this assessment to be correct, it is tempting to conclude, "In the Columbia case, violence was justified." But this conclusion is *totally wrong,* for it implies that a line can be drawn between legitimate and illegitimate forms of protest, the latter being justified only under special conditions and when all else has failed. We would all agree, I think, that under a dictatorship men have the right to defy the state or even to attack its representatives when their interests are denied and their needs ignored—the only rule that binds them is the general caution against doing more harm than they accomplish good. My purpose here is simply to argue that a modern industrial democracy, whatever merits it may have, is in this regard no different from a dictatorship. No special authority attaches to the laws of a representative, majoritarian state; it is only superstition and the myth of legitimacy that invests the judge, the policeman, or the official with an exclusive right to the exercise of certain kinds of force.

In the light of these arguments, it should be obvious that I see no merit in the doctrine of non-violence, nor do I believe that any special and complex justification is needed for what is usually called "civil disobedience." A commitment to non-violence can be understood in two different senses, depending on the interpretation given to the concept of violence. If violence is understood in the strict sense as the political use of force in ways proscribed by a legitimate government, then, of course, the doctrine of non-violence depends upon the assumption that there *are* or *could be* legitimate governments. Since I believe this assumption to be false, I can attribute no coherent meaning to this first conception of non-violence.

If violence is understood, on the other hand, as the use of force to interfere with someone in a direct bodily way or to injure him physically, then the doctrine of non-violence is merely a subjective queasiness having no moral rationale. When you occupy the seats at a lunch counter for hours on end, thereby depriving the proprietor of the profits he would have made on ordinary sales during that time, you are taking money out of his pocket quite as effectively as if you had robbed his till or smashed his stock. If you persist in the sit-in until he goes into debt, loses his lunch counter, and takes a job as a day laborer, then you have done him a much greater injury than would be accomplished by a mere beating in a dark alley. He may deserve to be ruined, of course, but, if so, then he probably also deserves to be beaten. A penchant for such indirect coercion as a boycott or a sit-in is morally questionable, for it merely leaves the dirty work to the bank that forecloses on the mortgage or the policeman who carries out the eviction. Emotionally, the commitment to non-violence is frequently a severely repressed expression of extreme hostility akin to the mortifications and self-flagellations of religious fanatics. Enough testimony has come from black novelists and psychiatrists to make it clear that the philosophy of non-violence is, for the American Negro, what Nietzsche called a "slave morality"—the principal difference is that in traditional Christianity God bears the guilt for inflicting pain on the wicked; in the social gospel the law acts as the scourge.

The doctrine of civil disobedience is an American peculiarity growing out of the conflict between the authority claims of the state and the directly contradictory claims of individual conscience. In a futile attempt to deny and affirm the authority of the state simultaneously, a number of conscientious dissenters have claimed the right to disobey what they believe to be immoral laws, so long as they are prepared to submit to punishment by the state. A willingness to go to jail for one's beliefs is widely viewed in this country as evidence of moral sincerity, and even as a sort of argument for the position one is defending.

Now, tactically speaking, there is much to be said for legal martyrdom. As tyrannical governments are perpetually discovering, the sight of one's leader nailed to a cross has a marvelously bracing effect on the faithful members of a dissident sect. When the rulers are afflicted by the very principles they are violating, even the *threat* of self-sacrifice may force a government to its knees. But leaving tactics aside, no one has any moral obligation whatsoever to resist an unjust government openly rather than clandestinely. Nor has anyone a duty to invite and then to suffer unjust punishment. The choice is simple: If the law is right, follow it. If the law is wrong, evade it.

I think it is possible to understand why conscientious and morally concerned men should feel a compulsion to seek punishment for acts they genuinely believe to be right. Conscience is the echo of society's voice within us. The men of strongest and most independent conscience are, in a manner of speaking, just those who have most completely internalized this social voice, so that they hear and obey its commands even when no policeman compels their compliance. Ironically, it is these same men who are most likely to set themselves against the government in the name of ideals and principles to which they feel a higher loyalty. When a society violates the very principles it claims to hold, these men of conscience experience a terrible conflict. They are deeply committed to the principles society has taught them, principles they have truly come to believe. But they can be true to their beliefs only by setting themselves against the laws of the very society that has been their teacher and with whose authority they identify themselves. Such a conflict never occurs in men of weak conscience, who merely obey the law, however much it violates the moral precepts they have only imperfectly learned.

The pain of the conflict is too great to be borne; somehow it must be alleviated. If the commitment to principle is weak, the individual submits, though he feels morally unclean for doing so. If the identification with society is weak, he rejects the society and becomes alienated, perhaps identifying with some other society. But if both conscience and identification are too strong to be broken, the only solution is to expiate the guilt by seeking social punishment for the breach of society's laws. Oddly enough, the expiation, instead of bringing them back into the fold of law-obeyers, makes it psychologically all the easier for them to continue their defiance of the state.

## III

The foregoing conclusions seem to reach far beyond what the argument warrants. The classical theory of political authority may indeed be inadequate; it may even be that the concept of legitimate authority is incoherent; but surely *some* genuine distinction can be drawn between a politics of reason, rules, and compromise on the one hand, and the resort to violent conflict on the other! Are the acts of a rioting mob different only in degree from the calm and orderly processes of a duly constituted court of law? Such a view partakes more of novelty than of truth!

Unless I very much misjudge my audience, most readers will respond roughly in this manner. There may be a few still willing to break a lance for sovereignty and legitimate authority, and a few, I hope, who agree immediately with what I have said, but the distinction between violence and non-violence in politics is too familiar to be so easily discarded. In this third section of my essay, therefore, I shall try to discover what makes the distinction so plausible, even though it is—I insist—unfounded.

The customary distinction between violent and non-violent modes of social interaction seems to me to rest on *two* genuine distinctions: the first is the *subjective* distinction between the regular or accepted and the irregular or unexpected uses of force; the second is the *objective* distinction between those interests which are central or vital to an individual and those which are secondary or peripheral.

Consider first the subjective distinction between regular and irregular uses of force in social interactions. It seems perfectly appropriate to us that a conflict between two men who desire the same piece of land should be settled in favor of the one who can pull more money out of his pocket. We consider it regular and orderly that the full weight of the police power of the state be placed behind that settlement in order to ensure that nothing upsets it. On the other hand, we consider it violent and disorderly to resolve the dispute by a fistfight or a duel. Yet what is the difference between the use of money, which is one kind of force, and the use of fists, which is another? Well, if we do not appeal to the supposed legitimacy of financial transactions or to the putative authority of the law, then the principal difference is that we are accustomed to settling disputes with dollars and we are no longer accustomed to settling them with fists.

Imagine how barbaric, how unjust, how *violent* it must seem to someone unfamiliar with the beauties of capitalism that a man's ability to obtain medical care for his children should depend solely on the contingency that some other man can make a profit from his productive labor! Is the federal government's seizure of my resources for the purpose of killing Asian peasants less violent than a bandit's extortion of tribute at gunpoint? Yet we are accustomed to the one and unaccustomed to the other.

The objective distinction between central and peripheral interests also shapes our conception of what is violent in politics. When my peripheral or secondary interests are at stake in a conflict, I quite naturally consider only a moderate use of force to be justified. Anything more, I will probably call "violence." What I tend to forget, of course, is that other parties to the conflict may find their primary interests challenged and, hence, may have a very different view of what is and is not violent. In the universities, for example, most of the student challenges have touched only on the peripheral interests of professors. No matter what is decided about ROTC, curriculum, the disposition of the endowment, or black studies, the typical philosophy professor's life will be largely unchanged. His tenure, salary, working conditions, status, and family life remain the same. Hence he is likely to take a tolerant view of building seizures and sit-ins. But let a classroom be disrupted, and he cries out that violence has no place on campus. What he means is that force has been used in a way that touches one of his deeper concerns.

The concept of violence serves as a rhetorical device for proscribing those political uses of force which one considers inimical to one's central interests. Since different social groups have different central interests and can draw on different kinds of force, it follows that there are conflicting definitions of violence. Broadly speaking, in the United States today, there are four conceptions of violence corresponding to four distinct socioeconomic classes.

The first view is associated with the established financial and political interests in the country. It identifies the violent with the illegal, and condemns all challenges to the authority of the state and all assaults on the rights of property as beyond the limits of permissible politics. The older segments of the business community adopt this view, along with the military establishment and the local elites of middle America. Robert Taft was once a perfect symbol of this sector of opinion.

The second view is associated with the affluent, educated, technical and professional middle class in America, together with the new rapidly growing future-oriented sectors of the economy, such as the communications industry, electronics, etc. They accept, even welcome, dissent, demonstration, ferment, and—within limits—attacks on property in ghetto areas. They look with favor on civil disobedience and feel at ease with extralegal tactics of social change. Their interests are identified with what is new in American society, and they are confident of coming out on top in the competition for wealth and status within an economy built on the principle of reward for profitable performance.

The "liberals," as this group is normally called, can afford to encourage modes of dissent or disruption that do not challenge the economic and social arrangements on which their success is based. They will defend rent strikes, grape boycotts, or lunch-counter sit-ins with the argument that unemployment and starvation are a form of violence also. Since they are themselves in competition with the older elite for power and prestige, they tend to view student rebels and black militants as their allies, up to the point at which their own interests are attacked. But when tactics are used that threaten their positions in universities, in corporations, or in affluent suburbs, then the liberals cry *violence* also, and call for the police. A poignant example of this class is the liberal professor who cheers the student rebels as they seize the administration building and then recoils in horror at the demand that he share his authority to determine curriculum and decide promotions.

The third view of violence is that held by working-class and lower-middle-class Americans, those most often referred to as the "white backlash." They perceive the principal threat to their interests as coming from the bottom class of ghetto dwellers, welfare clients, and non-unionized laborers who demand more living space, admission to union jobs with union wages, and a larger share of the social product. To this hard-pressed segment of American society, "violence" means street crime, ghetto riots, civil-rights marches into all-white neighborhoods, and antiwar attacks on the patriotic symbols of constituted authority with which backlash America identifies. Studies of the petty bourgeoisie in Weimar Germany suggest, and George Wallace's presidential campaign of 1968 confirms, that the lower middle class, when it finds itself pressed between inflationary prices and demands from the lower class, identifies its principal enemy as the lower class. So we find the classic political alliance of old established wealth with right-wing populist elements, both of which favor a repressive response to attacks on authority and a strong governmental policy toward the "violence" of demands for change.

The fourth view of violence is the revolutionary counterdefinition put forward by the out class and its sympathizers within the liberal wing of the established order. Two complementary rhetorical devices are employed. First, the connotation of the term "violence" is accepted, but the application of the term is reversed: police are violent, not rioters; employers, not strikers;

the American Army, not the enemy. In this way, an attack is mounted on the government's claim to possess the right to rule. Second, the denotation of the term is held constant and the connotation reversed. Violence is good, not bad; legitimate, not illegitimate. It is, in H. Rap Brown's great rhetorical flourish, "as American as cherry pie." Since the out class of rebels has scant access to the instruments of power used by established social classes—wealth, law, police power, legislation—it naturally seeks to legitimize the riots, harassments, and street crime which are its only weapons. Equally naturally, the rest of society labels such means "violent" and suppresses them.

In the complex class struggle for wealth and power in America, each of us must decide for himself which group he will identify with. It is not my purpose here to urge one choice rather than another. My sole aim is to argue that the concept of violence has no useful role to play in the deliberations leading to that choice. Whatever other considerations of utility and social justice one appeals to, no weight should be given to the view that *some* uses of force are prima facie ruled out as illegitimate and hence "violent," or that other uses of force are prima facie ruled in as legitimate, or legal. Furthermore, in the advancement of dissenting positions by illegal means no special moral merit attaches to the avoiding, as it were, of body contact. Physical harm may be among the most serious injuries that can be done to an opponent, but, if so, it differs only in degree and not in kind from the injuries inflicted by so-called non-violent techniques of political action.

## IV

The myth of legitimate authority is the secular reincarnation of that religious superstition which has finally ceased to play a significant role in the affairs of men. Like Christianity, the worship of the state has its fundamentalists, its revisionists, its ecumenicists (or world federalists), and its theological rationale. The philosophical anarchist is the atheist of politics. I began my discussion with the observation that the belief in legitimacy, like the penchant for transcendent metaphysics, is an ineradicable irrationality of the human experience. However, the slow extinction of religious faith over the past two centuries may encourage us to hope that in time anarchism, like atheism, will become the accepted conviction of enlightened and rational men.

## NOTES

1. What follows is a summary of analyses I have published elsewhere. The concept of political power is treated in Chapter III of *The Poverty of Liberalism:* Boston, Beacon Press, 1968. For an analysis of the concepts of legitimacy and authority, see *In Defense of Anarchism:* New York, Harper and Row, 1970.
2. See Robert A. Dahl, "The Concept of Power," *Behavior Science,* July 1957, for just such a classification.
3. See *In Defense of Anarchism.*

# PART

# II

# THE PERILS OF INDWELLING LAW

Daniel J. Boorstin

Of all terms used by social scientists today, "law" and "society" are perhaps the most vaguely interrelated. In some sense or other, law is a creature of society, and society is a creature of law. We generally think of a lawbreaker as a person who is antisocial. We cannot contribute to the improvement of our laws without at the same time contributing to the improvement of society. On the other hand, a person can be antisocial without being a lawbreaker; and a person is not always serving his society by obeying its laws.

"Society" is in some ways a much larger term than "law." Every society includes a system of law, yet "law" is somehow more durable, more chronologically extensive. "Roman society" calls to mind the way men lived at some particular time. But "Roman law" suggests ways of living that extended over generations. "Society" extends primarily in space; "law" primarily in time. The relation between "law" and "society" then must have something to do with the relations between the peculiar needs and habits of men in some particular place at a given time, and the persistent practices of a large group of men over generations.

I wish to focus not on the "real" relationship between a society and its laws, but rather on how people have thought of that relationship. My focus will be on the United States and on the attitudes of laymen, the consumers of the law.

In taking the layman's point of view, I will use no technical or philosophical definition but rather prefer the common dictionary definition of law: "All the rules of conduct established and enforced by the authority, legislation, or custom of a given community or other group." I will explore a few of the changing ways in which thoughtful laymen in America have come to look on the relation between these rules and all the rest of their social experience. How have literate, self-conscious Americans thought about the relation between their law and their society? What have they wanted to believe? I will be concerned with some examples, in this area, of what William James called the "Will to Believe," and it would not be inaccurate to say I am concerned with some "Varieties of Legal Experience."

## I. SOME PECULIAR PROBLEMS OF MAJORITY-MADE LAW

One of the difficulties of talking about the relation between law and society is that in law, as in all other deep human concerns, the demands we make of our world are contradictory. We wish to believe both that our laws come from a necessity beyond our reach, and that they are our own instruments shaping our community to our chosen ends. We wish to believe that our laws are both changeless and changeable, divine and secular, permanent and temporary, transcendental and pragmatic. These demands are perhaps no more contradictory than those we make of the world when we think of mortality, love, our personal choice of vocation, or our national destiny.

The progress of man, Alfred North Whitehead has shrewdly observed, depends largely on his ability to accept superficial paradoxes, to see that what at first looks like a contradiction need not always remain one. It must have seemed odd to the first man who tried a raft or a bridge that he should cross over a stream of water and not get wet. Now, in modern legal history, the paradox which modern man has learned to live with is that though he can somehow make his own laws, yet they can have an authority above and beyond him.

The discovery, or even the belief, that man could make his

own laws was burdensome. Formerly man could find authority for his laws in the mysterious sanction of ancient practice, "to which the mind of man runneth not to the contrary," or in a misty divinity. When, however, men came to see that they, or some majority of them, were the sources of the law, much of the charm melted away. Many men had doubted the wisdom of their kings or their priests. But nearly every man knew in his own heart the vagueness of his own knowledge and the uncertainty of his own wisdom about his society. Scrupulous men were troubled to think that their society was governed by a wisdom no greater than their own.

"Laws that emanate from the people," Orestes A. Brownson wrote in 1873, "or that are binding only by virtue of the assent of the governed, or that emanate from any human source alone, have none of the essential characteristics of law, for they bind no conscience, and restrain, except by force, no will." Brownson had been led to this conclusion by his interpretation of American history and his views of the American scene. He had taken an active part in the "Hard Cider" presidential campaign of 1840, on the side of the losing Democratic candidate, Martin Van Buren, whom he believed to be "the last first-class man that sat, or probably ever will sit, in the presidential chair of the United States." "What I saw served to dispel my democratic illusions, to break the idol I had worshipped, and shook to its foundation my belief in the divinity of the people, or in their will as the expression of eternal justice." In search of a higher authority, Brownson took refuge in the Roman Catholic Church.

Of course, most Americans have not been so deeply disturbed by this problem. They have preferred to believe that the trouble has not been in the source of the authority but in how the authority was exercised. That if the people were not yet able to make good laws for themselves, it was not because somebody else should make their laws for them but because the people were not yet literate enough, or wise enough, or pure enough in their motives.

The rise of self-conscious lawmaking has remained, however,

a parable of the peculiar problems of modern man. Man's growing control over nature has given him an unprecedented power to move about the earth, to reproduce the objects he needs, and to make images of nature. The Industrial Revolution in England and elsewhere in Europe and the American (or mass-production) system of manufacturing permitted man to surround himself with objects of his own making, to shape his environment to his own needs and desires, and even to his whims. And, incidentally, this allowed him to get in his own way or in the way of his neighbors, as he had never before imagined. In England this worried people like Ruskin and Matthew Arnold; in America it troubled fewer, but there were still some, like Brownson and Thoreau. The sentiment was summed up in Disraeli's aphorism that "Man is not the creature of circumstances. Circumstances are the creatures of men." The new sciences of sociology, psychology, and anthropology further heightened the self-consciousness of man's power to make himself.

Man's power to make his own laws was, despite everything, the most burdensome of his new responsibilities for himself and the universe. His new powers to make things and his powers over nature would have worried him much less if somehow he had felt confident that his laws were rooted outside his society. But in acquiring his mastery over nature he had acquired the guilty secret that his laws might be rooted only in his version of the needs of his time and place.

Now the two contrary beliefs which we still want to hold are (a) that our laws are immanent (or the mere symptom of an indwelling necessity) and (b) that our laws are instrumental (tools we shape to our chosen ends). These two emphases correspond roughly to the two great stages in the development of law which were described by Sir Henry Maine—the movement from customary law or divinely given codes to legislative law. I prefer to call these the successive stages of unself-conscious lawmaking and self-conscious lawmaking. But the rise of self-conscious lawmaking does not abolish the need for belief in immanence, it merely transforms that belief. It makes the need for that belief more acute. Now men are burdened not only because they make their particular laws but because they realize that they have the power to make their very concept of law.

This leads us to the most tantalizing problem—the mystery—of law in modern society. How retain any belief in the immanence of law, in its superiority to our individual, temporary needs, after we have adopted a wholehearted modern belief in its instrumentality? How continue to believe that something about our law is changeless after we have discovered that it may be infinitely plastic? How believe that in some sense the basic laws of society are given us by God, after we have become convinced that we have given them to ourselves?

How persuade ourselves that our laws can be both ancient and up to date, when almost nothing else we know has these contrary virtues? Under the older (immanent) view there were no good laws or bad laws, but only laws more or less established, more or less clearly revealed; under the later (instrumental) view there can be good laws, bad laws, better laws, worse laws, laws more effective or less effective. In the United States today we still want to believe that the laws of our community are somehow an inseparable part of our being, of the laws of the universe, of the order of nature, of God's plan for us. Yet we wish also to believe that these have been shaped primarily by our will—the will of the people—and that they are well shaped to the ends which our community has freely chosen.

## II. LEGAL IMMANENCE: TWO EARLIER AMERICAN EXAMPLES

In modern America, the subtlest problem has been how to retain a balanced sense of legal immanence. Many modern tendencies in social science push us toward extreme dogmas of the instrumental nature of law. Before describing the peculiar problems of finding legal immanence in twentieth-century America, I would like to illustrate what I mean by belief in the immanence of law by two examples. Both are taken from American history before the middle of the nineteenth century: before the flowering of modern social science and before the rise of pragmatism as an explicit philosophy (or substitute for philosophy).

### *1. Personal Perfectionism: The Quakers of Colonial Pennsylvania*

It is hard to find a better example of belief in an indwelling law than among the Quakers of Colonial Pennsylvania. For the English Quakers in the seventeenth century the law took its proper shape from the very nature of God, man, and society. This law was supposed to prevail against all the commands of the state. George Fox had exhorted, "My friends . . . going over to plant, and to make outward plantations in America, keep your own plantations in your hearts, with the spirit and power of God, that your own vines and lilies be not hurt." But William Penn, founder of Pennsylvania, was a very sensible man, a man of this world and no mean politician. His preface to his "Frame of Government for Pennsylvania" (1682) was one of the wisest political manifestos of the age. In it he warned against excessive faith in any form of government or of laws:

> Any government is free to the people under it (whatever be the frame) where the laws rule, and the people are a party to those laws, and more than this is tyranny, oligarchy, or confusion. But, lastly, when all is said, there is hardly one frame of government in the world so ill designed by its first founders, that, in good hands, would not do well enough . . . Governments, like clocks, go from the motion men give them; and as governments are made and moved by men, so by them are they ruined too. Wherefore governments rather depend upon men, than men upon governments. Let men be good, and the government cannot be bad; if it be ill, they will cure it. But if men be bad, let the government be never so good, they will endeavour to warp and spoil it to their turn.

Such an emphasis on the indwelling spirit of man as the shaper of society and its laws was the keynote of the Quaker colony. For the first half-century of its life, Quaker Pennsylvania flourished, and it remained decisively Quaker. Although sects struggled among themselves, the Quakers managed to rule.

But by the early decades of the eighteenth century, a great struggle had begun. Politically speaking, it was a struggle between the Quakers, settled mostly in Philadelphia and eastern Pennsylvania, and later immigrants who settled to the westward and were beginning to engulf the Quakers even in their Friendly City. It was also, however, a struggle between two concepts of law. On the one side was the Quaker view of an indwelling law, implanted in man and in society by God's beneficent spirit. On the other side was the view of an instrumental law, a man-shaped tool to protect the society against its enemies foreign and domestic.

The weightiest Quakers obstinately insisted on preserving the purity of the law which dwelt within them. They refused to take oaths, because the indwelling law forbade it; they refused to bear arms, or to support the purchase of arms, because their indwelling law was a law of peace; they refused to deal prudently and at arm's length with the threatening Indians, because their indwelling law of love commanded that the Indians were good, and that they be treated as brothers. The result is now a familiar story. The Quakers were driven from power in the Pennsylvania Assembly in 1756 and became strangers in their own colony. The government of the colony was taken over by non-Quakers and by the party of the shrewd Benjamin Franklin. From rulers of a society, the Quakers became prophets of a sect. Thereafter they gave most of their energy to reforming their own members, to building miscellaneous humanitarian institutions, and to stirring the larger community toward specific seemingly utopian reforms. They agitated against slavery and the slave trade, they worked to humanize prisons and insane asylums, they built hospitals, they opposed war on principle. Although a long political struggle had been needed to displace them from power, their fate had actually been sealed a century before when a Quaker yearly meeting had declared, "The setting up and putting down Kings and Governments is God's peculiar prerogative, for causes best known to himself."

The Pennsylvania Quaker experience in the eighteenth century dramatized on the American colonial stage both the strengths and the weaknesses of one extreme form of belief in the immanence of law. Rigid and changeless, it was a law of self-righteousness—of the righteousness of the self. But it was a law careless of its effects, more concerned for self than for community, blind to the needs of suffering women and children in the Indian-harried backwoods. It was a law of intransigent individuals. Inevitably Quaker law became a sectarian credo rather than the foundation of a large society.

Certain features of the Quaker law must be noted. The Quakers were an untheoretical, untheological, unlegislative people. Their law was untechnical. Their law consisted in a few general tenets: love, peace, no swearing, all men are good. Paradoxically, its very unsystematic, unwritten, untechnical character made the Quakers the more fearful of bending any provisions of their law to the needs of community.

These rigid, unrealistic qualities of Quaker law were not the necessary consequences of a belief in God, or in a divine foundation for society. Less than three hundred miles away were the New England Puritans. The laws of Puritanism were highly elaborated, very much written, and not lacking in technicality. In the long run the written, technical, elaborated laws of the bibliolatrous New England Puritans—God-based though they were—proved far more flexible than the unwritten, inarticulate, untechnical benevolent spirit which governed the Pennsylvania Quakers.

## 2. *Social Narcissism: The Ante-Bellum South*

Another, and in many ways contrasting, form of belief in immanent law developed in the Southern United States in the half-century before the Civil War. It shared many of the formal features of the Colonial Pennsylvanian law of the Quakers: it, too, was unwritten, inarticulate, untechnical, and unbending. But it differed in its content, its source, and its sanction.

The rise in the South of belief in immanent law must be explained by two dominant facts of Southern life in this period. The first was the institution of slavery; the second was the defensive spirit, the feeling that the whole Southern society was under attack from the outside.

The great planters ran their affairs by informal understandings, gentlemen's agreements, and pledges of honor. Surprisingly little legal paper was used in the conduct of the Southern plantation and Southern commerce in the early years of the nineteenth century. This is, of course, one of the reasons why it is hard to learn as much as we would like about the daily life of the time. The tendency to rely on unwritten rules was accentuated by the existence of slavery and by the very character of that institution. Slavery was a labor system in which the rules were local custom or the arbitrary decision of the master. Since the common law of England did not recognize the status of slavery, there was no developed body of law concerning slavery, the rights of the slave, or the duties of the master in the English slave-holding colonies. By contrast, as has often been noted, Latin America and the Caribbean areas, governed by the Roman law transmitted through Spain or Portugal, had a highly developed law of slavery with traditions and practices reaching back to ancient times.

An ironic result of the fact that English law favored liberty and refused to recognize slavery was thus that the Negro slave in the English colonies was a mere chattel, with virtually no recognizable legal personality, and few if any rights against his master. He was in many ways worse off than were slaves in a society that had inherited a long tradition of legalized slavery. The legal situation of the slave in the Southern United States was further worsened by the failure of Protestantism to take the strong religious-equalitarian stand of Catholicism, and by the indelible identification of race with the status of slavery. In Roman law, slavery was, of course, a legal status independent of race; and as the slave laws of Cuba, for example, developed, they recognized gradations of servitude and racial gradations (mulatto, quadroon, octoroon, etc.). But in the North American English colonies and in the states derived from them, slavery was an all-or-nothing proposition.

Another striking fact about the institution of slavery in the ante-bellum South is not merely the meager or nonexistent rights of the Negro slave but the meager amount of legal literature concerning the laws of slavery. Slave codes were sparse and did not purport to cover all possible situations. Even treatises on slavery were few and far between. The best legal treatises of the age on American Negro slavery (with the conspicuous exception only of Cobb's "Law of Negro Slavery," 1858) did not come from the South at all but were written in New York or Philadelphia.

When the Southerner confronted this fact of the sparseness of the formal legal rights of the Negro and the meagerness of written law, he began to discover, by the 1840's and 1850's, that these symbolized the virtues of the South's peculiar institution. Not only extremist defenders of slavery like George Fitzhugh, but other loyal Southerners as well, argued that this distinction between the legalistic, pettifogging, literal-minded, mean-spirited North—with its eye always on written record and the cash box—and on the other hand, the generous, chivalrous, kind-hearted, honor-hearted, honor-governed South expressed the whole difference between their institutions.

"Human Law," Fitzhugh explained in *Cannibals All! or, Slaves without Masters* (1857), "cannot beget benevolence, affection, maternal and paternal love; nor can it supply their places; but it may, by breaking up the ordinary relations of human beings, stop and disturb the current of these finer feelings of our nature. It may abolish slavery; but it can never create between the capitalist and the laborer, between employer and employed, the kind and affectionate relations that usually exist between master and slave." The essence of slavery, Southern defenders argued, was that it did not depend on explicit instrumental rules; and this was precisely its virtue. For, under slavery, they said, the laws of employment became one with the natural currents of social sentiment on both sides: kindness and generosity on the side of the employer, loyalty and industry on the side of the employed. "Experience and observation fully satisfy me," remarked Judge O'Neall of South Carolina in 1853, "that the first law of slavery is that of kindness from the master to the slave . . . slavery becomes a family relation, next in its attachments to that of parent and child."

To understand the Southern law of slavery, then, you could not look at the lawbooks but instead had to observe the actual ways of the community. The defense of slavery becomes more and more a defense of the unwritten law, the immanent law, the ways which dwelt in the going Southern society, or as it was sometimes said, in the Southern Way of Life.

The South then came to idealize the unwritten law, which was said to be the only proper law for a Christian society, an ennobling influence on all who allowed themselves to be ruled by it. Just as slavery made it possible for the relations between superior and inferior to be governed in this fashion, so too a code of "honor" made it possible for relations among equals to be similarly governed. And the gentlemen of the Southern ruling class spurned the letter of the law which, in the Southern states as elsewhere, forbade the duel and punished it as homicide. They actually made resort to the duel (the "code of honor") a symbol of their respect for the immanent as against the instrumental law of the community. In the South, in the half-century before the Civil War, there was hardly a leader in public life who had not fought a duel. Much as a war record nowadays attests a man's high devotion to his community, and is supposed to help qualify him for public office, so in those days, having fought an "affair of honor" proved a gentleman to be a "man of honor," for it showed that he held the immanent law of the society above its petty explicit rules.

The Southern defense of its immanent law, of the actual rules by which the South lived, against the attacks by literal-minded casual travelers and bookish Northerners who judged all societies by their written rules—this itself became a defense of the Southern Way of Life. Southerners were increasingly holistic and mystical in their praise of their institutions. Southern Ways, they declared, fitted together so neatly and so subtly that one dared not jar them by tinkering with the explicit rules.

Southerners became social narcissists. What were the proper virtues of any society, what were the laws by which any society should be ruled? Look at the South and you would see. Not at the rules in books, or the statutes passed by legislatures, or the decisions of judges (there were precious few of these anyway), but at the society itself, at how it actually worked. The proper laws of the South, it was said again and again, dwelt in the actual ways of the South. For the laws of its society the South came more and more to look in the mirror.

The consequences of this increasingly intransigent, increasingly narrow, increasingly inward and tautologous way of looking at law were, of course, to be far-reaching. They were tragic for the nation, and still remain tragic for the South. But we need not follow them out in detail to see that the South had developed an extreme and uncompromising belief in the immanence of law. The Southerners, we might say, had developed an odd kind of social Quakerism. The Quakers were a "peculiar people" (so they called themselves); the Southerners lived by their "peculiar institution." The Quakers lived by a law which dwelt in each individual and against which there could be no proper appeal to statute books, legislatures, or law courts. The Southerners too lived by a law which dwelt in their society and against which they believed there could be no appeal. Both societies had chosen to live by an immanent law: unwritten, inarticulate, untechnical, and unbending.

## III. LEGAL IMMANENCE: THE FEDERAL CONSTITUTION AND THE FOUR FREEDOMS

Belief in the immanence of law runs deep in our American tradition. In the story of the development of our institutions, what distinguishes both the Quakers of Colonial Pennsylvania and the ante-bellum Southerners is not their belief in some form of legal immanence but the extreme and intransigent shape of their belief.

A striking feature of our history is how few examples we offer of individuals or communities embracing a radically instrumental theory of law. Jeremy Bentham, therefore, is one of the most un-American of English thinkers. Few nations have legislated more than the United States, or put more faith in legislation; few have put less faith in any explicit theory of legislation. Traditional legal learning has sometimes been overvalued here because of its scarcity, but it has generally commanded the same naïve respect accorded to all ancient lineages in raw countries.

In this New World, where men have so often boasted of their opportunity to make a New Beginning, movements to codify or new-fashion laws have made surprisingly little headway. In the early nineteenth century, which was an age of codes and radical legislation in Western Europe, we were making constitutions and elaborating an American common law. Even in England, much of the legal history of the nineteenth century can be written around movements self-consciously to change society by using law as a tool; in the twentieth century there have been triumphs of intricate and subtle codification, like the Real Property Act of 1928. But in the United States, while we have codified some of our procedure and made some headway toward Uniform State Laws, even in this century our distinctive contributions have been our modest efforts to draw the private law together and to make it accessible rather than boldly to reshape it to serve new social needs. Perhaps our most distinctive contributions have been our extralegal devices for indexing, key-numbering, and collecting cases. Our great twentieth-century effort to reformulate the law has produced informal "restatements" rather than sweeping revisions or codifications.

We have been a nation, then, of many laws, but of few law reforms. The circumstances of our American Revolution had encouraged belief that the laws of our nation were not malleable instruments to attain specific social purposes but were part of our very being. We inherited a legal system which was brought here in the very minds of the settlers. We had no self-conscious "reception" of the common law comparable to that which agitated the European continent. Our legal theory could thus remain impressively inarticulate, while Continental legal thinkers asked again and again how laws could be used to serve social ends. What, they asked, was the proper relation between law and society? What were the healthiest roots of laws?

Savigny and Jhering remained even more exotic than Bentham; to this day they are hardly known among American lawyers. Here there was no widespread open battle between legal systems. Our battle was only among jurisdictions. Our common law had come with us. Since no conscious act of adoption or acceptance was ever needed, we continued to see a certain inevitability about our whole system of law. The common law and its tradition of constitutionalism seemed part of the very fiber of our social being. We embraced the Blackstonian view (which in England even by the time of our Revolution was coming to seem obsolete) that the common law was a providential embodiment of Reason and Nature. We inherited a great legal literature, which summed up the general rules without our ever having been required to make those rules, or even to make the effort of "discovering" them.

One symptom of the relatively minor role we have given legislation as an instrument for social change is the extraordinary importance we have given to constitutions. What Willard Hurst calls our tradition of "constitution worship" has embodied the still deeper tradition that our laws must somehow be the expressers rather than the shapers of our society.

American tradition has, of course, given a mystic role to the framers of the Federal Constitution. They have been adored for what we suppose to have been a declaratory rather than a creative act. Again and again we have held that they surely revealed the innermost spirit of the new American nation and embodied it in words.

"The system is no invention of man," a nineteenth-century writer observed, "is no creation of the [Constitutional] convention, but is given us by Providence in the living constitution of the American people." The merit of the statesmen of 1787 is that they did not destroy or deface the work of Providence but accepted it and organized the government in harmony with the real order, the real elements given them. They suffered themselves in all their positive substantial work to be governed by reality, not by theories and speculations.

When Justice Samuel F. Miller of the Supreme Court spoke in 1887 at the centennial celebration of the framing of the Federal Constitution, he recalled George Bancroft's description of the last hours of the Convention: "The members were awestruck at the results of their councils, the Constitution was a nobler work than anyone of them had believed possible to achieve." Justice Miller himself expressed his satisfaction that the Constitution had originally been intended to establish a truly national government. This tradition, of course, continues. W. W. Crosskey's weighty *Politics and the Constitution* (1953) again aims to prove that the providential foresight of the framers envisioned precisely the kind of national government which was most convenient to handle the problems of the national economy under Franklin Delano Roosevelt.

For us, the idea of a constitution—a fundamental law which in some strange way is less changeable than the ordinary instruments of legislation—has had a peculiar therapeutic attraction. Since 1776, there have been over two hundred state conventions to adopt or revise constitutions. Yet we have seldom amended our Federal Constitution and it remains the oldest working written constitution in the Western world. We retain an incurable belief that constitutions are born but not made, and this despite the carelessness, prolixity, crudity, and proven ineptitude of many of our state constitutions.

The two great armed conflicts on our soil, the American Revolution and the Civil War, were both victories for legal orthodoxy, for traditional legal doctrines—at least according to the victors. We have a remarkable continuity in our political and legal history. Any decisive innovations in our institutions (for example, those induced by the Depression of 1929) have sooner or later been hallowed by the Supreme Court. The Court certifies that the laws required by newly emerging problems somehow were implied and authorized in the very charter of our national existence. The continuous power and dignity of the Supreme Court makes the Court a distinctive American embodiment of belief in the immanence of our laws. Despite everything, we insist on believing that what the Court does is not to make the law but to declare it: not *jus dare* but *jus dicere.*

Never yet have we experienced a forcible deflection of our national institutions by arms, by *coup d'état,* or the seizure of power by one party or one class. Thus we have never really been jolted into seeing laws as the mere instruments of power. But in this, as in so many other ways, the South has been an exception.

Since the earliest years of the twentieth century events on the international scene have pushed us as a nation toward an increasing belief in legal immanence. More and more we have come to believe that a nation's laws are not mere instruments toward ends but are themselves essential to the character of the society, inseparable from the society, an indwelling expression of a nation's purposes.

This movement toward a wider belief in the oneness of a society's laws with its ends is illustrated by the contrast between our stated national objectives in World War I and in World War II. There is a striking contrast between the kind of objectives stated by President Woodrow Wilson in his Fourteen Points (Annual Address to Congress, January 8, 1918) and those stated by President Franklin Delano Roosevelt in his Four Freedoms (Annual Address to Congress, January 6, 1941). President Wilson itemized a number of objectives on the international scene. These were quite specific political and economic readjustments —for example, reduction of armaments, the impartial settlement of colonial claims, the evacuation of Russia, the restoration of Belgium, the freeing of invaded portions of France, the adjustment of the frontiers of Italy, the autonomy of the peoples of Austria-Hungary, etc. Such objectives required laws for their accomplishment, but the objectives were plainly separate from the laws.

President Roosevelt's Four Freedoms speech, on the other hand, described perils to "the democratic way of life," which was "assailed in every part of the world." His "four essential human freedoms"—freedom of speech and expression, freedom of every person to worship God in his own way, freedom from want, and freedom from fear—were called way-of-life objectives. They were not political aims to be attained by legal tools. Rather the aims themselves were as much legal as political. A nation's laws now were the touchstone. Laws were assumed to be not a mere instrument but the primary expression of its way of life. From the American point of view the conflict was between law-loving, law-fearing societies, and others.

In the three decades after our entry into World War I, leading Americans had ceased to believe that on the international scene the United States was concerned merely with the preservation of a political system. What had to be defended, we heard again and again, was a "Way of Life." The terrors of totalitarian democracies—of dictatorships which actually could claim to express the will of the majority of their people—revealed that the mere fact that a government represented a current majority was no guarantee of decency or of respect for human rights. Only slowly did Americans abandon the political fallacy. They hung on to their belief—which many have not yet abandoned—that if a government outraged decency then, *ex hypothesi,* it could not express the will of the majority of its people. But it has lately dawned on more and more of us that political democracy is only one element and not enough in itself to insure decent institutions. Way of life means much more. It includes a society's laws, and its attitude toward its laws. The traditional American distrust of legal instrumentalism has been expressed anew in a popular antipathy to "isms": fear of any concept of society that would abstract and dogmatize national objectives, and then use its laws as mere tools to those ends.

## IV. TEMPTATIONS TO A MIRROR VIEW

As I remarked at the outset, the balance between legal immanence and legal instrumentalism is the mysterious balance of law in society. It is one of the subtlest problems of every age. We face it once again in our time—in the pressures all around us to believe that force successfully exerted by small groups within our society must be accepted as law.

We have seen that the kind of immanence which people find in the law, and which can satisfy their belief that the law is not arbitrary or purely instrumental, varies a great deal. It is far too narrow to identify this belief exclusively with natural law or with a belief in God. In the Soviet Union, and perhaps in other communist countries, it seems possible for people to have this satisfaction of a belief in legal immanence by seeing their laws as a manifestation of rules indwelling in history, as expounded in the gospel according to Marx, Lenin, Stalin, and their followers. In Nazi Germany, people secured it by belief in a racial destiny, an indwelling "law of the folk"—expounded by the gospel according to Hitler, Rosenberg, and Goebbels. We are too ready from our provincial point of view to view totalitarianism as a barefaced unhallowed instrumentalism, in which rulers use the law for their own ends. But this is not how such systems look to their supporters, from the inside. These peoples have not given up the need to find some immanence—some transcendental-indwelling validity in their laws. Rather they find forms of immanence unfamiliar to us. We have yet to see a government that has ruled a society effectively without providing its people with some persuasive way of believing that their laws come from some higher, deeper, indwelling source.

In the United States the kind of belief in immanence which has been growing in the last half-century bears, superficially at least, some discomfiting similarities to that which I have described in the Southern states before the Civil War. Although the content is very different, the formal character of the beliefs and some of the surrounding circumstances are quite comparable. Our belief in legal immanence has arisen out of a dominant—one might almost say fetishistic—belief in the peculiar virtue and perfection of political democracy as we know it, and as it is practiced in the United States. And *our* belief, too, has been a kind of response to outside attack. In order to strengthen ourselves against the threat of communist conspiracy and totalitarian subversion we take a holistic view. While Southerners came to see the institution of slavery as the lifeblood of all social good, nourishing the peculiar virtues of political, social, economic, and cultural life in the South, so we see our institution of political democracy informing our political, social, economic, and cultural life. Just as the Southerners saw a peril, not only to their political system and their economy, but to their own Way of Life, so with us. With the increase of Northern threats the intransigence of Southern belief in themselves and their peculiar institution hardened. Their belief in immanence was expressed in their faith in a law which was unwritten, untechnical, and unbending. And so is ours.

I have characterized the ante-bellum Southern belief in immanence as a tendency toward "social narcissism." The society came to worship itself. Reform movements virtually disappeared. Southern thinkers came to confuse sociology with social morality. They looked into the mirror to see what they should be. Certain tendencies in American life today suggest that we too are in danger of finding our immanence in the mirror, being tempted to allow brute power, wherever displayed or threatened, to become the measure of law.

In the last half-century, the predominant fact of intellectual history shaping our thinking about law and society has been the rise of the social sciences and the idea of social science. Only two decades ago courses in sociology in our better colleges were still entitled "The Prevention of Poverty." They were primarily concerned with such topics as crime, delinquency, and "the social evil." But nowadays sociology is concerned with "techniques of social control," the structure of society, the functions of cities, and the roles of social classes and races. The study of government has become "political science"; political economy has become the "science of economics." Even history has become more and more social-scientific. *An American Dilemma: The Negro Problem and Modern Democracy,* a collaborative work in social sciences by Gunnar Myrdal and many others, was published in 1944. The unanimous Supreme Court decision declaring racial segregation in the public schools unconstitutional came exactly ten years later, in 1954. The "future" which Justice Holmes in his "Path of the Law" (1897) predicted would belong to "the man of statistics and the master of economics"—that future has now arrived.

The conviction grows—and is expressed in the curricula of our best law schools—that the lawyer must not only know law. He must know the facts of life, the facts of our society, the laws of social behavior inherent in society itself. Only recently have we begun to act on the truism that one cannot know society's laws without knowing the society. There are obviously many advantages, for the lawyer, and for the society.

But with this belief comes the tendency to find the immanence of the law in the supposedly inevitable tendencies of the society itself. It has often been remarked that Justice Holmes's description of the object of legal study as "prediction, the prediction of the incidence of the public force through the instrumentality of the courts," while helpful to the practicing lawyer, is not very useful to the legislator, the citizen, or the social scientist trying to decide how legal development should be directed. The great danger of the social-science emphasis in the training of lawyers, the great danger of finding the immanence of our law in the very processes of our society is that we should make law into tautology. The predictive theory of law could lead us to make all our society's laws nothing but self-fulfilling prophecies. Obviously, our laws cannot ignore the facts of our social life, but they must do more than merely reflect them. Intelligent citizens cannot be guided by what their opinion polls tell them is their opinion.

We suffer ever stronger temptations to social narcissism. In a beleaguered world we are even more tempted to be satisfied that our laws should reflect a society which we define as *ex hypothesi* good. But to do so is to deprive our laws of the normative role which, in the common-law tradition, has made them a bulwark for each generation against the specious urgencies of its own age.

One of the most difficult problems in our society today is to get a message in from the outside. We believe in our power to make ourselves. The more we see our laws as a reflection of norms indwelling in current social practice, pressures, and disorders, the more we deprive ourselves of an opportunity to make law a means of communication between the past and the present. For this purpose the preservation of a tradition of professionalism, of technicality, is essential. Here we must more than ever rely on what Coke—against the arbitrary James I, the amateur lawyer who said he knew all he needed to know of the law—said was not natural reason but "the artificial reason and judgment of the law, which law is an art which requires long study and experience, before that a man can attain to the cognizance of it."

## V. LAW AS PROPAGANDA

The temptations to tautology, to a mirror view of the law, to a doctrine of immanence which finds the purposes and forms of the law in the most pressing needs of our own day, are increased by the pressures we feel from abroad. Our temptation is to make the social sciences a body of knowledge for fashioning the law into a better mirror of what our society already is. But the challenge of totalitarianism and the desire to confront the world with our "Way of Life" press us to make our law an instrument of propaganda.

The use of international trials, under cover of law, as an instrument of political persuasion and diplomacy is an example. Such trials are a peculiar feature of our age. After World War II, the "War Crimes Trials"—designed, among other things, to dramatize our Way of Life and contrast it with totalitarian ways—made law into propaganda.

When future generations read the proceedings of the Nuremberg Trials, where the criminals were prosecuted by a Justice of the United States Supreme Court who had stepped down from his bench specifically for this purpose and where the accused were adjudged by representatives of the victorious powers, it is doubtful if they will see it as a triumph of law. Although the background in each case was of course very different, and the truth of the charges varied vastly, it is more likely that the War Crimes Trials of 1946 will be classed with the Reichstag Fire Trial (1933–1934), the so-called Trial of the Trotskyite-Zinovievite Terrorist Center (1936), the Moscow Trials of the "Anti-Soviet 'Bloc of Rights and Trotskyites'" (1938), the Japanese War Crimes Trials (1946–1948), and the Eichmann Trial (1961) as examples of use of the forms of legality for political and propaganda purposes. The readiness of a country like Israel to use kidnaping to bring international criminals before the bar of "legality" illustrates where the modern propagandistic use of law can lead us. We move toward an unalloyed legal instrumentalism, in the name of a higher law.

Our position before the world makes it increasingly difficult for us to satisfy our need for an immanent law without giving in to the temptations to make our law unwritten, untechnical, and unbending. How can we satisfy our need to find immanence in our law without making it a mere name for lawlessness? Our lawyers can help by perpetuating their professional esprit and their pride of specialized knowledge. But here is also a problem for the laymen. Every society is apt to think too well of itself, to exaggerate its urgencies against the claims which the past has on it, or the debt it owes to the future. How can our society find and preserve that mysterious balance between the implicit and the explicit, the immanent and the instrumental, which our legal tradition requires of us? Only such a balance can preserve our tradition of a society ruled by law.

# VIOLENCE, MORALITY, AND REVITALIZATION

Anthony F. C. Wallace

In the literature on revitalization movements, it has repeatedly been noted that such movements, at the outset optimistic of achieving social and cultural reform by peaceful persuasion, often fall into a position of violent confrontation with an established system. Superficially it is easy to explain away the violent outcome either as the inevitable consequence of an irreconcilable conflict of interests, or as a result of the overly rigid or even paranoid character of either the visionary reformers or the blindly repressive conservatives. But a more complex process is often—perhaps usually—involved, and it is by this process that non-violent confrontation is transformed into revolutionary and counterrevolutionary violence.

I have observed that a large part of military violence is impersonal, in the sense that those wreaking destruction on a foreign enemy are mobilized by a sense of duty to the institutions of their own society and by a feeling of loyalty to the members of their own group rather than by any personal hatred of those whom they coerce, injure, or kill. Domestic violence is another matter, for it is more apt to be motivated by personal animosities. But in both situations violence rarely if ever occurs in a moral vacuum. To the contrary: one may speak of a moral structure of violence, meaning that assembly of values and codes of conduct which define the proper means, objects, and occasions of violence, both domestic and international. The kinds of change in these moral structures which revitalization movements generally encourage, and the escalation of fearful fantasies of violence which these changes in turn entail, can be seen as the essential element in the process of transformation to violence.

## MORAL STRUCTURES OF VIOLENCE

Every culture includes a set of rules for violence. These rules prescribe the weapons (including the parts of the body) which may be used, the injuries which may be inflicted, the persons who may attack or be attacked, and the provocations which justify, or even require, the threat or actual use of force. In our society, such rules are embedded in a large mass of law and of explicitly recognized custom and these in turn in a still larger mass of values and beliefs. These values and beliefs relating to violence are endlessly explained, illustrated, and rationalized in popular literature, i.e., in newspapers, magazines, books, radio, and, of course, television, much of whose fictional and news fare is devoted to depicting violence interpreted in a context of folk morality. This literature answers, for both children and adults, such questions as When is it all right to kill someone? What kinds of people are dangerous because they may become violent without legitimate occasion? To whom can one turn for help when threatened with violence? What kinds of weapons are legitimate to use? The answers invoke rather simple abstract principles: It is all right to kill if someone is about to kill you, your kinfolk, or your friends; people who have been frustrated for a long time may suddenly become vicious; police and registered private investigators are usually helpful, but some of them turn bad; weapons which threaten mass destruction should not be used in domestic situations, even in a legitimate cause, because they can injure innocent bystanders, but they may be used in war; criminals should be brought to justice and if violence is needed to do it, then as much violence as is required should be used; and so on into the night.[1]

But the moral structure we have been talking about so far is the traditional structure. It is geared largely to the maintenance and defense of traditional values and traditional institutions. Groups critical of the established institutions are apt to advocate a moral structure of violence rather different, in certain ways, from that congenial to the conservative. This difference is apt to take the form of sanctioning certain types of non-compliance with law or custom, and even of violence to property and to persons who occupy official positions, on the grounds of tactical necessity in the movement to change society for the better. Some kinds of violence which are acceptable in tradition and law, as threats or even in application, are defined as hypocritical or even criminal because their net effect is to help to maintain a social system defined as iniquitous.

The difference in the kinds of moral structure surrounding the ideas of violence promulgated by the "System" and the "Movement" is not merely a matter of detail. It is a difference that approaches the distinction between two ideal types of morality which I shall call procedural morality and teleological morality. I suggest that this difference is characteristic of the contrast between the morality of the existing order and the morality of revitalization in any culture; but I shall speak largely of our own society. The distinction, too, probably applies to other domains of moral concern than the structure of violence alone; but I shall largely confine my discussion to the issue of force and the threat of force.

## PROCEDURAL MORALITY

The premise of the conservative position, in contrast to that of the revitalization movement, is that human wants, including justice (however it may be locally defined), can in principle be achieved by or for everyone if everyone follows procedures already available or implied in the culture. Hence, following proper procedure is morally justified by the virtue of the ends to which it is the efficient means. Some modification, of course, will be needed from time to time (in fact, tinkering with institutions by "reorganizing" may be a standard procedure), and application must be flexible enough to meet local contingencies. But if something is wrong, it is basically because someone did the wrong thing: the procedures, including procedures for procedural modification, have not been properly followed. To follow correct procedure is not merely the responsibility of the individual in attempting to satisfy his own wants; it is also the responsibility of each individual with whom he interacts. And responsibility for the consequences of failure to follow proper procedure is individual not collective.

This being the case, great moral importance attaches to "doing things right." "Doing things right" is not, in this point of view, a matter of filling out forms correctly in six bureaucratic copies or of meticulous observance of empty religious ritual, although these exercises may be a part of it. It is essentially a feeling of responsibility for keeping things going: taking care of equipment, seeing that the traffic moves, keeping lines of communication open, not killing game out of season, ensuring that the city water supply is adequate, and so on. All this is felt to be *important*. Similarly important is the use of correct procedure in matters involving violence—and this means the legal system. Aggrieved persons ought not to "take the law into their own hands" but complain to proper authorities; they should not express generalized resentment by peculiarities of speech, dress, grooming, or manner; and the authorities must follow proper procedures in turn in order to ensure that no one is subjected to violence who is innocent. "Due process" must be followed.

In our society the conservative position (if I read it correctly) is that any failure to follow proper procedure injures, or threatens, the interests of others who are following the rules. Furthermore, such injury is apt to ramify among its victims in unanticipated ways. And still further, if the initial violation is not immediately detected and either punished or corrected, it may tempt the violator, or those who observe him, into repetition and into even more serious violations. Thus, the acceptable rationalization for the continuance of stringent sanctions against the use of marijuana is that it leads to the use of more and more dangerous and expensive drugs by more and more people; it is viewed as the portal, relatively innocuous in itself, to a series of increasingly serious violations by an increasingly large number of persons. Paralleling the conception that a seemingly trivial misdeed may have terrifying functional consequences is the principle that in the apprehension and punishment of the offender, no matter how minor his initial misdemeanor, any amount of force, including the use of lethal weapons, may in graduated steps be applied. Thus, a person who receives a ticket for parking five minutes overtime is at the threshold of a possible sequence of situations of increasing gravity. If he fails to plead guilty and pay the three dollars, he may receive a summons; if then he fails to plead guilty and pay the fine and court costs, a warrant may be issued for his arrest; if he thoughtlessly runs from the policeman who comes to arrest him (perhaps eighteen months later), he may be chased, told to stop, and if he fails to stop, he may be shot, charged with resisting arrest, jailed . . . and so on.

In view of the large number of petty regulations of which anyone may run afoul, much is overlooked by everyone and the horrifying escalations of misdemeanor and retributive violence are relatively rare (although no doubt not uncommon). But the fact that they are considered to be possible and do in fact occur is a reflection, perhaps, of an accurate folk awareness of the functional interdependence of the elements of custom in society. It is not entirely naïve to ask, when the wisdom of some police practice like chasing speeding cars is questioned, "What if everyone did this?" Procedural morality thus sees even minor violations as *in principle* invalidating the customary rights of others in domains of experience far removed from that of the violation, not so much by the possible ramifying effects of a single act, as by setting a precedent which, if followed, would entail serious changes in structure. Such issues are given very formal expression in the concept of due process in court procedure, but they are just as basic at humbler levels. The enraged traffic officer scolding a motorist who turns left in the face of a "No Left Turn" sign is correct in pointing out to the offending driver that if everyone drove like him, no one could drive at all. Massive disregard of traffic signs and driving regulations would indeed probably lead to an increased frequency of accidents, and certainly to such massive traffic jams in urban areas that the transportation systems of whole cities would be rendered completely non-operative in their present form. Not only would no cars move, but no trucks or surface trolley cars would move either, and passengers would be unable to get to railroad stations and bus terminals and airports to use other means of transport.

Furthermore, the functional argument is present even when it is not expressed. The anthropologist's informant who, when asked why a certain custom is followed, answers, "Because we've always done it this way" is giving a very good answer. The consequences of doing it any other way, or of not doing it at all, are often difficult to calculate, and the function of the custom furthermore may have changed since earlier times, so that the formal rationalization is not really relevant any more. The best reason for retaining, let us say, the rule for driving on the right hand side of the road, or a non-metric system of weights and measures, or the seven-day week, is indeed that we've always done it this way, that we have to have *some* standard way, and that changing it will probably lead to all sorts of unanticipated undesirable consequences.

But no one will argue—not even most revolutionaries—about things like traffic rules and weights and measures and other customs of public places (provided they are fairly enforced), and hence they come most easily to mind when arguing the case for procedural morality. Argument is more apt to center on the merits of the morality when it concerns economic matters, administrative structures, human relations, and private behavior. But the procedural moralist is perfectly consistent: the same kind of explication is applied here too. It is always the *consequence* of the violation, whether in its ramifications in the individual case or in the invalidation of the customary procedures of other people, that is invoked.

A procedural morality easily takes a view of alien customs as perverse or criminal (and again, in a sense, with reason). Just as a violation of his own custom is condemned because of its functional consequences, as if it were an alternate custom, so an alien custom, disfunctional (in his view, at least) in his own culture, is quite properly defined as wrong. In a sense, then, the procedural moralist lives in a world of custom alternatives, of which some are moral because they fit, and others are immoral because they don't fit, into an ideal functional model of the system.

It should not be supposed that the procedural moralist is in principle opposed to change in procedure. Indeed, he is accustomed to think in terms of possible cultural alternatives and he condemns violations of procedure in large part because he thinks of them as alternate customs whose functional consequences are undesirable. And he is also used to asking whether existing customs may not have undesirable consequences, and to weighing the merits of modifications, deletions, and substitutions. But the process of decision is apt to be slow and agonizing because it must involve elaborate step-by-step consideration of possible functional consequences in a complex social and cultural system which is not fully understood by anyone.

## TELEOLOGICAL MORALITY

The members of revitalization movements—groups who seek to establish a new and more satisfying culture in place of an old, evil way of life—may initially have been conscientious procedural moralists disillusioned with the existing system because they observed too many instances in which procedures were not followed. Eventually they have come to believe that even when correctly followed the procedures are at least selectively advantageous to some and disadvantageous to others, or even damaging to all. But the transformation from outraged conservative to ardent revolutionary requires more than this: it requires a shift in moral emphasis from the process to the goal. The goals, indeed, may not really change much; the conservative and the revitalizer generally say that they are in favor of the same obviously good things like human love, social justice, freedom, education, material comfort, self-fulfillment, peace, brotherhood, mental health, and so forth. But, having lost confidence in due process, the revitalizer now is convinced that the traditional due process itself is responsible for preventing the realization of these aims. His moral conversation therefore focuses on asserting and defining the importance of these goals, and *any* process which will bring them nearer becomes legitimate; the end not merely justifies the means, the end morally requires means adequate to its achievement. Furthermore, he sees responsibility—and guilt—as collective rather than individual because it is the system itself which is at fault.

Violence, then, in the short term is justified for the movement by the end it seeks rather than by its procedural legitimacy. But in the long term, the movement generally looks forward to a new, stable order in which, it is fondly hoped, a new system will be perfected and in which accordingly a procedural morality will be required. The movement thus is, as it were, an uneasy phase of revolutionary teleological morality sandwiched between an old procedural morality which it defines as immoral, and a new procedural morality for which the rules have not yet, except for the procedural morality of combat groups, been established (and which, furthermore, once established, will become at once conservative).

Like the procedural moralist, the teleological moralist sees the conventions of society as an intricate functional fabric which will begin to unravel if a thread is cut anywhere. But this awareness leads not to a cautious and slow step-by-step surgical procedure but to enthusiastic assault on any vulnerable part in the hope of setting in motion a general disintegration. The tactics by which these attacks are mounted are not viewed so much as alternate customs which the revolutionary moralist views as inherently desirable. The revolutionary rarely recommends blowing up buildings, burning books, assassinating enemies, and disrupting traffic as the way of life to which his movement aspires;

he is not likely to feel that human dialogue should be permanently couched in a language of insult and threat. He may even have some admiration for certain components of the system which he is bent on destroying and he may proceed with the task of destruction with private feelings of regret for the pain and inconvenience which it is necessary for him to cause. Furthermore, he may even experience a sense of outrage that his opponents, loyal to the old system, are less pure in their own procedural morality than they ought, by their own standards, to be —and not merely because these betrayals of convention may be threatening to him.

But the teleological moralist must take the view, in contrast to that of the proceduralist, that the new fabric of convention has to be rewoven all at once, rather than be changed strand after strand. Where the conservative is afraid that violation may become alien new custom, and that new custom even if sanctioned may work the same ills as traditional violations, the revolutionary leaps beyond the difficulty of change and postulates that only a whole new pattern of procedures, instituted in accordance with a plan, all at once, will obviate the distressing difficulties of piecemeal transformation.

Furthermore, the teleological moralist even while he is functioning within the old system (which is, in fact, what he does most of the time) attends less to the merely possible ill effects of procedural change than to what he regards as the presently inevitable ill effects of conventional rightness. If he looks at the traffic control situation, he perceives that it can in fact be used as a device for selectively harassing and restricting the movements of members of minority groups. If he looks at a mental hospital, he sees that the patient with family, education, and money can be treated and released—or even saved from incarceration—while the disturbed individual without these advantages is unable to use available procedures to protect himself from loss of civil and social rights.

In modern society, at least—and perhaps to a greater extent in traditional societies than one might think—the individual's welfare depends upon the errorless performance of a complex chain of procedures in any link of which an error may occur. Such errors—unintended violations of procedure by man or machine—can have disastrous consequences. An IBM card puncher's error, checking the wrong box on a personnel form, delay in the mails, a mistaken diagnosis, misunderstood legal advice, and so forth and so on can plunge student, employee, welfare recipient, taxpayer—anyone at all—into a crisis which if not quickly resolved may have serious consequences. To the procedural moralist, error is regrettable but unavoidable; to the teleological moralist, in a sense, such error is an attribute of the system and because it is discriminatory it is as much a fault as an accident. Such errors probably do, in fact, injure the poorer, the less educated, and the more isolated individual, even without design, for he has fewer resources with which to examine the situation, locate the mistake, and ensure that it is corrected.

It is in the moral analysis of error, indeed, that the teleologist reaches the extreme of ramifying suspiciousness which the proceduralist achieves in the analysis of minor intentional violation. Whereas the proceduralist views violation as the gateway to catastrophic innovation (and comes therefore to fear innovation itself), the teleologist sees error as an inherent mechanism by which the system prevents its victims (social classes, or ethnic and religious, or the aged, or the young) from realizing the ends to which the system professes its procedures are adequate means. At the pure and paranoid extremes, the proceduralist fears that if anyone is allowed to "get away with" anything, the whole world will crumble, and the teleologist fears that he individually may be destroyed "accidentally on purpose" by a malevolent system.

## THE CLIMATE OF VIOLENCE

Most of the time, most people cannot be really pigeonholed as pure proceduralists or pure teleologists; we generally alternate stances depending on personal interests, circumstances, mood, and affiliation. The conservative businessman, confronted by a tangle of governmental regulations, may feel that the System is trying to ruin him personally; and the angry militant, unable to maintain discipline in his column of the Movement, may at times despair of reaching utopia with such a band of irresponsibles. But there are times when, with respect to the major institutions of the society, people do tend to identify themselves with one moral attitude or the other. It is at such times that issues of violence come to the fore of conscious moral attention.

Once a moral confrontation between the System and the Movement has been realized by both groups, a climate of violence is almost certain to develop, irrespective of peaceful professions on both sides. On the Movement side, this climate is often nourished by the apocalyptic world-destruction fantasies of a prophet and his disciples, by the destructive aim of the Movement with regard to old institutions, and by the fear of retaliation by an already punitive System which will even abandon its own procedural morality in order to destroy its enemies. On the System's side, the fear of being destroyed by self-righteous opponents who seem intent on wrecking what they do not understand, who have publicly declared their refusal to accept the traditional procedural morality, and whose professions of brotherly love are belied by the bellicose assaults which they launch whenever their solicitations to conversion are rejected, prompts the conservative to look to his defenses and to wonder whether he indeed may not temporarily have to abandon the old procedural morality as it applies to violence.

In such a climate as this, where the Movement denies the validity of traditional sanctions on violence and where the System is tempted to abandon them too, it becomes more difficult, and at the same time crucially important, for both participants and observers to evaluate private motives. In the traditional situation, motivation to violence is in a sense irrelevant, provided the procedures are scrupulously followed; if they are not followed, however, the evaluation of the act depends largely upon an evaluation of individual motives. In the climate of violence, where the traditional norms are suspended, it becomes necessary to judge the morality of private motives in terms of ultimate values, in order to estimate the desirability of the probable consequences of a person's acts, including violent acts. But even this has its dark side too, for on both sides it promotes a general suspiciousness and suggests tests of loyalty and the regulation of ordinarily private conduct, and spreads the lack of trust still further. Apprehension nourishes a proliferation of more or less bizarre fantasies of impending violent assault. There may occur, in this process of escalating distrust, a kind of flash point at which both groups perceive (often falsely) or anticipate a sudden increase in illegitimate violence. The conservative, who regards his own violence as legitimate, is frightened by the appearance of new and added forms of violence on the part of the Movement; these he regards as criminal. In opposition, the Movement member increasingly sees the use of force to preserve "law and order" as criminal and thus as an addition to the total amount of violence in the society, while at the same time he does not see his own acts as anything of the sort, since they are for him morally justified. When this climate of mutual apprehension of a sudden outbreak of unrestrained and illegitimate violence is reached, the groups are on the verge of war, where mobilization processes will take over and intergroup violence becomes impersonal.

## ILLUSTRATIONS

The climate of violence that is implicit in the revitalization situation, whether or not it culminates in organized revolution or civil war, can be readily illustrated in the records of well-known revitalization movements. I shall briefly mention relevant data about two such movements among American Indians: the new religion of Handsome Lake among the Iroquois and the Ghost Dance on the Plains.[2] The reader will, I think, be readily able to supply others from his own experience.

Handsome Lake's mission among the Iroquois lasted from

1799 until his death (which was murder by witchcraft, according to his followers, instigated by the relatives of a woman he had earlier executed for witchcraft) in 1815. He was known among the whites as the "Peace Prophet" because he opposed Indian involvement in the War of 1812. He sought to bring about a world of harmony and tranquility for the Indians, in which tribal factions and domestic quarrels would be unknown, and worked to suppress the use of alcohol, the practice of witchcraft, and the sale of land, which he felt were the principal obstacles to the achievement of this goal. But he believed that there was a conspiratorial establishment composed of witches, whiskey sellers, and drunken chiefs who were working to destroy the Indian people. Because their ceremonies contributed to the use of alcohol, he attempted to disband the traditional medicine societies, but in this he was unsuccessful. More significantly, he also attempted to suspend some of the traditional norms with regard to violence, assuming for himself the right to identify and condemn any and all witches, to demand confession, and if necessary to prescribe punishment, including death, at the hands of persons other than the witch's kinsmen.

Although few witches were actually killed, rumor soon had it that he was exterminating all of those opposed to his policies, whether or not they were really guilty of witchcraft, and his political pretensions were quickly rejected. The fearful fantasies of his political opponents were nourished by an atmosphere of violence that attended his reported visions: prognostications of a fiery end of the world, dire warnings of the subversive activities of the witches, and graphic descriptions of the bloody tortures waiting in hell for those who committed various sins and refused to confess, repent, and accept *Gaiwiio,* his message. But the critical instigation to violence was his handling of witchcraft. The old procedural morality in matters of suspected deaths by witchcraft was to discourage such accusations in the first place, on the grounds that the bereaved person's mind was not clear; if evidence were convincing, and the witch refused to confess, then to convince if possible some kinsmen of the witch to kill him, in order to prevent any possibility of a blood feud by aggrieved kinfolk who did not believe the charge. If kinsmen remained who could not be convinced, the witch could not comfortably be executed. By refusing to follow this principle, on the grounds of teleological morality, Handsome Lake left many members of the population feeling that they were exposed to arbitrary condemnation by a self-righteous self-appointed censor who was not interested in evidence beyond his own intuition and who would not recognize the protection normally given the innocent by their kin group. He nearly precipitated a real war between the Seneca and the Delaware Indians by insisting on a principle of collective guilt in a case of witchcraft which he personally had diagnosed. Some of the bitterness engendered by these violations of procedural morality has survived to this day, long after witchcraft has ceased to be a matter of major public concern.

The reverse problem—non-procedural violence by the System—occurred in the course of the development of the Ghost Dance among the Sioux. The Ghost Dance doctrine itself, as promulgated by the prophet Wovoka, did not advocate violence by Indians against each other or against whites. It urged upon the Indians simple, ultimate moral virtues like honesty and kindness and prescribed a dance ritual by which a person might in a vision see and speak with his beloved dead. But it did express moral indifference to white regulations, which were to be obeyed only as a matter of temporary convenience rather than as necessary means to important goals, and it did contain an apocalyptic theme—the imminent cataclysmic destruction of the existing world, and of most of the white people in it, and the return of the Indian dead to those who mourned them. Among the Sioux, as among many other tribes on new reservations, this doctrine was congenial. The Sioux were in the midst of profound internal dissension about the course of acculturation and about their relations with Indian agency and military personnel near their reservations in the Dakotas. The new religion looked forward to a time when the oppressions of the whites, and the divisions among themselves, would be suddenly and happily ended. Sioux inclined to resist white demands further interpreted the doctrine to mean that the whites would be powerless to injure them if they wore the accouterments of the Dance and that therefore they could with impunity violate normal procedures in relations with whites.

The whites, and Sioux who identified with white policy, however, responded more to the climate of violence implicit in the indifference to administrative regulations and in the apocalyptic theme of the Ghost Dance religion than to the actual peaceableness of the Ghost Dancers. Anticipating "trouble" from disaffected Ghost Dancers, Indian police first precipitated a gunfight at Sitting Bull's residence, in an effort to confiscate guns and arrest Sitting Bull. Later a cavalry regiment armed with Hotchkiss guns slaughtered several hundred men, women, and children who were on their way to surrender weapons and take up quarters near the Sioux agency. The provocation offered by the Indians at Wounded Knee was minimal and perhaps nonexistent; the murderous response by the surrounding troops was a clear breach of the procedural morality of the military, determined partly no doubt by a pervasive antipathy to Indians, but precipitated at that moment by the aura of anticipated illegitimate violence associated with the spread of the apocalyptic Ghost Dance doctrine.

## CONCLUSION

One of the ingredients of the revitalization situation is a loss of confidence in procedural morality and a consequent increased estimation of teleological morality. The abandonment of procedural morality by the Movement, however, arouses extreme anxiety in those who remain loyal to the System, and who value the procedural morality highly, since they feel that they can no longer predict what if any restraints on violence will be employed by their opponents, and they in turn tend to abandon procedure and to focus on ends rather than on means. This situation leads to a climate of violence in which both sides see the other as bent on illegitimate violence, in which a new procedural morality is undefined by the Movement and the old is being constantly abrogated by the System, and in which therefore mutual trust becomes difficult, since mere mutual professions or even a common teleological morality do nothing to provide a basis for cooperative action. To this climate of violence, the frequently apocalyptic character of revitalization fantasies also contributes. One is tempted to point out that even after mobilized warfare has developed, such different conceptions of morality remain to make negotiation for peace extremely difficult.

It is no doubt a perception of the danger inherent in permitting the climate of violence to develop which has led some leaders of revitalization movements to insist on non-violence, a tactic which permits only such violations of procedural morality which do not include physical assault and destruction. A complementary insistence by the System on strict adherence to its own procedural morality by police, courts, and the military has a similar purpose. Such devices, together with free communication of factual information to dispel at least gross fantasies of violence by "the other side," may hopefully combine to establish means for effecting change by negotiation and bargaining rather than by internal war. Mankind needs to find the cultural means for making violence unnecessary as a tactic for revitalization.

## NOTES

1. Whether this daily fare of fantasied violence also incites acts of violence is open to question; one doubts that crime in the streets, riots, and police brutality—or racism, poverty, and war either—would all disappear or even substantially decline if the television screens of America were given over to variety shows and domestic comedies. The high rates of certain kinds of violence in America are older than TV and grow from other sources than the character of popular drama. America is no different, indeed, from any other society, insofar as it attempts to express the moral structure of violence in law and literature. But in response to

widespread concern, the National Institute of Mental Health has appointed a committee to consider the possible relations between television and social behavior, including violence.

2. For more detailed description of these events, see James Mooney, *The Ghost Dance Religion and the Sioux Outbreak of 1890,* first published in 1896 and substantially reprinted in 1965 by the University of Chicago Press; and Anthony F. C. Wallace, *The Death and Rebirth of the Seneca:* New York, Knopf, 1970.

# THE RULE OF LAW VERSUS THE ORDER OF CUSTOM

## Stanley Diamond

CREON: Knowest thou the edict has forbidden this?
ANTIGONE: I knew it well. Why not? It was proclaimed.
CREON: But thou didst dare to violate the law?
ANTIGONE: It was not God above who framed that law,
Nor justice, whispering from the underworld,
Nor deemed I thy decrees were of such force
As to o'er ride the sanctities of heaven;
Which are not of today or yesterday.
From whom—whence they first issued, no one knows.
I was not like to scant their holy rites
And brave the even justice of the gods
For fear of someone's edict.

—SOPHOCLES, *Antigone*

The lowest police employee of the civilized state has more "authority" than all the organs of gentilism combined. But the mightiest prince and the greatest statesman or general of civilization may look with envy on the spontaneous and undisputed esteem that was the privilege of the least gentile sachem. The one stands in the middle of society, the other is forced to assume a position outside and above it.

—ENGELS, *Origin of the Family, Private Property and the State*

There's too much due process of law. The electric chair is a cheap crime deterrent to show these criminal elements that law and order is going to triumph.

—Detective Sergeant John Heffernan, current vice-president of the International Conference of Police Associations and head of the New Jersey State Police Benevolent Association

## I

We must distinguish the rule of law from the authority of custom. In a recent effort to do so (which I shall critically examine because it is so typical), Paul Bohannan contends, under the imprimateur of the *International Encyclopedia of the Social Sciences,*[1] that laws result from "double" institutionalization.* He means by this the lending of a specific force, a cutting edge to the functioning of "customary" institutions: marriage, the family, religion. But, he tells us, the laws so emerging assume a character and dynamic of their own. They form a structured legal dimension of society; they do not merely reflect, but interact with given institutions. Therefore, Bohannan is led to maintain that laws are typically out of phase with society and it is this process which is both a symptom and cause of social change. Thus, the laws of marriage, to illustrate Bohannan's argument with the sort of concrete example his definition lacks, are not synonymous with the institution of marriage. They reinforce certain rights and obligations while neglecting others. Moreover, they subject partners defined as truant to intervention by an external, impersonal agency whose decisions are sanctioned by the power of the police.

Bohannan's sociological construction *does* have the virtue of denying the primacy of the legal order, and of implying that law is generic to unstable (or progressive) societies, but it is more or less typical of abstract efforts to define the eternal essence of the law, and it begs the significant questions. Law has no such essence but a definable historical nature. Thus, if we inquire into the structure of the contemporary institutions, which according to Bohannan stand in a primary relation to the law, we find that their customary content has drastically diminished. Paul Radin made the point as follows: "A custom is in no sense a part of our properly functioning culture. It belongs definitely to the past. At best, it is moribund. But customs are an integral part of the life of primitive peoples. There is no compulsive submission to them. They are not followed because the weight of tradition overwhelms a man. . . . A custom is obeyed because it is intimately intertwined with a vast living network of interrelations, arranged in a meticulous and ordered manner. They are tied up with all the mechanisms used in government." [2] And, "What is significant in this connection," as J. G. Peristiany indicates, "is not that common values should exist, but that they should be expressed although no common political organization corresponds to them." [3] No contemporary institution functions with the kind of autonomy that permits us to postulate a significant dialectic between law and custom. We live in a law-ridden society; law has cannibalized the institutions which it presumably reinforces or with which it interacts.

Accordingly, morality continues to be reduced to or confused with legality. We tend to assume that legal behavior is the measure of moral behavior, and it is a matter of some interest that a former Chief Justice of the Supreme Court proposed, with the best of intentions, that a federal agency be established in order to advise government employees, and those doing business with the government, concerning the legal/ethical propriety of their behavior. Any conflict of interest not legally enjoined would thus become socially or morally acceptable. These efforts to legislate conscience by an external political power are the antithesis of custom: customary behavior comprises precisely those aspects of social behavior which are traditional, moral, and religious, which are, in short, conventional and nonlegal. Put another way, custom *is* social morality.[4] The relation between custom and law is, basically, one of contradiction, not continuity.

The customary and the legal orders are historically, not logically related. They touch coincidentally; one does not imply the other. Custom, as most anthropologists agree, is characteristic of primitive society, and laws of civilization. Robert Redfield's dichotomy between the primitive "moral order" and the civilized "legal" or "technical" order remains a classic statement of the case.

"The dispute," writes William Seagle, "whether primitive societies have law or custom, is not merely a dispute over words. Only confusion can result from treating them as interchangeable phenomena. If custom is spontaneous and automatic, law is the product of organized force. Reciprocity is in force in civilized communities too but at least nobody confuses social with formal legal relationships." [5] Parenthetically, one should note that students of primitive society who use the term "customary law" blur the issue semantically, but nonetheless recognize the distinction.

It is this overall legalization of behavior in modern society which Bohannan slights. In fascist Germany, for example, laws flourished as never before. By 1941, more edicts had been proclaimed than in all the years of the Republic and the Third Reich. At the same time, ignorance of the law inevitably increased. In a sense, the very force of the law depends upon ignorance of its specifications, which is hardly recognized as a mitigating circumstance. As Seagle states, law is not definite and certain while custom is vague and uncertain. Rather, the converse holds. Customary rules must be clearly known; they are not sanctioned by organized political force, hence serious disputes about the nature of custom would destroy the integrity of society. But laws may always be invented, and stand a good chance of being enforced: "Thus, the sanction is far more important than the rule in the legal system . . . but the tendency is to minimize the sanction and to admire the rule." [6]

In fascist Germany, customs did not become laws through a process of "double institutionalization." Rather, repressive laws, conjured up in the interests of the Nazi party and its supporters, cannibalized the institutions of German society. Even the residual customary authority of the family was assaulted: children were encouraged to become police informers, upholding the laws against their kin. "The absolute reign of law has often been synonymous with the absolute reign of lawlessness." [7] Certainly, Germany under Hitler was a changing society, if hardly a progressive one, but it was a special case of the general process in civilization through which the organs of the state have become increasingly irresistible. It will be recalled that Bohannan takes law as opposed to custom to be symptomatic of changing societies. But the historical inadequacy of his argument is exactly here: he does not intimate the overall direction of that change and therefore fails to clarify the actual relation between custom and law. Accordingly, the notion that social change is a function of the law, and vice versa, implies a dialectic that is out of phase with *historical* reality.

Plato understood this well enough when he conceived the problem of civilization as primarily one of *injustice,* which he did not scant by legalistic definition. His remedy was the thorough restructuring of society. Whether we admire his utopia or not, the *Republic* testifies to Plato's recognition that laws follow social change and reflect prevailing social relationships but are the cause of neither.

Curiously, this view of the relationship between law and society accords with the Marxist perspective on the history of culture. Customary societies are said to precede legal societies, an idea which, semantics aside, most students of historical jurisprudence would accept. But Marxists envision the future as being without laws as we know them, as a return to custom, so to speak, on a higher level, since the repressive and punitive functions of law will become superfluous. Conflicts of economic and political interest will be resolved through the equitable reordering of institutions. Law for the Marxists and most classic students of historical jurisprudence is the cutting edge of the state—but the former, insisting on both a historical and normative view of man, define the state as the instrument of the ruling class, anticipating its dissolution with the abolition of classes, and the common ownership of the basic means of production. But whatever our view of the ultimate Marxist dynamic, law is clearly inseparable from the state. Sir Henry Maine equates the history of individual property with that of civilization: "Nobody is at liberty to attack several property and to say at the same time that he values civilization. The history of the two cannot be disentangled. Civilization is nothing more than the name for the . . . order . . . dissolved but perpetually reconstituting itself under a vast variety of solvent influences, of which infinitely the most powerful have been those which have, slowly, and, in some parts of the world much less perfectly than others, substituted several property for collective ownership."[8] In the words of Jeremy Bentham, "Property and law are born together and die together."

Law, thus, is symptomatic of the emergence of the state; the legal sanction is not simply the cutting edge of institutions at all times and in all places. The "double institutionalization" to which Bohannan refers is, where it occurs, primarily a historical process of unusual complexity. And it occurs in several modes. Custom—spontaneous, traditional, personal, commonly known, corporate, relatively unchanging—is the modality of primitive society; law is the instrument of civilization, of political society sanctioned by organized force, presumably above society at large, and buttressing a new set of social interests. Law and custom both involve the regulation of behavior but their characters are entirely distinct; no evolutionary balance has been struck between developing law and custom, traditional—or emergent.

## II

The simple dichotomy primitive society/civilization does not illustrate the passage from the customary to the legal order. The most critical and revealing period in the evolution of law is that of archaic societies, the local segments of which are the cultures most often studied by anthropologists. More precisely, the earlier phases of these societies, which I call proto-states, represent a transition from the primitive kinship-based communities to the class-structured polity. In such polities, law and custom exist side by side; this gives us the opportunity to examine their connections, distinctions, and differential relationship to the society at large. The customary behavior typical of the local groups—joint families, clans, villages—maintains most of its force; the Vietnamese still say: "The customs of the village are stronger than the law of the emperor." Simultaneously, the civil power, comprising bureaucracy and sovereign, the dominant emerging class, issues a series of edicts that have the double purpose of confiscating "surplus" goods and labor for the support of those not directly engaged in production while attempting to deflect the loyalties of the local groups to the center.

These archaic societies are the great historical watershed; it is there that Sir Henry Maine and Paul Vinogradoff located the passage from status to contract, from the kinship to the territorial principle, from extended familial controls to public law. One need not be concerned with the important distinctions among archaic societies, or with the precise language or emphases of those scholars who have recognized their centrality for our understanding of the law. The significant point is that they are transitional. Particularly in their early phase, they are the agencies that transmute customary forms of order into legal sanction. There we find "double institutionalization" functioning explicitly: we can witness, so to speak, the actual shift of a customary function into its own opposite as a legal function. The following example from the archaic proto-state of Dahomey, prior to the French conquest in 1892, will make this process clear.

Traditionally, in Dahomey, each person was said to have three "best" friends, in descending order of intimacy and importance. This formal institution, a transfiguration of kin connections, of the same species as blood brotherhood, reinforced the extended family structure, which continued to exist in the early state, but was being thrown into question as a result of the political and economic demands made by the emerging civil power. So, for example, the best friend of a joint-family patriarch would serve as his testator, and name his successor upon the latter's decease to the assembled family. It seems that the ordinary convention of succession no longer sufficed to guarantee the family's integrity, since the central authority was mustering family heads as indirect rulers. In this instance, the institution of friendship was assimilated to the form and purpose of customary behavior. On the other hand, the best friend of a man charged with a civil "crime" could be seized by the king's police in his stead. However, these traditional friendships were so socially critical and so deeply held that the person charged, whether or not he had actually committed a civil breach, would typically turn himself in rather than implicate a friend in his punishment. The custom of friendship was thus given a legal edge and converted by the civil power into a means of enforcing its will. This example of "double institutionalization" has the virtue of explicitly revealing the *contradiction* between law and custom; but there are others in which law appears as a *reinforcement* of customary procedure.

In eleventh-century Russia, for instance, Article 1 of the codified law states, "If a man kills a man . . . the brother is to avenge his brother; the son, his father; or the father, his son; and the son of the brother [of the murdered man] or the son of his sister, their respective uncle. If there is no avenger [the murderer] pays 40 grivna wergeld . . ." [9] Similarly, circa A.D. 700 the law of the Visigoths states, "Whoever shall have killed a man, whether he committed a homicide intending to or not intending to [*volens aut nolens*] . . . let him be handed over into the potestas of the parents or next of kin of the deceased . . ." [10] In these instances, a custom has been codified by an external agency, thus assuming legal force, and *its punitive character sharpened*. Such confirmation is both the *intimation* of legal control and the *antecedent* of institutional change beyond the wish or conception of the family. "Whatever princes do, they seem to command," or, as Sir Henry Maine put it, "What the sovereign permits, he commands." [11] Maine had specifically in mind "the Sikh despot who permitted heads of households and village elders to prescribe rules, therefore these rules became his command and true laws, which are the 'solvent' of local and domestic usage." Simpson and Stone explain this apparent reinforcement of custom by the civil power as follows: "Turning then to the role of law in the emergent political society . . . it is true that political institutions, independent of the kin and the supernatural, had risen to power; yet these institutions were young, weak and untried. Their encroachment on the old allegiance was perforce wary and hesitating. Social cohesion still seemed based on non-political elements, and these elements were therefore protected. It is this society which Pound has perceived and expressed when he says that the end of law envisaged in his 'period of strict law' is the maintenance of the social *status quo*. In modern terminology this means the primacy of the interest in the maintenance of antecedent social institutions." [12]

This sort of confirmation, which betrays the structural opportunism of the early civil power, inheres in the limitations of sovereignty, and is further apparent in the sovereign's relation to the communally held clan or joint-family land. In Dahomey, for example, where the king was said to "own" all property, including land, it is plain that such ownership was a legal fiction and had the effect of validating the pre-existent joint-family tradition. That is, the king "permitted" the joint families, by virtue of his fictional ownership, to expand into new lands and continue transmitting their property intact, generation after generation. The civil power could not rent, alienate, or sell joint-family property, nor could any member of a joint family." [13] This is borne out by A. I. Richards, who informs us that in Northern Rhodesia [Zambia] the statement that " 'all the land is mine' does not mean that the ruler has the right to take any piece of land he chooses for his own use . . . I have never heard of a case where a chief took land that had already been occupied by a commoner." [14] The same point is made by Rattray on the Ashanti,[15] and Mair on the Baganda,[16] among others. Civil validation, then, expresses the intention but not yet the reality of state control. We might more realistically formulate Maine's epigram as: What he cannot command, the sovereign permits.

Ultimately, the local groups maintained their autonomy because their traditional economies were indispensable to the functioning of the overall society. They could be hedged around by restrictions, harassed by law, or, as we have seen, they could be "legally" confirmed in their customary usage; but, just so long as the central power depended on them for support, in the absence of any alternative mode or source of production, their integrity could be substantially preserved. This was particularly the case during the early phases of state organization in the classic nuclear areas (e.g., Egypt, Babylonia, Northern India) before the introduction of large-scale irrigation and analogous public works, and held throughout pre-colonial Africa. But in *all* archaic societies, whether incipient, as in sub-Saharan Africa, florescent, as in the ancient peasant societies of the Middle East or China, or in cognate contemporary societies which probably still embrace most of the world's population, the extensive kin unit was more functional, in spite of varying degrees of autonomy, than the family in commercial/industrial civilization.

As the state develops, according to Maine, "the individual is steadily substituted for the family as the unit of which civil laws take account." [17] And in Jhering's words, "The progress of law consists in the destruction of every natural tie, in a continued process of separation and isolation." [18] The legal stipulation that spouses may not testify against each other is perhaps the last formal recognition of familial integrity, and the exception that proves the historical case. Clearly, the nuclear family in contemporary urban civilization, although bound by legal obligations, has minimal autonomy. It is a reflex of society at large. Obviously, the means of education, subsistence, and self-defense are outside the family's competence. It is in this sense that, given the absence of mediating institutions having a clearly defined independent authority, the historical tendency of all state structures vis-à-vis the individual may be designated as totalitarian. If "totalization" is *the* state process, totalitarianism cannot be confined to a particular political ideology but is, so to speak, *the* ideology, explicit or not, of political society.

This etatist tendency has its origins in archaic society; we can observe it with unusual clarity in the proto-states of sub-Saharan Africa. In East Africa, pastoralists, competing for land, and in West Africa, militaristic clans, catalyzed by the Arab and, later, the European slave trade, conquered horticulturalists, thereby providing the major occasions for the growth of civil power. Since the basic means of exploiting the environment in these polities remained substantially unchanged, and, to some extent, survived under colonialism, we can capture, through chronicles extending back for centuries and by means of contemporary field work, the structure of early state controls, which evolved in the absence of writing and the systematic codification of law. The absence of writing *should* relieve the scholar from that dependence on official records that has so thoroughly shaped our sense of European history; unfortunately, rubbing shoulders with the upper class in a preliterate state creates equivalent distortions.

In such societies, Rattray tells us, referring to Ashanti, "the small state was ever confronted with the kindred organization which was always insidiously undermining its authority by placing certain persons outside its jurisdiction. It could only hold its own, therefore, by throwing out an ever-widening circle to embrace those loyalties which were lost to it owing to the workings of the old tribal organization which has survived everywhere." [19] Further, "the old family, clan and tribal organization survived in the new regime which was ever striving to make territorial considerations, and not the incidence of kinship, the basis of state control." Rattray concludes that "corporate responsibility for every act was an established principle which survived even the advent of a powerful central public authority as the administration of public justice." [20] Nadel asserts, concerning the Islamized Nupe of the Nigerian Middle Belt, that what emerged from his analysis was "a much more subtle development and a deeper kind of antagonism [than interstate warfare], namely, the almost eternal antagonism of developed State versus that raw material of the Community which, always and everywhere, must form the nourishing soil from which alone the state can grow." [21] And Engels refers to the "irreconcilable opposition of gentile society to the state." [22]

I have documented this conflict in detail in a study of the Dahomean Proto-state. There, as elsewhere, it is apparent that the contradictory transition from customs to specified laws, "double institutionalization," if you will, *is by no means the major source of law*. Whether the law arises latently, in confirmation of previous usage, or through the transformation of some aspect of custom, as in the example of the "best friend," neither circumstance brings us to the heart of the matter. For we learn by studying intermediate societies that the laws so typical of them are *unprecedented;* they do not emerge through the process of "double institutionalization." They arise in opposition to the customary order of the antecedent kin or kin-equivalent groups; they represent a new set of social goals pursued by a new and unanticipated power in society. These goals can be reduced to a single complex imperative: the imposition of the interrelated census-tax-conscription system. The territorial thrust of the early state, along with its vertical social entrenchment, demanded conscription of labor, the mustering of an army, the levying of taxes and tribute, the maintenance of a bureaucracy, and the assessment of the extent, location, and numbers of the population being subjected. *These were the major direct or indirect occasions for the development of civil law.*

The primary purpose of the census is indicative. Census figures (in preliterate societies, pebbles, for example, would be used as counters) provided the basis on which taxes were apportioned to the conquered districts and tribute in labor exacted from the constituent kin units. The census was also essential for conscripting men into the army. This information was considered so important in Dahomey that each new king, upon his enstoolment, was escorted by his two leading ministers to a special hut in the royal compound and there admonished as he knelt, "Young man, all your life you have heard Dahomey, Dahomey, but you have never until today seen the true Dahomey, for Dahomey is its people and here they are." [23]

With this declaration, the two elders pointed to sacks of pebbles, each pebble representing a person, each sack representing a sex or age. The young king was then told that he must never allow the contents of the sack to diminish and that every year the pebbles would be counted to see whether their number had increased or declined. He was then given an old gun (in earlier times a hoe handle) and advised, "Fight with this. But take care that you are not vanquished." [24]

The census figures represented the potential power of the state and were carefully guarded, perhaps they were the first state secret. The act and intent of the census turned persons into ciphers, abstractions in civil perspective; people did all they could to avoid being counted. Suspicion persists; even in the United States the authorities during the period of census taking find it necessary to assert that census information will not be used to tax or otherwise penalize the individual, and, in fact, to do so is said to be against the law.

The double meanings of certain critical terms in common English use—"custom," "duty," and "court"—reveal this conflict between local usage and the census-tax-conscription system of the early state. We have been speaking of custom as traditional or conventional non-legal behavior, but custom also refers to a tax routinely payable to the state for the transportation of goods across territorial borders. All such taxes are clearly defined legal impositions, frequently honored in the breach, and they do not have the traditional command of custom. In Dahomey, the "Grand Customs" held at the unveiling of a new king, presumably in honor of his ancestors, were the occasion for the payment of taxes, the large-scale sentencing and sacrifice of criminals, and the prosecution of other state business. Camus has Caligula describe such an event in a passage that could have been extrapolated from a Dahomean chronicle: "It's only the Treasury that counts. The fountain-head of all. Ah, now at last I'm going to *live*. And living is the opposite of loving . . . and I invite you to the most gorgeous of shows, a sight for gods to gloat on, a whole world called to judgment. But for that I must have a crowd—spectators, victims, criminals, hundreds and thousands of them. Let the accused come forward. I want my criminals, and they are all criminals. Bring in the condemned men. I must have my public. Judges, witnesses, accused—all sentenced to death without a hearing. Yes, Caesonia, I'll show them something they've never seen before, the one free man in the Roman Empire." [25] Along with the annual "customs," the "Grand Customs" paralleled the form of local ceremonies, but the substance was entirely changed. Fiscal or legal coercion, political imposition were not the purpose of these ancestral ceremonies which ritually re-enacted reciprocal bonds. The "customs" of the sovereign were laws, the ceremonies of the kin groups were customs.

Similarly, the term "duty" implies a moral obligation on the one hand and a tax on the other. Naturally, we assume that it is the duty of citizens to pay taxes: the paradox inherent in the term becomes more obvious, as one might imagine, as we examine archaic civilizations.

The term "court" is analogously ambivalent. On the one hand, it refers to the residence or entourage of the sovereign; on the other, to a place where civil justice is dispensed, but at their root the functions fuse. The prototypical juridical institution was, in fact, the court of the sovereign where legislation was instituted, for which no precedent existed on the local level. Peristiany, speaking of the Kipsigis, sharpens the latter point: One of the most significant differences between the . . . council of elders and a European judicature is to be found in the relation between officer and office. The council elders do not hold their office from a higher authority. They are not appointed . . ." [26] As Seagle, among others, indicates, the court is the first, most important, and perhaps the last legal artifact. In Montaigne's words, "France takes as its rule the rule of the court." [27] Put another way, the court is a specialized legal structure and it embraces all those particular and determinate legal bodies which are peculiar to civilization.

Clearly, the function of the court was not primarily the establishment of order. In primitive societies, as in the traditional sectors of proto-states, there already existed built-in mechanisms for the resolution of conflict. Generally speaking, as Max Gluckman, among others, has shown, in such societies, conflicts generated by the ordinary functioning of social institutions were resolved as part of the customary ritual cycle integral to the institutions themselves.

With regard to more specific breaches, we recall Rattray's observation on the Ashanti: "Corporate responsibility for every act was an established principle which survived even the advent of . . . the administration of public justice." That is to say, the kin unit was the juridical unit, just as it was the economic and social unit. Furthermore, "Causes which give rise to the greater part of present 'civil' actions were practically nonexistent. Inheritance, ownership of moveable and non-moveable property, status of individuals, rules of behavior and morality were matters inevitably settled by the customary law, with which everyone was familiar from childhood, and litigation regarding such matters was . . . almost inconceivable. Individual contract, moreover, from the very nature of the community with which we are concerned, was also unknown, thus removing another possible, fruitful source of litigation." [28]

The primary purpose of the historically emerging court, the sovereign's entourage and habitation, was to govern. The distinguished British jurist Sir John Salmond has observed, "Law is secondary and unessential. . . . The administration of justice is perfectly possible without law at all." [29] And Sir William Markby writes, "Tribunals can act entirely without law." [30] The perhaps unintended point here is that justice, commonly defined, is neither deducible from the law, nor was the legislation of the court a measure of justice, but of the political thrust of the early state, and *that* flowed from the implementation of the census-tax-conscription system.

In the census-tax-conscription system, every conceivable occasion was utilized for the creation of law in support of bureaucracy and sovereign. We observe no abstract principle, no impartial justice, *no precedent,* only the spontaneous opportunism of a new class designing the edifice of its power. Stubbs writes about the Norman kings that "It was mainly for the sake of the profits that early justice was administered at all." [31] Burton relates that at Whydah, in native Dahomey, in the event of a financial dispute the Yevogan, the leading bureaucrat in the district, sat in judgment. For his services, he appropriated half of the merchandise involved, in the name of the king, and another quarter for various lesser officials. The remainder presumably went to the winning contestant in the judicial duel." [32] Among the Ashanti, the central authority relied on the proceeds of litigation as a fruitful means for replenishing a depleted treasury. Litigation, Rattray notes, came actually to be encouraged.[33]

Tolls were an important source of revenue. In Ashanti, the king had all the roads guarded; all traders were detained until inquiries were made about them, whereupon they were allowed to pass on payment of gold dust.[34] W. Bosman writes that in early eighteenth-century Whydah, the king's revenue "in proportion to his country is very large, of which I believe, he hath above one thousand collectors who dispose themselves throughout the whole land in all market roads and passages, in order to gather the king's toll which amounts to an incredible sum, for there is nothing so mean sold in the whole kingdom that the king hath no toll for it . . ." [35]

The punishment for the theft of property designated as the king's was summary execution by "kangaroo courts" organized on the spot by the king's agents.[36] This is echoed in the code of Hammurabi: "If a man steals the property of a god [temple] or a palace, that man shall be put to death; and he who receives from his hands the stolen [property] shall also be put to death." [37] Where the king's property was concerned, no judicial duel was possible. In these instances, which could be endlessly multiplied, we witness the extension of the king's peace, the primary form of the civil "order," actually the invention and application of sumptuary law through the subsidiary peaces of highway and market. In Maitland's words, "The king has a peace that devours all others." If, in these proto-states, the sovereign power is not yet fully effective, it nonetheless strives to that monopoly of force which characterizes the mature state.

The purpose and abundance of laws inevitably provoked breaches. The civil authority, in fact, continually probed for breaches and frequently manufactured them. In Dahomey, for example, a certain category of the king's women were distributed to the local villages and those men who made the mistake of having intercourse with them were accused of rape, for which the punishment, following a summary trial, was conscription into the army.[38] Thus, rape was invented as a *civil* crime. If rape had, in fact, occurred in the traditional joint-family villages, and such an occurrence would have been rare, as indicated by the necessity of civil invention, the wrong could have been dealt with by composition (the ritualized giving of goods to the injured party), ritual purification, ridicule, and, perhaps for repeated transgressions, banishment—or other customary machinery would have gone into effect automatically, probably on the initiative of the family of the aggressor. Such instances as this only sharpen the point that in early states, crimes seem to have been invented to suit the laws; the latent purpose of the law was punishment in the service and profit of the state, not prevention or the protection of persons, not the *healing* of the breach. As Seagle indicates, "The criminal law springs into life in every great period of class conflict."

In its civil origins, then, a correlation existed between law and crime which partook of entrapment. One may even state that the substantial rationale for law developed *after* the fact of its emergence. For example, civil protection of the marketplace or highway was certainly not necessary to the degree implied in the archaic edicts at the time they were issued. Joint-family markets and village trails were not ordinarily dangerous places, if we are to believe the reports of the earliest chroniclers, along with those of more contemporary observers. Moreover, if trouble had developed, the family, clan, or village were capable of dealing with it. But, in an evolving conquest state, the presence of the king's men would itself be a primary cause of disruption. Indeed, as M. Quénum, a descendant of Dahomean commoners, informs us in a remarkable work, the soldiers were referred to as bandits and predators who victimized many people. Sometimes their forays were confined to a single compound, where someone resided who had spoken badly of the sovereign or whom the king suspected, whether man, woman, or child.[39] In common parlance, the very names of the elite army units became insults; one would mean "nasty person," another "arrogant person," and one would say of a tragic event that it was worthy of yet another military cadre. It is, therefore, understandable that the peace of the highway became an issue.[40]

As the integrity of the local groups declined, a process which, in the autochthonous state, must have taken generations or even centuries, conditions doubtless developed which served as an ex post facto rationalization for edicts already in effect. In this sense, laws became self-fulfilling prophecies. Crime and the laws which served it were, then, co-variants of the evolving state system.

Just as entrapment was characteristic of early civil law, the idea of protection, in the sense of protection racket, also inheres in its origins. In Dahomey, we are told by Norris and others, prostitution was encouraged by the civil power and prostitutes were distributed through the villages, the price of their favors being set by civil decree. They were obliged to offer themselves to any man who could pay the moderate fee and once a year were convened at the "annual customs," where they were heavily taxed.[41] Skertchly notes that the prostitutes were licensed by the king and placed in the charge of the Mew, the second leading bureaucrat, who was entrusted with the task of "keeping up the supply." [42] Bosman observes at Whydah that "for every affair that can be thought of, the king hath appointed a captain overseer." [43] *What the king permits, he commands; what he "protects," he taxes.*

The intention of the civil power is epitomized in the sanctions against homicide and suicide, typical of early polities; indeed they were among the very first civil laws. Just as the sovereign is said to own the land, intimating the mature right of eminent domain, so the individual is ultimately conceived as the chattel of the state. In Dahomey, persons were conceived as *"les choses du monarque."* Eminent domain in persons and property is, of course, the cardinal prerequisite of the census-tax-conscription system. We recall that Maine designated the individual the unit of which the civil law steadily takes account. Seagle stated the matter as follows: "By undermining the kinship bond, they [the early civil authorities] made it easier to deal with individuals, and isolation of the individual is a basic precondition for the growth of law." [44]

Homicide, then, was regarded as an offense against the state. In Rattray's words, "The blow which struck down the dead man would thus appear to have been regarded as aimed also at the . . . central authority." [45] In Ashanti, it was punishable by death in its most horrible form; in Dahomey, by death or conscription into the army. There is a nuance here which should not be overlooked. By making homicide, along with the theft of the king's property, a capital offense, the sovereign power discouraged violent opposition to the imposition of the civil order.

Traditionally, murder in a joint-family village was a tort—a private, remediable wrong—which could stimulate a blood feud, not to be confused with the *lex talionis,* until redress—which did not imply equivalent injury—was achieved. But a breach was most often settled by composition. As Paul Radin put it: "The theory of an eye for an eye . . . never really held for primitive people . . . rather it was replacement for loss with damages." [46] And this is echoed by Peristiany: ". . . they claim restitution or private damages and not social retribution." [47] In any case, the family was fully involved. "The family was a corporation," said Rattray, "it is not easy to grasp what must have been the effect . . . of untold generations of thinking and acting . . . in relation to one's group. The Ashanti's idea of what we term moral responsibility for his actions must surely have been more developed than in peoples where individualism is the order of the day." [48] This more or less typical anthropological observation makes it clear that the law against homicide was not a "progressive" step, as if some abstract right were involved which the state, coming of age, finally understands and seeks to establish. "Antisocial conduct [is] exceptional in small kinship groups," writes Margery Perham of the Ibo.[49] Crimes of violence were rare,[50] Richard Burton reports of Dahomey, and "murder virtually unknown." [51] Of course, as with other crimes defined by civil law, they may have increased as the social autonomy, economic communalism, and reciprocity of the kin units weakened. But this is much less important than Dalzel's observation that in Dahomey "many creatures have been put to death . . . without having committed any crime at all," [52] thus exemplifying the power of the sovereign literally to command the lives of his citizens. The threat and example of summary execution, especially but by no means exclusively evident at the mortuary celebrations or "Grand Customs" on the enstooling of a king, encouraged obedience to civil injunctions.

The law against suicide, a capital offense, was the apotheosis of political absurdity. The individual, it was assumed, had no right to take his own life; that prerogative was, presumably, the state's alone, whose property he was conceived to be.

The fanatical nature of the civil legislature in claiming sole prerogative to the lives of its subjects is conclusively revealed among the Ashanti, where, if the suicide was a murderer, "the central authority refused to be cheated thus and the long arm of the law followed the suicide to the grave from which, if his kinsmen should have dared to bury him, he was dragged to stand trial." [53] (One recalls Antigone's defiance.) It can hardly be argued that the purpose of the civil sanction against suicide was to diminish its incidence or to propagate a superior moral consciousness. Dare we say, as with other crimes, that attempts at suicide increased as society became more thoroughly politicized? The law against suicide reveals, in the extreme, the whole meaning and intent of civil law at its origins. In the proto-state, the quintessential struggle was over the lives and labor of the people, who, still moving in a joint-family context, were nonetheless conceived to be *"les choses du monarque."*

## III

If revolutions are the acute, episodic signs of civilizational discontent, the rule of law, in seven millennia of political society, from Sumer or Akkad to New York or Moscow, has been the chronic symptom of the disorder of institutions. E. B. Tylor stated, "A constitutional government, whether called republic or kingdom, is an arrangement by which the nation governs itself by means of the machinery of a military despotism." [54]

The generalization lacks nuance but we can accept it if we bear in mind Tylor's point of reference: "Among the lessons to be learnt from the life of rude tribes is how society can go on without the policeman to keep order." [55] When he alludes to constitutional government, Tylor was not distinguishing its ultimate sanction from that of any other form of the state: all political society is based on repressive organized force. In this he was accurate. For Pharaohs and presidents alike have always made a public claim to represent the common interest, indeed to incarnate the common good. Only a Plato or Machiavelli in search of political harmony or a Marx in search of political truth has been able to penetrate this myth of the identity between ruler and ruled, of equality under law. The tradition of Plato and Machiavelli commends the use of the "royal" or "noble lie," while that of Marx exposes and rejects the power structure (ultimately the state) that propagates so false a political consciousness. On this issue, I follow Marx.

Tylor distinguishes the civilized from the primitive order. Such a distinction has been made at every moment of crisis in the West but nowhere so pertinently as in Montaigne's contrast of a primitive society with Plato's ideally civilized republic: "This is a nation, I should say to Plato, in which there is no sort of traffic, no knowledge of letters, no science of numbers, no name for a magistrate or for political superiority, no custom of servitude, no riches or poverty, no contracts, no successions, no partitions . . . no care for any but common kinship. . . . How far from this perfection would he find the Republic he imagines." [56] The issue of law and order implicit in Montaigne's contrast between primitive and civilized societies has been a persistent underlying theme for the most reflective and acute minds of the West. The inquiry into the nature of politics probably demarcates most accurately the boundaries of our intellectual landscape. The evolution of the state toward what Max Weber called maximally politicized society, the unprecedented concentration of bureaucratic and technological power which economically and culturally dominates the rest of the world, creates a climate in which all problems cast a political shadow. We may flee from the political dimension of our experience or we may embrace it in order to do away with it, but we are obsessed by politics. It was perhaps Plato's primary virtue that, at the very origin of the Western intellectual tradition, he understood that, in civilization, all significant human problems have a political aspect and he insisted upon the solution of the latter as a coefficient of the creative resolution of the former. The *Republic* is the first civilizational utopia, and it maintains its force both as a model of inquiry and as antithesis to all projections of the nature of primitive society. Any contrary view of the possibilities of human association must take the *Republic* into account.

The legal order, which Plato idealized, is, as Tylor maintained and Marx understood, synonymous with the power of the state. "The state," writes Paul Vinogradoff, "has assumed the monopoly of political co-ordination. It is the state which rules, makes laws and eventually enforces them by coercion. Such a state did not exist in ancient times. The commonwealth was not centered in one sovereign body towering immeasurably above single individuals and meting out to everyone his portion of right." [57] And Engels, reflecting on the origins of the state, asserts, "The right of the state to existence was founded on the preservation of order in the interior and the protection against the barbarians outside but this order was worse than the most disgusting disorder, and the barbarians against whom the state pretended to protect its citizens were hailed by them as saviors." [58] Moreover, "The state created a public power of coercion that did no longer coincide with the old self-organized and [self] armed population." [59] Finally, in a passage that epitomizes the West's awareness of itself, he writes, "The state, then, is by no means a power forced on society at a certain stage of evolution. It is the confession that this society has become hopelessly divided against itself, has estranged itself in irreconcilable contradictions which it is powerless to banish. In order that these contradictions, these classes with conflicting economic interests may not annihilate themselves and society in a useless struggle, a power becomes necessary that stands apparently above society and has the function of keeping down the conflicts and maintaining 'order.' And this power, the outgrowth of society, but assuming supremacy over it and becoming more and more divorced from it, is the state . . ." [60] In a word, the state is the alienated form of society: and it is this process which has fascinated the Western intellect and which may, in fact, have led to the peculiar intensity of the reflective, analytic, and introspective consciousness in the West, to our search for origins and our inexhaustible concern with secular history. A knowledge of one's present, as Montaigne maintained, implies not only a knowledge of one's past but of one's future.

However we project, imagine, or reconstruct the past, we recognize the division, the objective correlate of the division within ourselves, between primitive and civilized society, between moral and civil order, between custom and law. Interpretation of the nature of the primitive and the civilized has, of course, not been uniform. Hobbes versus Rousseau is paradigmatic. But most theorists tend to see civilization as a kind of fall from a "natural," or at least more natural, to a legal or more repressive order. No matter how the virtues of civilization are weighed, the price exacted is inevitably noted. This is as true of Plato as of Freud or Engels. Plato, for example, notes, however inadequately, a condition of existence prior to the city-state, a type of rusticity which he views nostalgically and whose destruction he maintains was socioeconomically determined. I suspect that even the great majority of anthropologists, despite professional illusions of dissociated objectivity, sense that primitive are somehow closer than civilized societies to the realization of "natural" law and "natural" right. I believe this emphasis in the Western tradition to be the sounder, and it serves as the basis of my own thinking. There is, as Montaigne noted, an "amazing distance" between the primitive character and our own. In the contrast between these two sides of our historical nature, which we existentially reenact, we come to understand law as the antonym and not the synonym of order.

## IV

I agree with Nadel that in the transition from primitive to political society the means of control and integration employed were, in a wider sense "all . . . deliberately conceived and [executed]: they are agencies of an assimilation conscious of itself and of the message which it carries." [61] Finally, we are led to ask, as did Nadel about the Nupe: "What did the tax-paying, law-abiding citizen receive in return for allegiance to king and nobility. Was extortion, bribery, brutal force, the only aspect under which the state revealed itself to the populace? The people were to receive, theoretically, on the whole, one thing: security—protection against external and internal enemies, and general security for carrying out the daily work, holding markets, using the roads. . . . We have seen what protection and security meant in reality. At their best, they represented something very unequal and very unstable. This situation must have led to much tension and change within the system and to frequent attempts to procure better safeguards for civil rights." [62]

The struggle for civil rights, then, is a response to the imposition of civil law. With the destruction of the primitive base of society, civil rights have been defined and redefined as a reaction to drastic changes in the socioeconomic structure—the rise of caste and class systems, imperialism, modern war, technology as a means of social exploitation, maldistribution and misuse of resources, racial hatred. The right to socially and economically fruitful work, for example, which did not come into question in a primitive society or in a traditional sector of an early state (and therefore was not conceived to be a stipulated right), becomes an issue under capitalism. The demand implies a need for deeply changing the system and indicates that our sense of the appropriately human has very ancient roots indeed. However, we are reminded, in the struggle for civil rights, that legislation alone has no force beyond the potential of the social system that generates it. From the study of proto-states we also learn that the citizen must be constantly alert to laws which seek to curb his rights in the name of protection or security. Restrictive legislation is almost always a signal of repressive institutional change, but is, of course, not the cause of it.

The major focus of the defense of the citizen as a person can only be on procedure or, as we call it in our own society, due process. Quénum reports, of the early state of Dahomey, "There was no penal code promulgated . . . punishment had no fixity . . . the Miegan [leading bureaucrat, chief judge, and executioner] would become restive if capital punishment would be too long in coming." [63] In the words of Dalzel, "There was a vast disproportion between crimes and punishments." [64] And in early states, most, if not all, civil breaches were what we would define as crimes, just as, in primitive societies, "civil crimes" were considered, where they were not unprecedented, torts or private remediable wrongs. As every intelligent lawyer knows, the substance of the law can hardly be assimilated to morality. It is clear, therefore, why Jhering insisted that "Form is the sworn enemy of unlimited discretion [of the sovereign power] and the twin sister of freedom." [65] The degrees of theft or homicide, the question or double jeopardy, habeas corpus, the right to counsel, the question of legitimate witness, trial by jury and the selection of jurors, protection against summary search and seizure, the very division between civil and criminal law—these intricacies of procedure are the primary, but far from absolute, assurance of whatever justice can be obtained under the rule of law.

For example, the only way dissidents in Russia can defend themselves against summary punishment and make their cases universally understandable is by calling attention to abuses of procedure. The spirit of the laws, mummified in the excellent constitution of 1936, is irrelevant, abstract. The tribunal that discharges the intentions of the state can discard, suspend, reinterpret, and invent laws at will. The court, not the constitution, is the primary legal reality. And the politically inspired charge of insanity, which can remove dissidents from the body politic altogether, is the ultimate etatistic definition of the person—a non-being incapable of autonomy. And that, I should note, is foreshadowed in the consummate anti-Socratic Platonism of the Laws, the heavenly city brought to earth, wherein the ordinary citizen is "to become, by long habit, utterly incapable of doing anything at all independently."

Procedure is the individual's last line of defense in contemporary civilization, wherein all other associations to which he may belong have become subordinate to the state. The elaboration of procedure, then, is a unique, if fragile, feature of more fully evolved states, in compensation, so to speak, for the radical isolation of the individual. In the proto-states, the harshness of rudimentary procedure was countered by the role of the kinship units which, as we recall, retained a significant measure of functional socioeconomic autonomy and, therefore, local political cohesion.

But "law has its origin in the pathology of social relations and functions only when there are frequent disturbances of the social equilibrium." [66] Law arises in the breach of a prior customary order and increases in force with the conflicts that divide political societies internally and among themselves. Law *and* order is the historical illusion; law versus order is the historical reality.

In the tradition of Rousseau, Lévi-Strauss declares, "We must go beyond the evidence of the injustices and abuses to which the social order gives rise, and discover the unshakable basis of human society . . . Anthropology shows that base cannot be found in our own civilization, ours is indeed perhaps the one furthest from it." [67]

The progressive reduction of society to a series of technical and legal signals, the consequent diminution of culture, i.e., of reciprocal, symbolic meanings, are perhaps the primary reasons why our civilization is the one least likely to serve as a guide to "the unshakable basis of human society."

## NOTES

1. Paul Bohannan. "Law," *International Encyclopedia of the Social Sciences*. New York, 1968, pp. 73–78.
2. Paul Radin. *The World of Primitive Man*. New York, 1953, p. 223.
3. J. G. Peristiany. *The Institutions of Primitive Society*. Glencove, Illinois, 1956, p. 45.
4. Sydney P. Simpson and Julius Stone. *Law and Society in Evolution,* Book I. Saint Paul, 1942, p. 2.
5. William Seagle. *The History of Law*. Tudor, 1946, p. 35.
6. Ibid., pp. 19–20.
7. Ibid.
8. Sir Henry Maine. *Village Communities and Miscellanies*. New York, 1889, p. 230.
9. G. Vernadsky. *Medieval Russian Laws*. New York, 1947, pp. 26–27.
10. Quoted by Simpson and Stone, p. 78.
11. Maine, *Early History of Institutions*. 1897, p. 383.
12. Simpson and Stone, p. 177.
13. Stanley Diamond. *Dahomey, a Proto-state in West Africa*. Ann Arbor, Microfilm, 1951, p. 109.
14. Quoted by Max Gluckman. "Studies in African Land Tenure," *African Studies,* Vol. III, 1944, pp. 14–21.
15. R. S. Rattray. *Ashanti, Law and Constitution*. London, 1929.
16. L. P. Mair. "Baganda Land Tenure," *Africa,* Vol. VI, 1933.
17. Maine. *Ancient Law*. P. 140.
18. R. von Jhering. *Geist des Romischen Recht* 1866, Vol. II, p. 31.
19. Rattray, p. 80.

20. Ibid., p. 286.
21. S. F. Nadel. "Nupe State and Community," *Africa,* Vol. VIII, p. 303.
22. Friedrich Engels. *Origin of the Family, Private Property and the State.* Chicago, 1902, p. 133.
23. M. J. Herskowitz. *Dahomey, an Ancient West African Kingdom.* New York, 1938, p. 73.
24. Ibid.
25. Albert Camus. *Caligula and Three Other Plays.* New York, 1958, p. 17.
26. Peristiany, *op. cit.,* p. 42.
27. Michel de Montaigne. *The Complete Essays.* Stanford, 1965, p. 197.
28. Rattray, p. 286.
29. Sir John Salmond. *Jurisprudence.* 1920, p. 13.
30. Sir William Markby. *Elements of Law.* 1905, p. 21.
31. William Stubbs. *The Constitutional History of England.* London, 1890, Vol. I, p. 48.
32. Burton, Captain Sir Richard F. *A Mission to Gelele, a King of Dahomey.* London, 1864, Vol. II, p. 211.
33. Rattray, p. 292.
34. Ibid., p. 111.
35. W. Bosman. *A New and Accurate Description of the Coast of Guinea.* London, 1705, p. 362.
36. R. Norris. *Reise nach Abomey, der Hofstadt des Königs von Dahomey an von Guinea im jahr 1772.* Leipzig, 1790, p. 221 ff.
37. *Code of Hammurabi,* Harper translation. 1904, paragraph 6, p. 13.
38. A. Le Herisse. *L'Ancien Royaume du Dahomey.* Paris, 1911, p. 72.
39. M. Quénum. *Au Pays des Fons.* Paris, 1938, p. 7.
40. Quénum, p. 21–22.
41. Norris, p. 257.
42. Skertchly. *Dahomey As It Is.* London, 1874, p. 283.
43. Bosman, p. 361.
44. Seagle, p. 64. Quénum had a poor opinion of the ethnographers who claimed to understand and interpret his country. They failed, he believed, because of inadequate sources of information and (or) ignorance of social customs. "Most of our ethnographers," he wrote, "have had as collaborators princes and ex-ministers of state and have believed their tales." He adds that ignorance of the native language and deficient sympathy compounded the problem. The point to note here is that Qué-

num is objecting to the view from the top, which is a critical issue in the writing of all political history.

45. Rattray, p. 295.
46. Radin, *op. cit.*, p. 252.
47. Peristiany, *op. cit.*, p. 43.
48. Radin, *op. cit.*, p. 62.
49. Margery Perham. *Native Administration in Nigeria.* London, 1962, pp. 229 ff.
50. Acts of violence must be distinguished from *crimes* of violence. The incidence, occasions for, and character of violence in primitive, as opposed to civilized, societies is a subject of the utmost importance, which I have discussed elsewhere (see footnote 52). But the question here has to do with crimes in which violence is used as a means for, e.g., the theft of property. In contemporary societies, unpremeditated acts of personal violence which have no ulterior motive, so-called crimes of passion, may not be penalized or carry minor degrees of guilt, that is, their status as legally definable crimes is ambiguous. This would seem to reflect a historically profound distinction between crime and certain types of violence. In primitive societies violence tends to be personal, structured, nondissociative, and, thereby, self-limiting.
51. Burton, p. 56.
52. A. Dalzel. *The History of Dahomey, An Inland Kingdom of Africa;* compiled from authentic Memoirs, with an introduction and notes. London, 1793, p. 212.
53. Rattray, p. 299.
54. E. B. Tylor. *Anthropology,* Vol. II. London, 1946, p. 156.
55. Ibid., p. 134.
56. Michel de Montaigne. *The Complete Essays,* translated by Donald Frame. Stanford, 1965, p. 153. In ignorance of Montaigne's contrast between primitive society and Plato's ideal republic, I published an article, "Plato and the Definition of the Primitive," *Culture in History,* New York, 1960, which explicates some of the points briefly noted above. For a more comprehensive model of primitive society see my "The Search for the Primitive" in *Man's Image in Medicine and Anthropology,* New York, 1963, edited by I. Galdston, pp. 62–115. In order to understand the functioning of custom in primitive society fully, one should have such a model in mind. Unfortunately, in this article, I can only suggest its outlines.
57. Paul Vinogradoff. *Outlines of Historical Jurisprudence,* Vol. I. London, 1920, p. 93.

58. Friedrich Engels. *Origin of the Family, Private Property and the State*. Chicago, 1902, p. 179.
59. Ibid., p. 207.
60. Ibid., p. 206.
61. S. F. Nadel. *A Black Byzantium*. London, New York, Toronto, 1942, p. 144.
62. Nadel, "Nupe State and Community," *Africa,* Vol. VIII, p. 287.
63. Quénum, p. 22.
64. Dalzel, p. 212.
65. Jhering, Vol. II, p. 471.
66. Seagle, p. 36.
67. Claude Lévi-Strauss. *A World on the Wane*. New York, 1961, p. 390.

* The double institutionalization, to which Bohannan refers, needs redefinition. As this article attempts to show, it cannot be regarded as the simple passage of custom into law. Nevertheless, I have retained the phrase for semantic convenience, while critically elaborating the concept for which it stands.

# PART

# III

# PHILOSOPHY AND THE CRITIQUE OF LAW

Ronald Dworkin

There is just now great dissatisfaction with law and its enforcement in the United States. Criticism comes from two sides. Critics of the law accuse it of being archaic, unjust, and discriminatory; they cite the draft laws that supply men for the Vietnamese war, the scheme of property that forces the very poor to live in ghettos, and the political structures that deny large numbers of people effective participation in the institutions that govern them. Critics of law enforcement, on the other hand, are offended by the tolerance that legal officials—ranging from attorneys general to college presidents—sometimes show to those who break the law.

Both sets of critics present the issues they raise as part of a larger issue, namely the issue of whether law, as an abstract institution, is a good or poor thing, and the extent to which citizens have a moral or political obligation to obey it. The radicals believe that the injustice of particular laws reflects defects in the nature of law, and they oppose the assumption that society should be governed in accordance with fixed general rules that are necessarily, in their opinion, blind to moral discriminations and so unnecessarily restrictive of human freedom. The conservatives, for their part, see in particular acts of disobedience a challenge to the general authority of law, and they therefore believe that tolerating dissent is the same thing as condoning lawlessness.

So the assumption, that these political disputes necessarily involve a trial of the value of law, is common ground. It is also, I think, a common mistake, and one that is dangerous because it obscures the disputes and hides certain forms of accommodation that are in fact attractive. In this essay I want to show how much the common assumption depends upon one particular theory about the nature of law, a theory that both radicals and conservatives seem to accept. I mean the positivist theory that has been set out, in different forms, by the great legal philosophers John Austin, Hans Kelsen, and H. L. A. Hart. According to this theory the law of a community is a set of rules adopted in accordance with stipulated constitutional procedures—in the United States this means rules enacted by state or federal legislatures, or adopted by courts, or established by custom, in conformity with the rules of the state or federal constitution. These rules are always more or less vague, and in any event they cannot anticipate all cases that may arise; it follows that in some cases the law, so conceived, will provide no clear answer to some novel legal question. In such cases the judges and other officials who enforce the law must supplement the rules, even though retroactively, with a piece of fresh legislation.

The law, on this conception, is morally neutral, in the sense that any rule adopted by the proper institution or official will be law without regard to its moral quality. In the United States, this last statement is qualified by the fact that the Federal Constitution invalidates statutes that offend constitutional rules, and some of these constitutional rules, like the rule that the government cannot abridge freedom of speech, happen to have a moral quality. But the constitutional rules are themselves vague and leave open the issue of whether in close cases a statutory rule is valid; it may be doubtful, that is, whether obscenity laws do abridge freedom of speech. In such cases the judge must also legislate to close the gap, and his decision becomes law without regard to its moral quality.

Some readers will be surprised that I describe this positivist view of law as generally accepted. After all, a great many American lawyers, inside the law schools and out, have rejected Austin, Kelsen, and Hart as unrealistic. But this rejection is deceptive, for the disagreement runs to complementary issues and not the theory of law I sketched. Some American lawyers (particularly those who think of themselves as "Realists") believe that Hart, for example, underestimates the degree of vagueness of most legal rules and the extent to which judges who cite these rules are actually enforcing their own social or political theories. The Realists think that judicial legislation is more frequent and broader than Hart allows, a difference that at least in part reflects a difference between American and English practice. But when they speak of the law or of legal rules, even to reject the idea that these play a dominant role in influencing official decisions, they use Hart's positivist conception of what the law is, and so do those more numerous lawyers and citizens who debate the merits of civil disobedience even though they have never reflected on abstract questions about law and morals.

## I. SOCIAL OBLIGATION

In order to show the power that the positivist theory has exercised in the political debates, I shall outline an alternative theory of law, and then consider how the debates would differ if this alternative, rather than the positivist theory, were generally accepted. I shall not provide arguments to show that this alternative theory is a better theory of law than positivism, though in fact I think that it is. I am interested here in the contrast between the two theories, and the bearing of each theory on the political debates.

I shall begin my outline of this alternate theory by trying to clarify two central concepts that the theory employs. These are the concepts of a social right and a social obligation. They combine what I shall treat here as two separate ideas: the idea of a moral right or obligation, in the strong sense of those terms, and the idea that at least some moral rights and obligations arise out of social conventions or institutions. (When I speak of the "strong sense" of right and obligation I mean the sense in which these terms are used to make a specially forceful sort of moral judgment. Saying that someone has an obligation to do something, in this strong sense, means that he must do it, which is more than saying simply that he ought to do it, or that it would be generous of him to do it. Saying that someone has a right to something, in this sense, means that he is entitled to it and may properly demand it, not merely that he ought to have it or would be better or happier if he did.)

It is a familiar idea that claims that men make about rights and obligations are often based on the authority of social conventions, like the conventions of promising, personal security, and privacy. The claims that someone has a right not to have his mail read or his person touched or that someone has an obligation to keep his word are examples of such claims, which I shall call judgments of social obligation. I do not mean to argue that all claims of right or obligation, in the strong sense, are judgments of social obligation, that is, that they all depend on social convention in this way. That may be so, as some philosophers think, but the theory I shall describe assumes only that some judgments of right and obligation are based on social practice in this way; it is these judgments that the theory describes as playing a role in legal reasoning. The theory holds, for example, as I shall explain, that judges must take into account the principles and excuses of promising when deciding difficult contract cases, the conventional principles of privacy in novel tort cases, the conventional principles of property in fundamental cases of title, and so forth.

But some judgments of social right and obligation are a great deal more complex than simple appeals to acknowledged social conventions like promising and privacy, because these conventions are not the only social practices that are relevant to such judgments. In addition to these first-order practices (as I shall call them) the members of our community follow second-order practices that furnish conventions for criticizing and applying first-order practices. Some of these conventions deal with hard or uncertain cases. They provide, for example, that if it is unclear whether someone has an obligation under a particular practice, it is relevant, in reaching a decision, to consider the point of the practice, that is, the principles or policies the practice might be said to serve, and also to consider the impact of other policies to which the community is committed. So if the question arises whether I am entitled to spy on someone else for his own good, I would be expected to support my view with some appeals to the point of the conventions at stake, and the point of whatever other responsibilities towards him I may claim to have.

Other second-order conventions are critical and furnish grounds for disavowing obligations. One of these, for example, is the rule that a pointless first-order practice cannot impose genuine social obligations, even though those who follow the practice believe that it is binding on others. Suppose that the community follows the practice that each man must participate in rain dances, or play his part in some defense scheme, but a minority thinks these practices pointless (they think, that is, that the practices cannot achieve the policies they aim at). Members of that minority will not believe that they have any duty to follow the practices, though they may do so out of politeness or fear. Most members of the majority will agree with the minority to this extent: they will agree that *if* the minority were right as to the pointlessness of the practice in question, then the minority would be right on the issue of obligation as well. Another critical convention is the principle of fairness, though this is much harder to explicate. One aspect of this principle is the proviso that if some group is systematically excluded from the benefits of a practice, through no fault or because of no relevant disability of theirs, then the practice cannot impose genuine obligations upon members of that group. So if a frontier community follows a practice of mutual defense, which stops short at a certain distance from the town, the community cannot expect those who live beyond the area of defense to participate in protecting those who live within.

These critical principles are most important when their application is controversial, that is, when the bulk of the community thinks that a practice does serve some point or does benefit a minority group, but others disagree. The critical principles exist because the majority respects them in the abstract; but they would serve no function unless it were generally recognized that the majority might be wrong in judging whether they apply in particular cases. If this were not generally recognized, the critical principles would be superfluous. If the majority's view settled the question of when a critical principle applied, then the existence of a social practice—whether rain dances or racial segregation or the demand that those outside the defense perimeter help protect those within—would prove that it infringed no such principles.

These second-order practices insure that some arguments about social obligation cannot be settled by one side proving beyond question that the other is wrong. There is no master rule or test that can be used to demonstrate mathematically that a given critical principle applies to a given case. Each man must make and act on his own judgment and must apply his own understanding of the principles and policies in question. That does not mean that individuals have discretion to act as they please in hard cases. It means rather that the institution of social obligation (by which I mean the general practice of making and responding to particular claims of social right or duty) requires individuals to assume that they have rights and obligations even when these cannot be proved with certainty, and to act on their judgment that the case in favor of a particular obligation is stronger than the case against, even when others will disagree. It is true that this institution would fail and lapse unless the range of disagreement in understanding within the community were relatively small. The range must be sufficiently small so that particular disagreements can be argued against a background of general agreement about what is a good and what is a poor argument. Disagreements must for the most part be disagreements about where a balance should be struck, not about what should be weighed. The former sort of disagreement may be as bitter as the latter, of course, because opponents will see each other not as representatives of alien cultures but as men blind to discriminations within their own.

## II. AN ALTERNATE THEORY

This is hardly an adequate account of the concepts of social right and social obligation, but it may be sufficient to allow me to describe the most important differences between positivism and the alternate theory I want to present. That theory offers a substantially different account from positivism of the reasoning involved in deciding whether someone has a particular *legal* right or obligation on particular facts. According to positivism, this question is decided by checking to see whether the appropriate legal institutions have enacted a rule that fits these facts, or whether such a rule has been developed by custom. If a rule with that pedigree is found, the legal rights and duties are as that rule provides; if the rule is unclear, or it is not clear whether it fits these facts, then the judge deciding the case exercises his discretion to clarify the rule or invent a new one. On this view the question of whether a particular legal right exists cannot be uncertain, in the sense in which a question of history or economics can be uncertain. If the rule is clear and clearly applies, then the question is settled; if not, then there is no legal right, and anyone who claims that there is must mean that there should be, or must be predicting that a judge will exercise his discretion retroactively to create one.

On the alternate theory, reasoning about legal rights and obligations is more complex, at least in those hard cases in which no clear rule is available. The theory provides that one must approach these hard cases like doubtful cases of *social* right or obligation, by attempting to identify the principles and policies that the established rules serve, and then interpreting these rules, or designing new rules, in that light. The correct decision is that which best accommodates the medley of these principles and policies, some of which, of course, will conflict with others.

There may well be no way of demonstrating beyond question which of several different accommodations is the best, just as there is no way of demonstrating which analysis of historical data is the soundest or which of alternate economic programs is the wisest. Each man who must decide a difficult issue of legal rights, because of his personal situation or official responsibilities, must make and act on his own judgment. It is important to notice that on this theory difficult issues of law are genuinely uncertain, because it makes sense to claim that a legal right exists even when one cannot demonstrate that claim by an iron proof. The theory does not hold, with positivism, that a right does not exist unless it clearly exists; it provides that a claim of right is proper when the argument supporting the claim is stronger than the opposite argument, even when this is a matter of judgment.

It is true that a positivist might say that judges look to the principles and policies I mentioned for guidance when exercising their discretion. But the alternate theory insists, on the model of social obligation, that the judge must proceed in this way, and it treats the judgment he reaches not as an act of individual discretion but as an attempt to establish the existence of a legal right or duty. This, as I shall try to show, is a crucial difference.

So the alternate theory uses reasoning about social obligations as the model for reasoning about legal obligations. But it also, and independently, provides for a more intimate connection between these institutions. It provides that the first-order and critical principles that the community follows in making judgments of social right and obligation are among the standards that a judgment of legal obligation must try to accommodate. The weight that must be given to these principles, as opposed to the principles and policies derived from strictly legal sources, varies from case to case, but it is greatest on two sorts of occasions. The first are cases in which the rules established by legislation and precedent seem conflicting and uncertain, and these difficulties are not entirely removed by an inspection of the principles or policies the rules exemplify. The second are cases in which the legal rules make moral considerations relevant, like the provision of the Uniform Commercial Code that "unconscionable" contracts are unenforceable, or the provisions of the United States Constitution, such as the "due process" and "equal protection" clauses, that assume that citizens have inalienable rights but do not specify what these are.

Even in these cases, however, the influence of principles drawn from social obligation is limited by what might be called exclusionary principles. I mean principles, themselves established by legislation or precedent, or drawn from practical features of the process of adjudication, that provide affirmative reasons for not giving legal effect to moral or social rights. The principle that the law does not recognize mental suffering as a legal injury, and that the courts should not tackle "political questions" (that is, questions of political controversy better left to other institutions to resolve) are both examples of exclusionary principles. These principles are not flat rules separating distinct domains of law and morality. They are principles; one who appeals to them to exclude considerations of social obligation must make an affirmative case for the principle he wants to invoke, and he must recognize that any such principle can be overcome when these social considerations are especially strong or the point of the exclusionary principle only marginally relevant. (In the segregation cases the principle about not recognizing mental suffering or insult was overcome for the first reason, and in the reapportionment cases the political question exclusion was overridden by the second.)

I shall close this brief summary of the alternative theory with two illustrations. A case I used elsewhere, in a criticism of positivism, illustrates the role the theory assigns to social practices in reasoning about commercial law. The case is *Henningsen* v. *Bloomington Motors,* and the question at issue was whether an automobile manufacturer should be allowed to limit its liability for defects by inserting a clause to that effect in its standard contract.

The precedents seemed to give effect to such a waiver, but

they were not clear and in any event this result seemed unfair. The judge decided not to enforce the waiver. Two judgments of social obligation figured in his decision. The first was the judgment that manufacturers of dangerous objects like cars have a heavier social obligation to take care than do manufacturers of neckties, for example, so that the fact that the latter are allowed to exclude liability is not decisive that the former should be allowed to do so. The second was the judgment that an institution has a duty to keep not only the promises it makes in explicit terms but also those it makes implicitly by its conduct; it follows from this that an automobile manufacturer should be held to the impressions made by its advertising as well as the letter of its contracts.

These are not exotic or even very controversial judgments, and the crux of the case was not whether they do represent social practice but whether competing principles, including exclusionary principles, barred them from having any effect. The exclusionary principle most relevant was the principle that only relatively precise agreements count in determining legal obligation; this time-honored principle, which works toward increasing the efficiency of lawsuits, might bar consideration of the vague promises implied in general advertising. But the judge argued, through a careful study of recent precedents in related areas of law, that the force of this exclusionary principle was waning, and was overcome by the powerful effect of institutional advertising, at least on the facts of the present case. It does not follow that the principle would not bar the admission of vague promises in another sort of case.

Almost any controversial case involving the Bill of Rights would illustrate the role assigned to social practices in constitutional reasoning. In the recent case of *Griswold* v. *Connecticut,* for example, the issue posed was whether the Connecticut law forbidding the prescription of contraceptives violated the United States Constitution. A majority of the Supreme Court decided that it did. Different justices gave different grounds for this decision, but each of the majority opinions appealed to judgments of social right and obligation in some way, and two such judgments played a major part in the ultimate decision. The first of these made use of one of the critical principles I mentioned: several justices thought that the Connecticut law was pointless, because it served no point that could properly be attributed to the Connecticut legislature, given the rest of Connecticut's legislation, and given the principle of the First Amendment that a state may not establish obligations to serve a religious point. These justices held that the Constitution incorporates this critical principle through the provision that the state's criminal process must observe due process of law. The second (and much more far-reaching) judgment was that the Constitution invalidates state laws that conflict with social rights established by the most powerful first-order social practices. Some of the justices thought that the social institution of privacy was sufficiently powerful to invoke this constitutional protection and that the anticontraception statute infringed the social rights established by that institution, either directly, or indirectly because enforcement of the law would require invading these rights.

## III. POLITICAL ISSUES

That completes my outline of an alternative theory; I hope that some of the more obvious gaps will be filled by the discussion that follows. I want now to list and discuss the various issues, central to discussions about law reform and civil disobedience, that seem to me to depend on whether one accepts the positivist theory of law or this alternative.

(1) *What grounds should a judge have for changing the law, either by developing unclear or incomplete law in one direction rather than another or by repealing an old doctrine outright?* The positivist theory holds that a judge about to lay down a new rule is exercising his discretion and acting as a legislator. This characterization was originally thought to be liberal, because it recognized the judge's freedom to make new law. But in fact it has suggested, for a great many lawyers who hold the positivist

theory, substantial limitations on judicial authority, because the judge's right to act as a legislator is questionable under democratic theory.

Judges are often appointed rather than elected. When they are elected it is generally for a very long term, and in any event we do not expect them to be responsive to public opinion in reaching their decisions. So they do not have the same warrant to make law, under orthodox political theory, that senators or congressmen do. That fact is not relevant in the simple run-of-the-mill lawsuit, which a judge can decide by applying an established, uncontroversial rule of law. In that case the judge's decisions are justified not on democratic theory but of the ground that the defendant either did or did not have the legal obligation the plaintiff alleged. This is a different ground from democratic theory because it does not suppose that at the time of the decision either the majority of the people or their elected representatives thought that the defendant should have that obligation. (Perhaps the obligation was imposed originally by a statute, but the statute need not represent the will of the majority at the time it is applied by the judge; indeed it might have been repealed between the time of the transaction or event in question and the time of the actual lawsuit.)

But on the positivist theory this alternative justification—that the defendant did or did not have a legal obligation—is unavailable in a hard case, because in such a case, by definition, no such obligation exists. The judge must therefore act as a legislator in spite of the fact that he does not have the legislator's warrant, and that means that he must show deference to the legislature as an institution with superior title. That is, I think, the ground of Oliver Wendell Holmes's injunction that the judge must legislate interstitially, between the cracks of what the legislature has done, and of the popular theory that a judge faced with a hard case should decide as he supposes the legislature would decide. It is also a major source of the doctrine of judicial restraint in constitutional law, because according to positivism a judge interpreting an unclear passage of the Constitution is legislating just as much as a judge filling in the chinks of the Internal Revenue Code, and his warrant is even less clear because the legislature cannot overrule a constitutional decision it disapproves, as it can overrule a disagreeable interpretation of the tax law. Learned Hand, in his brilliant and pessimistic lectures on the Bill of Rights, spoke as a positivist when he criticized the Supreme Court for acting as a super legislature. He meant that if the court was to legislate constitutional law it must do so as a junior rather than a senior partner and must try to allow the legislature the last word on what the Constitution means.

This view of the court's function not only encourages restraint, but also affects substance. It presses the judge, when he does change or develop the law, to look to the majority's interests or inclinations, because the legislature is the creature of the majority. That is not necessarily a conservative bias. In the 1930's, when positivism made great advances in the law schools of this country, the existing law in many instances favored a privileged minority, and the goal of reform was majoritarian equality. The theory that judges should decide novel cases with the interests of the majority at heart was therefore attractive to liberals.

Just now, however, those who worry about social justice are not concerned with recognizing the majority's title to rule but with protecting the rights of minorities against a majority bent on serving its own interest. Some liberals argue that this is a false contrast, and that the best interests of the majority lie in granting what the minorities ask. But that is a pious hope, and it rings false.

The alternate theory takes a very different view of the judge's role in hard cases. It does not draw a sharp line between easy and hard cases, as positivism does; instead it makes available for hard cases the same warrant the judge has in an easy case, that he is doing his best to enforce rights and obligations whose present power is independent of the majority's will. This warrant has the opposite force from the democratic warrant in the cases I just mentioned, when a minority is urging its social rights in its own terms, and the fact that the minority is unable to point to an established legal rule recognizing that right does not, for the reasons I gave, dispose of the issue. Even when the case is a constitutional one (as it may well be when the interests of a minority are at stake) a court may be bold, if it thinks the minority's claims are sound. The court should be sensitive to the views of the legislature and the public at large, on prudential grounds, and because it would be wrong to be arrogant in matters of judgment. But it need not consider itself a junior partner in the enterprise at hand. It need not fear being called a super legislature, because its warrant does not depend upon its being called a legislature at all.

(2) *What can it mean to say that a court, in a hard case, has made a mistake?* This second question need not detain us long, because its answer is governed by the answer to the first. On the positivist theory such a mistake cannot be a mistake of law, any more than a legislature's ill-advised statutes are mistakes of law. If the Supreme Court interprets the equal-protection clause of the Constitution in a way that disappoints me, I can give reasons why a different decision would have been fairer, or more efficient, but I cannot claim that the decision deprived me of anything to which I was legally entitled.

On the alternate theory, however, I can make this claim. I can say that the court made a mistake of law and deprived me of my rights, even though I have to admit that the issue was a close one and that reasonable men may agree with the court and disagree with me. I mean that the arguments supporting my view of the best accommodation of the various legal and social practices are stronger than the court's arguments. If I do take this view, however, then even under the alternate theory I must accept two caveats:

(a) Insofar as public officials (like the sheriff) must take a view of the law in dealing with me, they are obliged to proceed on the court's view rather than mine, not because the court's view is necessarily right, but because there exist independent rules of law that make the court's view count for these purposes, right or not. There are occasions, nevertheless, on which public officials may but need not take a position on the law; on these occasions they might well take into account the fact that I have a bona fide disagreement with the court as to what the law is. One such occasion arises when I have broken the law on the prosecutor's view but not on mine, and he must decide whether to exercise his discretion to prosecute me.

(b) Because of the practice of precedent, the court's view, even if wrong, becomes part of the sources which I must take into account in making fresh judgments of law in the future. When I make my calculations again, that is, I must take into account something that was not present before, namely the court's decision itself. Depending on the issue, and the rank of the court, this additional fact may or may not make the difference. If this issue was one of interpreting a provision of the tax law, and the Supreme Court found against me, then I would be forced to conclude that the decision, though wrong, had changed the law for the future. But if the issue was one of religious freedom, and the Supreme Court held that I might properly be forced to an act that infringed the tenets of my faith, I might well be justified in holding to my contrary view even after the court's decision. The difference between tax cases and civil rights cases is a difference established by the practice of precedent itself; the Supreme Court recognizes that it is bound by its own past decisions to a greater degree in tax cases than in cases affecting civil liberties.

(3) *When is it accurate to say that someone rejects the moral authority of law?* This is not a difficult question on the positivist theory. Under that theory one can draw a sharp distinction between legal and moral obligation and say that a man who disobeys a statute on moral principle is challenging the moral authority of law. There are two different postures such a man can take. He might recognize that the law generally imposes a moral as well as a legal obligation on him—he might accept, that is, a moral obligation to obey the law as such—but he might make exception from time to time and not regard a particular law as

morally binding if it is affirmatively objectionable on strong moral grounds. Or he might object to law as such and not recognize even in principle a moral obligation to obey it.

These distinctions, and the concepts they employ, have dominated discussions about civil disobedience and the challenge to law. The liberal, opposed to the war in Vietnam, thinks of himself as taking the first posture of disobedience. The radical, hating the institution of property, thinks of himself as taking the second. The conservative recognizes the distinction but claims it is irrelevant for purposes of punishment because in either case the law is the law and a dissenter is an outlaw. All three are aware of the fact that a law may be unconstitutional, but they regard this as a possibility to be excluded by hypothesis when civil disobedience is in issue. If the law being broken is unconstitutional, then it is no law, and the problem of civil disobedience does not arise. So the discussion must concentrate on these cases in which there is no doubt of constitutionality, or in which the courts have settled the issue in favor of the law.

But these distinctions cannot be made, at any rate so clearly, on the obligation theory. The root distinction between moral and legal obligation does not hold. Instead we must recognize a number of different sorts of cases of disobedience on principle. Suppose, for example, that a man believes that a statute is unconstitutional, even though the courts have held to the contrary. It is too simple to say that this man, if he refuses to obey the statute, is rejecting his legal obligations, and just as wrong to say that he evidences an attitude of hostility to law. On the alternate theory the court's decision does not necessarily make his view of the law wrong. To report his case with any accuracy, we should have to distinguish between his attitude toward law and toward the skill or, possibly, the authority of the courts. (I say "possibly" because, as I said, the courts themselves refuse to take their past decisions as necessarily controlling their future ones, particularly when important social rights are at stake.)

Suppose, to take a different case, that someone refuses to obey a statute on the ground that it infringes some fundamental social right, such as the right to privacy or security, and the Supreme Court has refused to consider whether the statute is constitutional. Or suppose the court has held the statute constitutional by appealing to an exclusionary policy, like the political question doctrine, or the doctrine that the courts should not adjudicate issues involving special competence in, say, military affairs. Even if the dissenter agrees that the court acted properly in disposing of the constitutional issue in this way, it is too simple again to say that he is rejecting the moral authority of law; we must say instead that he rejects the adequacy of adjudication, with its limitations of institutional competence, as a final guide to what his legal rights and duties are.

A positivist might want to say that this is nonsense, because the prudential exclusionary standards are also legal principles, and if a dissenter does not recognize these as binding on him as well as the courts, then he is challenging the law. It is true that exclusionary principles are legal, in the sense that a court must take them into account, but the alternate theory encourages us to distinguish the different strands that enter into a judicial judgment. It is important, when reporting someone's attitude about law, to distinguish policies that have to do with prudent adjudication from principles, drawn from statutes, precedents, and conventional morality, that express the nation's convictions about how its citizens shall behave and the rights they shall enjoy. If someone appeals to these latter standards to justify his behavior, it misses the heart of his attitude to say only that he is challenging the law on moral grounds. It is vital to add that his grounds are the fundamental principles of the law itself.

But what about the radical who takes the position that the whole of the law is rotten and deserves no respect? Surely it is accurate to say that this man is challenging the institution of law as such? I am not so sure, even here, because this flat statement might hide some important complexities. We must ask for the radical's grounds for condemning the law. Suppose that these involve the charge that our laws and institutions systematically deny important rights, like the right to equality, or dignity, or survival, or self-expression. Suppose, further, that his arguments in favor of these rights appeal to first-order or critical social practices, as they well might. He might appeal, for example, to the traditions of the nation, better exemplified in its earlier days. Or he might argue that the law fails to enforce rights recognized socially, or fails to extend to a minority group rights extended by the majority to its own members. If so, then on the alternate theory the radical's point is not well stated in the proposition that all law is corrupt. He is in fact arguing that the community's law is inconsistent, because a great many of its particular rules conflict with the social institutions and conventions on which the law is supposed to rest, and neither the courts nor the profession have recognized the conflict.

I know that the radical hates what he calls conventional morality as much as he hates what he calls law. But he may well mean by conventional morality only popular morality—the majority's views of what its rights and duties are—and not the complex social institutions and critical practices I tried to describe. Still, it would be wrong to define the thoroughgoing radical out of existence. I assume that there are at least some radicals who would take it as a point of pride to reject social practice of any sort as relevant to their claims, and in the next section I shall describe some of the difficulties I find in this ultraradical posture. I am sure, however, that many radicals do not take this posture, and that fewer would do so if they were not forced to choose between accepting popular morality and rejecting tradition and convention altogether.

I hope that no one will think that the argument has now become too speculative, or that I am playing with words in arguing that at least some radicals who denounce law are in fact paying great respect to its ideal. There are important practical issues at stake here. It is common opinion that those who oppose law are anarchists and outlaws who deserve to be treated as such. My point is that some of those who, on the positivist theory, must be regarded as hostile to law are in fact deeply committed to law in what I consider a more subtle and important sense. They are committed to the idea that government should be regulated by principle, and that those who have social power should extend to everyone the rights that they have consciously or habitually claimed for themselves. On the alternate theory that proposition is the heart of the rule of law; in any event it is the very opposite of anarchy. To call those who hold and act on these views outlaws is a distortion that must cripple our ability to understand and respond to what they say.

(4) *When is one justified in rejecting the authority of law?* We have been discussing when it is accurate to say that someone is challenging the law; now I want to discuss the different issue of whether someone is ever justified in doing so, and if so when. This is a very complex question, and I shall narrow it to this extent. I shall assume that the American community follows a social practice of obedience to law that would give rise, at least in the absence of some competing practice or some applicable critical principle, to a social obligation to obey the law binding on all its members. Many radicals claim that that social obligation has in fact been erased by some such competing practice or critical principle; I shall try to describe the impact of our two theories on that claim. I shall not consider the issue of whether one would have a moral obligation to obey the law, even if the social obligation had lapsed, or whether one has a moral right to disregard the social obligation, even if it has not lapsed. While each of these two last claims has been made, the bulk of the radical arguments now current, as I shall try to show, are aimed at proving that the normal social obligation to obey the law has been wiped away by one or another sort of political injustice.

The assumption I just named, that one has a social obligation to obey the law, unless that obligation has been removed by some critical principle, follows easily from both the positivist and the alternate theories. Positivism traces the authority of all law to a fundamental social practice, namely the practice of accepting and obeying rules created in accordance with the master rule. If there is law in a community, according to positivism, some such practice must exist, and if the law is at all stable, that practice must be spread throughout the bulk of the community. But if a general social practice of this sort exists, then members of the community have a social obligation to follow it, just as they have a social obligation to follow the practices of privacy or mutual defense, unless some critical principle applies. The alternate theory denies the existence of any one fundamental practice, but it traces the authority of law to the combination of several social practices: the distinctly legal practices of legislation and adjudication working in concert with the underlying practices of social obligation. It is therefore quite redundant, on the alternate theory, to say that one has at least a prima-facie social obligation to obey the law, for the law on this theory is the consequence of a set of social obligations. On both theories, however, the social obligations that the law represents can, at least in theory, be overcome if the law is unjust, and this is the background of most radical attacks on law. These attacks typically appeal to the critical principles of fairness; they argue that the institution of law constitutes a discrimination against minority groups within the community, pressing disadvantages on these groups for the sake of others.

The general acceptance of positivism affects these arguments in the following way. The notion that the authority of law rests on one fundamental rule has two consequences. First, it focuses the attack on law on the strictly legal practices and institutions that the master rule designates, for if these can be shown to be unfair it follows that one has no social obligation to obey any of the particular rules generated by these institutions, even those that are not unfair in themselves. Suppose a critic is persuaded, for example, that the legislature of his community is unfairly constituted, because his group is unrepresented, and that the courts, staffed by men from more affluent sectors, are insensitive to the special needs of that group. He might well feel justified in rejecting the practice that transforms the decisions of these institutions into social obligations, and treating that practice as we should treat any social practice we regarded as discriminatory.

If he were a positivist, disposed to rest the social obligation to obey the law on the authority of these institutions, he might conclude that this social obligation had been cut off at the source, and that he had no obligation by virtue of membership in the community to obey even those laws that he did not consider discriminatory, like the rules outlawing theft or violence to property.

Second, the assumption of a master rule neatly separates the social obligation to obey the law from other social rights and obligations, and so permits the radical consistently to reject the former while insisting on the full enforcement of the latter. He may argue that he has no duty to obey the laws of trespass, because the entire law is corrupt, and yet insist that society has the duty to recognize his right to security, privacy, or equality; indeed his arguments that the whole of the law is corrupt may depend in part on the claim that it does not recognize these rights. If legal and other social obligations were thought more interwoven than positivism allows, his position, while not necessarily inconsistent, would require him to show why the features that invalidate legal obligation do not also infect the other obligations he cites.

So positivism, which, as I argued in the last section, encourages the view that someone who disobeys a law on principle is challenging the authority of law wholesale, improves the case that one might have for making such a challenge. The alternate theory, on the other hand, discourages that characterization and complicates that case. If one accepts the alternate theory, he cannot argue, from the unfair composition or performance of any one institution, that the obligation to obey the law is cut off at the source. He must recognize that the legal institutions operate against a background of social practice and convention that supports and confines them, and guides the interpretation of what they do. If there were not an elaborate social system of respect for property, for example, structured by a set of rights and obligations independent of the law, then the law of trespass, for example, would constitute an inconceivable—and unconstitutional—infringement of personal liberty. If there were no statutes dealing with trespass, on the other hand, then the courts would still enforce at least the most important of the social rights at stake, not because a court is really a legislature, but because these rights are sufficiently important so that the courts would have to recognize them, on the alternate theory, notwithstanding the exclusionary principles. Of course the social practices of property are much strengthened by the fact that they have been codified in statutes and enforced by law, and perhaps they would no longer exist if legislatures and courts had tried to stamp them out. But that shows the historical interweaving of legal and social practice, not the formal dependence of one upon the other. So it is a fallacy to argue that because the legislature is unfair one has no social obligation to respect the law of property. That argument neglects the fact that the law of property is supported by a great deal more than the legislature's fiat.

This fact does not, by any means, prove that the laws of trespass represent genuine social as well as legal obligations. It does mean that there is no shortcut to proving the contrary. The conscientious radical, on the alternate theory, has two options if he wishes to deny that obligation. He may, on the one hand, dissect the social practices that support these laws, attempting to show that these social practices themselves conflict with other social rights or with critical principles the community has otherwise established. If he takes this tack, he will no longer seem so radical, because he will be accepting the fundamental principles of social obligation and criticizing particular features of that institution from within. Or he may, on the other hand, renounce the institution of social obligation altogether, relying on some personal or transcendental morality to condemn the very idea that social practice, even monitored by critical principles, can bind men. If he does this, however, then he runs the danger of undercutting his own position. He will then not be able, consistently, to make demands on the community by appealing to social rights or duties; he will not be able, for example, to argue that the community has an obligation, under its own conventions and critical standards, to improve the lives of minority groups. He may, of course, find other bases for argument—or he may not feel that he needs argument—but the appeal to social obligation has been the mainstay of political rhetoric for a long time.

It may seem naïve to suppose that effective radicals—or liberals or conservatives, for that matter—are sensitive to jurisprudential nuances, or that they will act or argue differently depending upon which theory of law gains their favor. It is impossible to say how much argument alters political convictions; this question, like other questions of individual and social motivation, is so entangled in conceptual confusion that it is not even clear how we might begin to answer it. It is clear, however, that persuading opponents to change their minds is not the only function of argument. Being prepared to reason and argue is part of the posture of having principles and acting on principle; one cannot claim to be a liberal, or a prohibitionist, or a Marxist unless he accepts a commitment to whatever has been shown to follow from these faiths. He may disagree that some particular proposition does follow from his principles, but he can hardly ignore arguments that it does. This fact may help to explain why the tradition of making and criticizing arguments has persisted, and why it has been thought an essential ingredient of principled government, in spite of wide suspicion that political argument changes few minds.

The point is of special consequence now. The United States is enforcing foreign and domestic policies supported by a majority but deeply resented by a large and powerful minority. We have not, as a nation, indulged in this stark form of majority rule very often, and our institutions and political maxims have not been developed to ease the tensions it generates. Men of good will sense the need for accommodation, but their principles, as they see them, stand in the way. Consistency to principle seems to demand that lawlessness be punished, on the one hand, and that no compromise be made with illegitimate authority, on the other. So political crises are deepened, not entirely because men are revolted by opposing ideologies, but in part because they feel committed by their own. It is important to discover whether in fact they are.

# HUMAN INTERACTION AND THE LAW

Lon L. Fuller

As it is used in my title, I mean the word "law" to be construed very broadly. I intend it to include not only the legal systems of states and nations but also the smaller systems—at least "law-like" in structure and function—to be found in labor unions, professional associations, clubs, churches, and universities. These miniature legal systems are, of course, concerned with the member's duties and entitlements within the association itself. They find their most dramatic expression when the erring member is called up to be tried for offenses that may lead to his being disciplined or expelled.

When the concept of law is given this broad coverage, it becomes apparent that many of the central issues of today are, in this extended sense, "legal" in nature. The pressure of our present predicament pushes us—as we have not been pushed for a long time—toward an effort at comprehension. We must come to perceive and understand the moral and psychological forces that underlie law generally and give it efficacy in human affairs.

## THE NATURE AND SIGNIFICANCE OF "CUSTOMARY LAW"

If in search of this understanding we turn to treatises on jurisprudence, we shall find that they commonly begin by distinguishing two kinds of law. On the one hand, there is enacted or authoritatively declared law—what may be called "made law"—

on the other hand, there is what is known as "customary law." Customary law is not the product of official enactment but owes its force to the fact that it has found direct expression in the conduct of men toward one another.

As between these two kinds of law the treatises commonly devote almost their entire attention to enacted or declared law, to the law that can be found in statutes, judicial decisions, bylaws, and administrative decrees. The discussion of customary law is largely confined to the question Why should it be thought to be law at all? After some discussion along this line, and some treatment of its function in primitive societies, customary law is generally dismissed as largely irrelevant to advanced civilizations. It tends to be regarded as a kind of museum piece offering an object for serious study only to anthropologists curious about the ways of tribal peoples.

This neglect of the phenomenon called "customary law" has, I think, done great damage to our thinking about law generally. Even if we accept the rather casual analysis of the subject offered by the treatises, it still remains true that a proper understanding of customary law is of capital importance in the world of today. In the first place, much of international law, and perhaps the most vital part of it, is essentially customary law. Upon the successful functioning of that body of law world peace may depend. In the second place, much of the world today is still governed internally by customary law. The newly emerging nations (notably India, and those in Africa and in the Pacific) are now engaged in a hazardous transition from systems of customary law to systems of enacted law. The stakes in this transition —for them and for us—are very high indeed. So the mere fact that we do not see ourselves as regulating our conduct toward fellow countrymen by customary law does not mean that it is of no importance to us as world citizens.

The thesis I am going to advance here is, however, something more radical than a mere insistence that customary law is still of considerable importance in the world of today. I am going to argue that we cannot understand "ordinary" law (that is, officially declared or enacted law) unless we first obtain an understanding of what is called "customary law."

In preparing my exposition I have to confess that at this point I encountered a great frustration. This arises from the term "customary law" itself. This is the term found in the titles and the indexes, and if you want to compare what I have to say with what others have said, this is the heading you will have to look under. At the same time the expression "customary law" is a most unfortunate one that obscures, almost beyond redemption, the nature of the phenomenon it purports to designate. Instead of serving as a neutral pointer, it prejudges its subject; it asserts that the force and meaning of what we call "customary law" lies in mere habit or usage.

Against this view I shall argue that the phenomenon called "customary law" can best be described as *a language of interaction.* To interact meaningfully, men require a social setting in which the moves of the participating players will fall generally within some predictable pattern. To engage in effective social behavior, men need the support of intermeshing anticipations that will let them know what their opposite numbers will do, or that will at least enable them to gauge the general scope of the repertory from which responses to their actions will be drawn. We sometimes speak of customary law as offering an unwritten "code of conduct." The word "code" is appropriate here because what is involved is not simply a negation, a prohibition of certain disapproved actions, but also the obverse side of this negation, the meaning it confers on foreseeable and approved actions, which then furnish a point of orientation for ongoing interactive responses. Professors Parsons and Shils have spoken of the function, in social action, of "complementary expectations";[1] the term "complementary expectations" indicates accurately the function I am here ascribing to the law that develops out of human interaction, a form of law that we are forced—by the dictionaries and title headings—to call "customary law."

Pursuing the comparison with language, let us suppose we were to open a treatise on linguistics and were to encounter the following statement as the first paragraph of the book:

> A spoken language consists of certain patterns of sound men make with their mouths. The forms of these patterns of sound are set by custom and tradition; such is the force of habit that within any given culture men will always be found to make the same general set of sounds that their ancestors did, with at most minor modifications and additions.

Surely, our reaction would be, this is a most curious way to open a discussion of language. We would be apt to say, "But this statement does not tell us what language is *for*. Plainly its purpose is *communication*. If that is its purpose, why then, of course, men will go on using generally the same sounds their fathers did and that their neighbors do now; the reason they do this is simply that they want to be *understood*." Yet in spirit and thought this imaginary introduction to linguistics is not far from what we find about customary law in treatises on jurisprudence. It will be well to turn briefly to some appraisals of customary law taken from the existing literature.

A much-quoted discussion is to be found in Holland's *Elements of Jurisprudence*.[2] He asserts that the characteristic which marks customary law is that

> it is a long and generally observed course of conduct. No one was ever consciously present at the commencement of such a course of conduct, but we can hardly doubt that it originated generally in the conscious choice of the more convenient of two acts, though sometimes doubtless in the accidental adoption of one of two indifferent alternatives; the choice in either case having been either deliberately or accidentally repeated till it ripened into habit.
>
> The best illustration of the formation of such habitual courses of action is the mode in which a path is formed across a common. One man crosses the common, in the direction which is suggested either by the purpose he has in view, or by mere accident. If others follow in the same track, which they are

> likely to do after it has once been trodden, a path is made.
> Before a custom is formed there is no juristic reason for its taking one direction rather than another, though doubtless there was some ground of expediency, of religious scruple, or of accidental suggestion. A habitual course of action once formed gathers strength and sanctity every year. It is a course of action which everyone is accustomed to see followed: it is generally believed to be salutary, and any deviation from it is felt to be abnormal, immoral. It has never been adjoined by the organized authority of the State, but it has unquestioningly been obeyed by the individuals of which the State is composed.

Now in the whole of this very lucidly written passage there is to be found, I submit, no hint that customary law originates in interaction or that it serves the purpose of organizing and facilitating interaction. Indeed, the picture of the lonely path maker seems almost deliberately chosen to rule out the complications involved when men attempt to achieve a reciprocal orientation of their actions.

In the first edition of the *Encyclopedia of Social Sciences,* the article on Customary Law begins by citing Holland, borrows his figure of the lonely path maker, and ends its first paragraph by explaining the role played by customary law in primitive societies as being due to "the force of habit" which "prevails in the whole early history of the race." [3]

Let me now quote briefly a passage from an author generally more favorable to—and, I would say, more perceptive about—customary law than those I have just quoted. Salmond in his treatise on *Jurisprudence*[4] discusses the question What reasons can justify a court in adopting customary practice as a standard of decision? One of these reasons he sees as consisting in the fact that

> custom is the embodiment of those principles which have commended themselves to the national conscience as principles of truth, justice, and public utility. The fact that any rule has already the sanction of custom, raises a presumption that it deserves to obtain a sanction of law also. . . . Speaking gen-

> erally, it is well that courts of justice, in seeking those rules of right which it is their duty to administer, should be content to accept those which have already in their favor the prestige and authority of long acceptance, rather than attempt the more dangerous task of fashioning a set of rules for themselves in the light of nature.

There is, of course, much wisdom—as well as a considerable measure of conservatism—in these remarks. But as touching the nature of customary law, the notion expressed seems to be that, just as a society may have rules imposed on it from above, so it may also reach out for rules by a kind of inarticulate collective preference. Men are seen as directing their interactions by a law that their society has, in some silent way, told them is just and proper. What is missing is any inquiry into the actual social processes through which this law came into being and by which it is sustained.

I might add other quotations from the literature of jurisprudence, but they would not introduce any substantial change in tone or substance into those I have just discussed. The point I wish to make here relates, in any event, not so much to what the writers say about customary law, but to what they do not say. They ask nearly every question that can be asked about customary rules but not such questions as What are the processes by which these rules are created? What functions did that law serve among those who brought it into being? Do the same functional needs exist in our society, and if so, how are we ourselves meeting them? Do we have processes going on around us that are similar to those which, before state-made law existed, brought customary rules into being?

These are questions to which I shall return later. Meanwhile, I should like to consider certain objections that may be raised against the proposal to view customary law as a language of interaction. In the process of answering these objections I may succeed in clarifying somewhat the view I am defending.

The first of these objections is that the customary law in primitive societies may lay down rules that have nothing to do with human interaction. There may be offenses against deities and spirits; a man may be punished, even by death, for an act committed out of the presence of other persons where that act violates some taboo. The answer to this is, I suggest, that animistic views of nature may vastly extend the significance one man's acts may have for his fellows. There is a passage in Walter Bagehot that is very much in point here. Bagehot observes that the "notion that the bad religion of A cannot impair, here or hereafter, the welfare of B is, strange to say, a modern idea." [5] The extent to which one man's beliefs and acts will be seen as affecting his fellows will depend upon the degree to which men see themselves as parts, one of another, and upon their beliefs about the intangible forces that unite them. Within the extended family the distinction between other-regarding and self-regarding acts will assume an aspect very different from that it has in our own society, composed, as that society is, largely of strangers with a strong disbelief in the supernatural.

A further objection to the conception of customary law as a language of interaction may be stated in these terms: Any such conception is much too rationalistic and attributes to customary law a functional aptness, a neatness of purpose, that is far from the realities of primitive practice. Customary law is filled with ritualistic routines and pointless ceremonies; these may cater to a certain instinct for drama, but they can hardly be said to serve effective communication or the development of stable expectations that will organize and facilitate interaction.

In answer I would assert, on the contrary, that a significant function of ritual is precisely that of communication, of labeling acts so that there can be no mistake as to their meaning. Erik Erikson has a fascinating discussion of the ritualism that develops in the interactions of a mother with her infant child.

> The awakening infant conveys a message to his mother and immediately awakens in her a whole repertoire of emotive, verbal, and manipulative behavior. She approaches him with smiling or worried concern, brightly or anxiously voicing a name, and goes into action: looking, feeling, sniffing, she ascer-

> tains possible sources of discomfort and initiates services to be rendered by rearranging the infant's condition, by preparing food, picking him up, etc. If observed for several days (especially in a milieu not one's own) it becomes clear that this daily event is highly formalized, in that the mother seems to feel obliged (and to be not a little pleased) to repeat a performance arousing in the infant predictable responses, which encourage her, in turn, to proceed.[6]

Erikson goes on to make the interesting observation that the formalization of this performance, the ritualistic element in it, is much more readily perceived by strangers to the participants, that is, by those who do not belong to the family, or the class, or the culture within which it develops. He ends by concluding that the purpose of the performance is to express a *mutuality of recognition;* its essential function is, in other words, *communication.* He goes on to refer to studies of ritualistic behavior among animals which indicate that such behavior has developed to "provide an unambiguous set of signals so as to avoid fatal misunderstandings" and concludes that with man "the overcoming of ambivalence is an important aim of . . . ritualization." Certainly among a people who have no state-kept official records to show who is married to whom, the elaborate wedding ceremonies found in some customary systems can be said to serve a purpose of communication and clarification.

To illustrate the points I have been making with regard to ritualism and, more generally, with regard to the communicative function of customary practices, I should like to refer briefly to a development that appears to be occurring in the diplomatic relations of Russia and the United States. Here we may be witnessing something like customary law in the making. Between these two countries there seems to have arisen a kind of reciprocity with respect to the forced withdrawal of diplomatic representatives. The American Government, for example, believes that a member of the Russian embassy is engaged in espionage, or, perhaps I should say, it believes him to be *over*engaged in espionage; it declares him *persona non grata* and requires his departure from this country. The expected response, based on past experience, is that Russia will acquiesce in this demand but will at once counter with a demand for the withdrawal from Russia of an American diplomatic agent of equal rank. Conversely, if the Russians expel an American emissary, the United States will react by shipping back one of Russia's envoys.

Here we have, for the time being at least, a quite stable set of interactional expectancies; within the field covered by this practice each country is able to anticipate with considerable confidence the reactions of its opposite number. This means that its decisions can be guided by a tolerably accurate advance estimate of costs. We know that if we throw one of their men out, they will throw out one of ours.

It should be noticed that the practice is routinized and contains (at least latently) ritualistic and symbolic qualities. Suppose, for example, that the American authorities were confronted with this dilemma: the Russians have declared *persona non grata* a high-ranking member of the American embassy in Moscow, and it turns out to be difficult to find an appropriate counterpiece for return to Russia. We may suppose, for example, that the Soviet representatives of equal rank with the expelled American are persons Washington would like very much to see remain in this country. In this predicament it could cross the minds of those responsible for the decision that they might, in order to preserve a proper balance, return to Russia five men of a lower rank than the expelled American, or perhaps even that the expulsion of ten filing clerks would be the most apt response.

Now I suggest that any responsible public official would reflect a long time before embracing such an alternative. Its danger would lie in the damage it would inflict on the neat symbolism of a one-to-one ratio, in the confusion it might introduce into the accepted meaning of the acts involved. This is a case where both sides would probably be well advised to stick with the familiar ritual, since a departure from it might forfeit the achieved gains of a stable interactional pattern.

The illustration just discussed may seem badly chosen because it represents, one might say, a very impoverished kind of customary law, a law that confers not a reciprocity of benefits but a reciprocity in expression of hostility. But much of the customary law of primitive peoples, it should be recalled, serves exactly the same function. Open and unrestricted hostilities between tribes often become in time subject to tacit and formalized restraints and may, in the end, survive only as a ritualistic mock battle.[7] Furthermore, in the diplomatic practice I have described here there may be present a richer reciprocity than appears on the surface. At the time of the *Pueblo* incident it was suggested that Russia and the United States may share an interest in being moderately and discreetly spied on by each other. We don't want the Russians to pry out our military secrets, but we want them to know, on the basis of information they will trust, that we are not planning to mount a surprise attack on them. This shared interest may furnish part of the background of the ritualistic and patterned exchange of diplomatic discourtesies that seems to be developing between the two countries.

I have already recorded my distress at having to employ the term "customary law" so frequently in this discussion. Both ingredients of the expression, the adjective and the noun, offer difficulties. I shall take up shortly the embarrassments created by the noun. Meanwhile, it would be well to explore more carefully than I have so far the problems involved in finding a satisfactory substitute for "customary." As I have already observed, the principal objection to this word lies in its suggestion that the mere repetition of some action by A will create in others a right that A shall repeat this action, with an added implication that the strength of this claim will vary directly with the duration in time of A's repetitive behavior. Of course, no theorist of customary law in fact embraces any such absurdity, however much the language employed may seem at times to suggest the contrary. My neighbor might for years have risen every morning precisely at eight, yet no one would think that this settled practice could create any obligation toward me unless it entered into some coordination of our activities, as it might if I had come to depend on him to drive me to work in his car. Instead, therefore, of speaking vaguely of an obligation arising through mere "custom" or repetition, it would be better to say that a sense of obligation will arise when a stabilization of interactional expectancies has occurred so that the parties have come to guide their conduct toward one another by these expectancies.

The term "interactional expectancy" is itself, however, capable of producing difficulties. We shall be misled, for example, if we suppose that the relevant expectancy or anticipation must enter actively into consciousness. In fact the anticipations which most unequivocally shape our behavior and attitudes toward others are often precisely those that are operative without our being aware of their presence. To take an example from a somewhat trivial context, experiments have shown that the distance at which people stand toward one another in carrying on ordinary conversations varies predictably among cultures and as between individuals. At the same time most people would not be able to state, without some preliminary testing, what they themselves regard as a normal conversational distance. My inability to define offhand a proper distance would not prevent me, however, from finding offensive the action of someone who projected his face uncomfortably close to mine, nor would it relieve my puzzlement and distress at the conduct of someone who kept retreating when I approached what seemed to me a normal speaking distance. Our conduct toward others and our interpretations of their behavior toward us are, in other words, constantly shaped by standards that do not enter consciously into our thought processes. The analogy of language is once again useful; often we only become aware of rules of grammar when they are broken, and it is sometimes their breach that leads us to articulate for the first time rules we had previously acted on without knowing it.

Any analysis in terms of "interactional expectancies" must also confront the problem of the man who is in some sense an outsider to the expectancies that organize the life of a particular group. He may be literally an outsider—a trader, for example, coming from a distance to sell his wares among a tribal people. Or, though born and raised within the group, he may be "alienated," too imperceptive to understand the system, or perhaps too perceptive to accept some of its built-in absurdities and anomalies. It would, of course, be impossible to undertake here any adequate analysis of the problems suggested. A guess may be hazarded, though, that it is to the intrusion of the true outsider—"the stranger" in Simmel's famous essay[8]—that we owe not only the invention of economic trade but the more general discovery that it is possible for men to arrange their relations with one another by explicit contract.

Now for the difficulties produced by the noun in the expression "customary law." If we speak of "a system of stabilized interactional expectancies" as a more adequate way of describing what the treatises call "customary law," we encounter the embarrassment that many of these expectancies relate to matters that seem remote from anything like a legal context. For example, rules of etiquette fully meet the suggested definition, yet one would scarcely be inclined to call rules of this sort rules of law.

This raises the question How much of what is called "customary law" really deserves the epithet "law"? Anthropologists have devoted some attention to this question[9] and have arrived at divergent responses to it, including one which asserts that the question is itself misconceived, since you cannot apply a conception interwoven with notions of explicit enactment to a social context where rules of conduct come into existence without the aid of a lawmaker. Among those who take the question seriously, the answer proposed by Hoebel has perhaps attracted the most attention; it will repay us to consider it for a moment.

Hoebel suggests that in dealing with stateless or primitive societies, "law may be defined in these terms: A social norm is legal if its neglect or infraction is regularly met, in threat or in fact, by the application of physical force by an individual or group possessing the socially recognized privilege of so acting." [10]

There are, I suggest, a number of difficulties with this solution. First, it seems to define "law" by an imperfection. If the function of law is to produce an ordered relationship among the members of a society, what shall we say of a system that works so smoothly that there is never any occasion to resort to force or the threat of force to effectuate its norms? Does its very success forfeit for such a system the right to be called by the prestigious name of "law"?

Again, can it always be known in advance whether the infraction of some particular norm will be visited with forceful reprisal? The seriousness of the breach of any rule is always in some measure a function of context. One might be inclined to hazard a guess that few societies would regularly punish with violence infractions of the rules of etiquette. Suppose, however, that a peacemaking conference is held by delegations representing two tribes on the verge of war; a member of one delegation uses an insulting nickname in addressing his opposite number; the result is a bloody and disastrous war. Is it likely that his fellow tribesmen would be content to visit on the offender some moderate measure of social censure? If this illustration seems contrived, it may be observed that in our free society it is an accepted legal principle that a man incurs no liability for expressing to another a low opinion of his intelligence and integrity. If a lawyer trying a case in court were to take advantage of this freedom in addressing the judge, he might very well find himself escorted forcibly from the courtroom to serve a jail sentence for contempt.

Perhaps the basic objection to Hoebel's proposal is that it ignores the *systematic* quality of primitive law. The law of the tribe or extended family is not simply a chart of do's and don't's; it is a program for living together. Some parts of the program may achieve articulation as distinct "norms" imposing specially defined "sanctions." But the basic logic of customary law will continue to inhere in the system as a whole. Lévi-Strauss may seem at times to drive this quality of primitive social orders to the point of caricature,[11] but if so, his efforts have provided a wholesome antidote to the tendency to assume that any customary system can be reduced to a kind of code book of numbered paragraphs, each paragraph standing forth as a little law complete in itself.

A recent controversy among anthropologists is worthy of consideration in this connection. In his famous book, *The Judicial Process among the Barotse of Northern Rhodesia,* Max Gluckman suggested that a key element of Barotse legal reasoning lay in the concept of "the reasonable man." The fact that this concept also plays a role in more "advanced" systems argued, so Gluckman concluded, for a certain unity in legal reasoning everywhere. This conclusion was rather emphatically rejected by a number of his professional colleagues.[12]

Perhaps it may help to clarify the issues by considering a rule of law, familiar to every reader, that is at least customary in origin. I refer to "the rule of the road" by which (over most of the world) one passes the oncoming vehicle on the right. Now it would seem redundant and even absurd to introduce into this context anything like the concept of the reasonable man; I pass on the right not because I am a reasonable man but because it is the rule. But suppose a situation is encountered in which the presuppositions underlying the rule no longer hold. For example, one is driving in a parking lot without marked lanes, where other vehicles are coming and going, backing and turning. Or, driving on a regular highway, one encounters an approaching vehicle careening back and forth across the road apparently out of control. In situations like these what is demanded is plainly something like the judgment and concern of "the reasonable man"; in such a context the rule of the road can furnish at most a kind of presumptive guide as to what to do when other factors in the situation offer no clear solution.

Primitive society, like vehicular traffic, is run by a system of interlocking roles. When one man steps out of his role, or a situation arises in which a familiar role forfeits some or all of its meaning, then adjustments will have to be made. There can be no formula to guide these adjustments beyond that of "reasonableness"—exercised in the light of the demands of the system as a whole. It is, therefore, no accident that Gluckman should report that he first perceived the significance of "the reasonable man" for Barotse law as he reflected on a controversy he designates as "The Case of the Biassed Father." [13]

Before proceeding to other matters it may repay us to pursue a little further the analogy between primitive legal systems and the laws of traffic. To that end, perhaps the reader will extend his indulgence to a somewhat uninhibited exercise in fantasy. We begin by supposing that an earthling is being interviewed by a visitor from outer space. In his astral home this visitor follows a profession we would designate as that of legal anthropology. In the pursuit of his speciality he has become fascinated with the earthly laws of traffic, a subject wholly unfamiliar to him because on his planet the movement of goods and living beings is accomplished automatically under the guidance of a computing center. He begins by asking what the rule is when two vehicles approach each other from opposite directions. The response is that each driver keeps to the right. The astral visitor asks, "Why to the right? Why not to the left?" The earthling replies that there is no special reason for the one rule or the other and that in some automotive cultures the rule is indeed that one keeps to the left. (At this point the anthropologist records in his notebook that the earthlings seem singularly incurious about the basic principles of their legal systems and are content to follow rules simply because they have been told they are the proper rules to follow.)

The interview is resumed, and the anthropologist asks, "What about the rule when you overtake another vehicle? I would suppose it would be the same, that is, that you pass on the right; this would keep the law simple and understandable." To the surprise of the astral visitor the earthling replies that the rule in this case is that you pass on the left. But why this anomaly? The earthling replies that it is not an anomaly at all but a logical corollary of the rule that you pass the oncoming vehicle on the right. At this point the anthropologist begins to lose his patience and demands that the earthling give him some simple, easily understood reason why the rule that you overtake on the left is the appropriate rule to go with the rule that you pass the oncoming vehicle on the right. Those of us who feel we might have some difficulty in producing a prompt response to this demand may take some consolation in the reflection that this incapacity of ours may help us to understand the difficulties natives sometimes have in explaining to outsiders the internal logic of their legal orders, particularly with respect to complex systems for reckoning kinship.

Some reflection on problems of traffic regulation may also be useful in another connection, that is, in helping us to understand the impact of "social change"—urbanization and industrialization, for example—on peoples used to ordering their lives by customary law. As every experienced driver knows, the old simplicity of "pass on the right, overtake on the left" has undergone substantial modification in accommodation to modern highway conditions. These changes reflect themselves in lengthening and largely unread paragraphs in the traffic code. Overtaking on the right may, for example, be permitted when driving on multilane divided highways, on one-way city streets, or when the driver ahead signals for a left turn. But these qualifications introduce their own special crop of uncertainties. Are you permitted to overtake on the right when on a very wide multilane highway that is not divided into two unidirectional sections? Again, the driver ahead signals for a left turn, you start to pass him on the right, then discover (before he does) that he is not permitted to turn left. Or, driving on a one-way street, you are about to take advantage of your privilege of overtaking on the right when you suddenly realize that the street is about to become two-way. The American driver caught in these perplexities is in a position to understand something of the plight of the African tribesman who tries conscientiously to live in town by one set of rules, in the country by another, and has some trouble at times in keeping the two systems apart.

## THE INTERACTIONAL FOUNDATIONS OF CONTRACT LAW

The brief account of contract law that follows has been included here primarily for the light it may shed on customary law, which is often and properly said to contain a "consensual element." In this shared aspect, contract law and customary law are indeed near cousins and a study of either will help to understand the other. In the course of the analysis that follows, I shall have occasion to revisit from a somewhat different perspective some of the questions already discussed, particularly that of knowing how to determine when patterns of interaction can properly be said to have created an obligation to persist in them.

In keeping with the general objective just outlined, we shall be concerned here with contract as a source of social order, as one means for establishing "stable interactional expectancies." As it is used in my subtitle, therefore, the term "contract law" refers primarily not to the law *of* or *about* contracts but to the "law" a contract itself brings into existence. This employment of the word "law" represents, of course, a considerable departure from the conventions we ordinarily follow in using the term.

Our reluctance to apply the word "law" to the obligation created by a contract is, however, in many ways an anomaly. In enforcing contracts, courts purport to derive the legal rights and duties of the litigants from the terms of their agreement, much as if a statute were being applied. The Romans did not hesitate, at least in certain contexts, to apply the word *"lex"* to contractual provisions, and the Latin word seems indeed to have taken its origin in a contractual context. Today international lawyers list treaties as the prime source of their kind of law. Though the term "customary law" has been regarded by some legal theorists as an abuse of language, today most writers seem to have overcome any qualms about that expression; the acceptance of "customary law" and the rejection of "contractual law" is all the more remarkable since if what is associated with "law" is something like an explicit legislative process, the contract comes much closer to fitting that model than do the silent processes through which customary law comes into being. Finally, as proof that lawyers do not reject the expression "law of the contract" because it conflicts with any basic demand of legal logic, I cite their readiness to accept the thought contained in the expression, provided it comes decently clothed in paraphrase. Thus, I doubt if any lawyer would be deeply perplexed (though he might be slightly intrigued) by the statement contained in Article 1134 of the French Civil Code that a contract "serves as law" between the parties. (*"Les conventions légalment formées tiennent lieu de loi à ceux qui les ont faites."*)

If we permit ourselves to think of "contract law" as the "law" that the parties themselves bring into existence by their agreement, the transition from customary law to contract law becomes a very easy one indeed. The difficulty then becomes, not that of subsuming the two kinds of law under one rubric but of knowing how to draw a clear line of division between them. We may say of course (using the jargon I have inflicted on the reader here) that in the one case the relevant interactional expectancies are created by words, in the other, by actions.

But this is too simple a view of the matter. Where words are used, they have to be interpreted. When the contract falls within some general area of repetitive dealings, there will usually exist a body of "standard practice" in the light of which verbal ambiguities will be resolved. Here, in effect, interactional regularities in the world outside the contract are written into the contract in the process of interpretation. In commercial law generally it is often difficult to know whether to say that by entering a particular field of practice the parties became subject to a governing body of customary law or to say that they have by tacit agreement incorporated standard practice into the terms of their contract.

The meaning of a contract may not only be determined by the area of practice within which the contract falls but by the interactions of the parties themselves after entering their agreement.

If the performance of a contract takes place over a period of time, the parties will often evidence by their conduct what courts sometimes call a "practical construction" of their agreement; this interpretation by deeds may control over the meaning that would ordinarily be attributed to the words of the contract itself. If the discrepancy between the parties' acts and the words of their agreement becomes too great to permit the courts to speak of a "practical construction," they may hold that the contract has been tacitly modified or even rescinded by the manner in which the parties have conducted themselves toward one another since entering the agreement.

Generally we may say that in the actual carrying out of a complex agreement between friendly parties, the written contract often furnishes a kind of framework for an ongoing relationship, rather than a precise definition of that relationship. For that definition we may have to look to a kind of two-party customary law implicit in the parties' actions, rather than to the verbal formulations of the contract; if this is true of contracts that are eventually brought to court, it must be much more commonly so in situations where the parties make out without resort to litigation.

If the words of a contract have to be interpreted in their interactional context, or in the light of the actions taken under them by the parties, the actions that bring customary law into existence also require to be interpreted, sometimes almost as if they were words. This problem of interpretation is at once the most crucial and most neglected problem of customary law; intrinsically difficult, it is made more so by inept theories about the nature of customary law, such as those explaining it as an expression of "the force of habit" that "prevails in the early history of the race."

The central problem of "interpretation" in customary law is that of knowing when to read into an act, or a pattern of repetitive acts, an obligatory sense like that which may attach to a promise explicitly spelled out in words. All are agreed that a person, a tribe, or a nation does not incur an obligation—

"legal" or "moral"—simply because a repetitive pattern can be discerned in his or its actions. All would probably also agree that the actions which create customary law must be such as enter into *inter*actions, though a complication ensues when we recall that under some circumstances inaction can take on the qualities of action, as when it becomes appropriate to call it "acquiescence" or "forbearance." Beyond this we encounter almost a vacuum of ideas.

Into this vacuum there is projected at least one articulate attempt at formulating a test. This is found in the doctrine of *opinio necessitatis*. According to this principle (which still enjoys some esteem in international law) customary law arises out of repetitive actions when and only when such actions are motivated by a sense of obligation, in other words, when people behave as they do, not because they want to, or because they act unreflectively, but because they believe they have to act as they do. This seems a curiously inept solution. In clear cases of established customary law, it becomes a tautology; in situations where customary law is in the process of being born, it defaults.

One might suggest that a better approach could be found in the principle contained in Section 90 of the American Law Institute's Restatement of Contracts. As formulated to fit the problem at hand this principle would run along these (unfortunately somewhat complex) lines: Where by his actions toward B, A has (whatever his actual intentions may have been) given B reasonably to understand that he (A) will in the future in similar situations act in a similar manner, and B has, in some substantial way, prudently adjusted his affairs to the expectation that A will in the future act in accordance with this expectation, then A is bound to follow the pattern set by his past actions toward B. This creates an obligation by A to B; if the pattern of interaction followed by A and B then spreads through the relevant community, a rule of general customary law will have been created. This rule will normally become part of a larger system, which will involve a complex network of reciprocal expectations. Absorption of the new rule into the larger system will, of course, be facilitated by the fact that the interactions that gave rise to it took place within limits set by that system and derived a part of their meaning for the parties from the wider interactional context within which they occurred.

The familiar phenomenon of the spread of customary law from one social context to another suggests a further distinction between customary law and contract law that deserves critical examination here. It may be said that a contract binds only the parties to it, while customary law normally extends its rules over a large and at times somewhat unclearly defined community. The first observation is that while this spread of customary law is a common occurrence it is by no means inevitable. Something that can be called two-party customary law can and does exist; it is, again, only a linguistic prejudice that makes us hesitant about this employment of the word "law."

Where customary law does in fact spread, we must not be misled as to the process by which this extension takes place. It has sometimes been thought of as if it involved a kind of inarticulate expression of group will; the members of Group B perceive that the rules governing Group A would furnish an apt law for them; they therefore take over those rules by an act of tacit collective adoption. This kind of explanation abstracts from the interactional processes underlying customary law and ignores their ever-present communicative aspect. Take, for example, a practice in the field of international relations, that of offering a twenty-one-gun salute to visiting heads of state. By a process of imitation this practice seems now to have become fairly general among the nations. One may say loosely that its appeal lies in the appropriateness of a resounding boom of cannon as a way of signalizing the arrival of a distinguished visitor. But why twenty-one guns instead of sixteen or twenty-five? It is apparent that once the pattern of twenty-one became familiar, any departure from it could generate misapprehension; spectators would spend their time not in enjoying the grandeur of cannon roar but in counting booms, attributing all sorts of meanings—intended and unintended—to any departure from the last allocation. Generally we may say that where A and B have become familiar with a practice obtaining between C and D, A is likely to adopt this pattern in his actions toward B, not simply or necessarily because it has any special aptness for their situation but because he knows B will understand the meaning of his behavior and will know how to react to it.

As for the proposition that a contract binds only those who made it, who actively and knowingly assented to its terms, a mere glance at modern contracting practice is sufficient to reveal how unreal and purely formal this proposition can become. Only a tiny fraction of the "contracts" signed today are actually negotiated or represent anything like an explicit accommodation of the parties' respective interests. Even contracts drafted by lawyers, and in theory specially fitted to the parties' situation, are apt to be full of traditional or "standard" clauses borrowed from other contracts and from general practice. These clauses are employed for a great variety of reasons—because the lawyer is in a hurry, or because he knows from the precedents how courts will construe them, or because the interests at stake are insufficient to justify the fee that would be appropriate to a more careful, specially tailored phrasing.

But the realities of contracting practice are much further removed from the picture of a "meeting of minds" than is suggested by a mere reference to standard clauses. In fact, the overwhelming majority of contracts are embodied in printed forms, prepared by one party to serve his interests and imposed on the other on a take-it-or-leave-it basis. In recent years American courts in dealing with such contracts have increasingly exercised the right to strike out clauses they regard as oppressive or grossly unfair. This practice stands in contrast with that of the homeland of the common law, where the courts are much more conservative in this matter, being inclined generally to enforce the contract "as written," that is, as printed from boiler plate. There is a certain irony in this, for from the time of Lord Coke the English courts have freely claimed the right to refuse enforcement to customary law deemed unreasonable and repugnant to the ordinary sense of fairness. If we were to search about in modern society for the nearest counterpart to the "repugnant" customary law of Coke's time, we might well find it in the standardized printed contract, drafted by one party and signed unread by the other.

There remains for discussion one further distinction that can be taken between contract law and customary law. This lies in the notion that a contract comes into effect at once, or when the parties stipulate it shall, while custom becomes law only through a usage observed to have persisted over a considerable period.

This is, again, too simple a view of the matter. The notion that customary law comes into effect gradually and only over a considerable period of time comes about in part because of mistaken implications read into the word "customary," and in part because it is true that normally it takes some time for reciprocal interactional expectancies to "jell." But there are circumstances in which customary law (or a phenomenon for which we have no other name) can develop almost overnight. As an authority in international law has observed,

> A new rule of customary international law based on the practice of States can emerge very quickly, and even almost suddenly, if new circumstances have arisen which imperatively call for regulation—though the time-factor is never wholly irrelevant.[14]

(The assertion sometimes encountered that to be accepted as law a custom must have existed "from time immemorial" is directed to a very special question, that is, When should custom be regarded as overriding provisions of the general law? This obviously can be something quite different from asking when custom should control an issue previously not regulated by law at all. The doctrine of *opinio necessitatis* probably originated in the same context, for it may make good sense to say that a man should not be held to have infringed at least some kinds of general law where he acted in the belief that a special or local customary law obligated him to conduct himself as he did.)

As for the notion that a contract binds at once, and before any action has been taken under it, this is again a misleading simplification, especially when the matter is viewed historically. It is, of course, dangerous to attempt generalizations about the historical course of legal development in all societies. Nevertheless, it is reasonably safe to say that the legal enforcement of contracts first emerges in two contexts. The first of these is that of the ritualistic promise, the promise accompanied by some traditional oath or the recital of a set verbal formula, for example. Here, indeed, the contract binds at once and without proof of any action under it. But the very formality of this process of "binding," and the distrust implied by an insistence on it, has no doubt always inhibited its use, as it does today in the case of its modern counterparts.

The second early legal manifestation of the contract principle involves the situation of the half-completed exchange. A delivers fish to B in return for B's promise of a basket of vegetables. B keeps the fish but refuses to deliver the vegetables. Plainly there is nothing mysterious about the fact that in this situation legal redress became available at an early period in history. It should be noted, however, that the obligation enforced rests not on mere words but primarily on the action (and inaction) that followed the words.

It appears likely that in all legal systems the enforcement of the executory bilateral contract is a development that comes quite late. This is the situation where A and B agree on the exchange, let us say again, of fish for vegetables; when A comes to deliver the fish, B refuses his offering and repudiates the agreement. The recognition that A has a legal claim in this situation seems generally to have occurred contemporaneously with the development of something like a market economy. But in such an environment there is likely to be action, at least in the sense of forbearance, in the very act of entering the contract. A, in seeking about for a chance to trade his fish for vegetables, forgoes, when he strikes his bargain with B, the chance to enter a similar trade with C, D, or E. So here once again the agreement becomes enforceable because its words have been underscored, as it were, by reliance on them; in this case, by an inferred neglect of other opportunities once the contract in question has been concluded.

Finally, it should be recalled that the promise of an outright gift retains to this day a somewhat uncertain legal status. There may exist cumbersome legal forms for making such promises enforceable, and the courts have sometimes shown remarkable ingenuity in finding tacit elements of exchange in what appears on its face as an expression of sheer generosity. In the United States there has emerged a doctrine (now known generally as the Section 90 Principle) whereby the promise may become enforceable when the promisee has seriously and reasonably taken its anticipated performance into account in the arrangement of his own affairs. As I have previously suggested (*supra,* p. 190), this principle is not far removed from one that underlies customary law generally.

## THE INTERACTIONAL FOUNDATIONS OF ENACTED LAW

Early in this essay I stated my intention to advance a thesis "more radical than a mere insistence that customary law is still of considerable importance in the world of today. I am going to argue that we cannot understand 'ordinary' law (that is, officially declared or enacted law) unless we first obtain an understanding of what is called 'customary law.' " The time has come to attempt some fulfillment of the commitment implied in this statement.

In the pages that have gone before I have treated both customary law and contract law as interactional phenomena. I have viewed them as arising out of interaction and as serving to order and facilitate interaction. Can anything like this be asserted of enacted law, as typified, for example, by the statute? Can we regard enacted law itself as dependent on the development of "stable interactional expectancies" between lawgiver and subject? Does enacted law also serve the purpose of ordering and facilitating the interactions of citizens with one another?

It cannot be said that there are no traces of ideas like these in the literature. What can be said is that it requires some diligence to find them. As for the general purpose of enacted law, the standard formula—both in jurisprudence and sociology—is to the effect that "law serves as an instrument of social control." Sometimes this conception is coupled with the notion that the necessity for law arises entirely from man's defective moral nature; if men could be counted on to act morally, law would be unnecessary. As for the way law is conceived to come into existence, it is by an exercise of authority and not from anything like an interplay of reciprocal expectancies. The law does not invite the citizen to interact with it; it acts upon him.

Let us test the question whether enacted law serves to put in order and facilitate human interaction by inquiring how this conception applies to some actual branches of the law. First, consider the law embraced under the following headings: contract, agency, marriage and divorce, property (both private and public), and the rules of court procedure. All of these vital branches of the law serve primarily to set the terms of men's relations with one another; they facilitate human interaction as traffic is facilitated by the laying out of roads and the installation of direction signs. To say that these branches of law would be unnecessary if men were more disposed to act morally is like saying that language could be dispensed with if only men were intelligent enough to communicate without it. The fact that the branches of law just listed include restraints as well as enabling provisions in no sense detracts from their facilitative quality; there is no more paradox here than there is in the proposition that highway traffic can be expedited by signs that read, "No Left Turn," "Stop, Then Enter."

An interactional theory of law can hardly claim acceptance, however, simply because it seems apt when applied to certain branches of the law, such as contracts, property, agency, and marital rights. The law of crimes, for example, presents a quite different test, for here an interactional view encounters an environment much less congenial to its premises. There would, for example, be something ludicrous about explaining the rule against murder as being intended to facilitate human interaction by removing from men's confrontations the fear that they may kill one another. Murder, we are likely to say, is prohibited because it is wrong, not because the threat of it can detract from the potential richness of man's relations with his fellows.

Viewed from a historical perspective, however, the matter assumes a very different aspect. Students of primitive society have seen the very inception of the concept of law itself in limitations on the blood feud. A member of Family A kills a member of Family B. In a primitive society the natural response to this act is for the members of Family B to seek revenge against Family A. If no limits are set to this revenge, there may ensue a war to the death between the two families. There has, accordingly, grown up in many primitive societies a rule that blood revenge on the part of Family B must, in the case supposed, be limited to one killing, though the injured family is regarded as being entitled as of right to this degree of counterkill. A later development will normally prohibit blood revenge and require instead compensation in the form of "blood money" for the life of the man whose life was taken. Here, plainly, the law of murder serves to regulate interaction and, if you will, to facilitate interaction on a level more profitable for all concerned than killing and counterkilling.

Today the law against murder appears on the surface to have become entirely divorced from its interactional origins; it is seen as projecting its imperative, "Thou shalt not kill," over the members of society generally and without regard to their interrelations. But what has in fact happened is that interactional issues that were once central have, as the result of legal and moral progress, been pushed to the periphery, where they remain as lively as ever. The most obvious example is offered by the plea of self-defense; a man is still legally privileged to kill an aggressor if this is necessary to save his own life. But how shall we interpret "necessary" in this context? How far can we expect a man to run some risk to his own life in order to avoid taking the life of another? Again, there is the question of reducing the degree of the offense when a man kills in "hot blood," as when he comes upon another making love to his wife. Finally, there are the disputed issues of killing to prevent a felony or to stop a fleeing felon. In all these much debated cases the rule against homicide may be modified, or punishment reduced, by a reference to the question What can reasonably be expected of a man in these interactional situations?

I trust it is clear that I am not advancing here the thesis that law, in its actual formulation and administration, always serves exclusively the purpose of ordering and facilitating human interaction. There are, certainly, some manifestations of law which cannot readily be forced into this frame of thought. Perhaps the most significant of these lies in that portion of the criminal law relating to what have been called "crimes without victims." Included here are laws forbidding the sale of intoxicants and contraceptive devices, the use of marijuana, homosexual practices, prostitution, and gambling. Assuming that those involved are of sound mind, and that there is no deception—the roulette wheel has not been "rigged," for example—these laws, far from facilitating interaction, have as their purpose preventing forms of interaction desired by the participants and not directly designed, at least, to injure others.

It is no accident, I think, that it is in this area—the area precisely where legal restraint appears most unequivocally as an "instrument of social control"—that the grossest failures of law have everywhere occurred. It is an area characterized by corruption, selective and sporadic enforcement, blackmail, and the open tolerance of illegality. There is no need to argue here that this body of law requires critical re-examination. The problem is to know by what guiding principle to direct that re-examination.

We should begin by asking ourselves why the law fails so notably in this general area of "crimes without victims." The usual answer is that you cannot enforce morality by law. But this is not so. Keeping promises may be a moral obligation, yet the law can and does successfully force people to keep their promises. Not only that, but the legal enforcement of promises, far from weakening the moral sense of obligation, tends to strengthen it. Suppose, for example, a situation where men associated in some business enterprise are discussing whether they ought to perform a disadvantageous contract. Those who believe they are morally bound to do so are in a position to remind their less principled associates that if the contract is broken they will all be brought to court and will subject themselves not only to the cost but also to the opprobrium of an adverse judgment. There are areas of human concern, then, where the cliché that you can't make men act morally by law does not hold. These are, I believe, precisely the areas where the law's sanctions reinforce interactional expectancies and facilitate a respect for them.

In dealing with primitive systems a distinction is sometimes taken between wrongs and sins.[15] A wrong is an act that inflicts a palpable damage on the fabric of social relations; a sin is thought to work a more diffuse harm by spreading a kind of corruption. Typically in primitive societies wrongs and sins are dealt with by different standards and different procedures, formalized "due process" being not uncommonly relaxed in the case of sins. While I would not recommend a resort to sorcery or ostracism as a way of dealing with modern sins, I think we might profitably borrow from primitive society some of the wisdom displayed in the basic distinction between wrongs and sins. Perhaps we might also add to that wisdom the insight that the best way for the law to deal with at least some modern sins is to leave them alone.

In this discussion of "the interactional foundations of enacted law" I have so far been chiefly concerned with the question whether enacted law can properly be regarded as putting in order and facilitating human interaction. It is time now to turn to what may seem the more basic question: Does enacted law itself depend for its existence on the development of "stable interactional expectancies" between lawgiver and subject?

To answer this question in the affirmative—as I shall here—is to run counter to an assumption now generally accepted in jurisprudence and sociology, the assumption, namely, that the essential characteristic of law lies simply in the fact that it is an exercise of *authority*. But we must ask, Authority to do *what?* Many men enjoy authority without being empowered to make law. Both an Army colonel and the director of a government printing office have "authority" in that they are thought of as rightfully exercising a control over those committed to their direction. They are not, however, considered to make law. How, then, do we distinguish between the functions performed by, let us say, a boss and those performed by a lawgiver? These two figures plainly represent distinct kinds of "social control." But how do we define the difference between them?

An ancient answer to this question—rather lost from view in contemporary discussions—is that the basic characteristic of law lies in its *generality*. Law lays down *general* rules; managerial direction may proceed by specific orders: "Here, do this." "A, change places with B." "Report tomorrow at eight-thirty." The difficulty here is that managerial direction also often proceeds by general rules or "standing orders." Would a managerial director so gifted with foresight and a capacity for apt phrasing that he never had occasion to issue anything but general orders become by that token a lawgiver?

To perceive the distinction between the office of boss and that of lawgiver we have to go behind the quality of generality and ask *why* it has been thought that law must take the form of general rules. The answer is a relatively simple one: The law does not tell a man what he should do to accomplish specific ends set by the lawgiver; it furnishes him with base lines against which to organize his life with his fellows. A transgression of these base lines may entail serious consequences for the citizen —he may be hanged for it—but the establishment of the base lines is not an exercise in managerial direction. Law provides a framework for the citizen within which to live his own life, though, to be sure, there are circumstances under which that framework can seem so uncomfortably lax or so perversely constrictive that its human object may believe that straightforward managerial direction would be preferable.

If we accept the view that the central purpose of law is to furnish base lines for human interaction, it then becomes apparent why the existence of enacted law as an effectively functioning system depends upon the establishment of stable interactional expectancies between lawgiver and subject. On the one hand, the lawgiver must be able to anticipate that the citizenry as a whole will accept as law and generally observe the body of rules he has promulgated. On the other hand, the legal subject must be able to anticipate that government will itself abide by its own declared rules when it comes to judge his actions, as in deciding, for example, whether he has committed a crime or claims property under a valid deed. A gross failure in the realization of either of these anticipations—of government toward citizen and of citizen toward government—can have the result that the most carefully drafted code will fail to become a functioning system of law.

It is a curious fact of history that although the older books are full of discussions of the principle that law implies general rules, there is almost no explicit recognition that the enactment of general rules becomes meaningless if government considers itself free to disregard them whenever it suits its convenience. Perhaps there is here illustrated a phenomenon already discussed,[16] that the anticipations which most firmly direct our actions toward others are often precisely those that do not rise to consciousness. Such anticipations are like the rules of grammar that we observe in practice without having occasion to articulate them until they have been conspicuously violated. Perhaps there is also operative here a confusion arising from the fact that we realize that normally a lawgiver can change any of his laws simply by repealing it and providing a quite different law for the governance of events thereafter happening. It seems curious that the agency that can rewrite the whole book of laws should be held to respect the most insignificant of its enactments in judging the events that occurred while it was still in effect. There is the paradox here, in Simmel's words, of "interaction within an apparently one-sided and passive submission." [17] Yet without that paradox the notion of enacted "law" would become empty and meaningless.

What are the practical implications of the twin requirements that law be expressed in general rules and that government abide by its own rules in acting upon the citizen? The short answer is that these implications are subtle and complex—so much so that they cannot be adequately explored in the present context. Certainly there is no intention here to suggest that the ordinary citizen should go about with a code book in his hand ascertaining whether government is conforming to its own rules. Normally, and by and large, the citizen must of necessity accept on faith that his government is playing the game of law fairly. But precisely because this faith plays so important a role in the functioning of a legal system, a single dramatic disappointment of it, or a less conspicuous but persistent disregard of legality over a whole branch of law, can undermine the moral foundations of a legal order—both for those subject to it and for those who administer it.

In speaking here of the moral aspects of the problem, there is no intention to imply that the preservation of legality does not make demands on the intellect as well as on good intentions. For example, a legislature passes a law authorizing the construction of a park in the city of Zenith. Does this enactment violate the principle that laws must be general in form? We may dismiss this problem as involving nothing more than a pun on the word "law," but in other cases, since government normally exercises managerial and administrative functions as well as legislative ones, the problem can become more perplexing. Again, suppose the absurd situation of a government that has only one law in the books: "Do right and avoid evil." Here the rule is "general" in a way that undermines legality more thoroughly than any number of "special" laws could do. These examples can only suggest some of the complexities that arise in the actual realization of the Rule of Law.[18] When these complexities are taken into account, the task of creating and administering a legal system will be seen as a very different kind of enterprise than is suggested when it is described simply as an exercise of "authority" for the purpose of effecting "social control."

In the analysis now being concluded, three distinct kinds of law have been passed in review: customary law, contract law, and enacted law. This list omits a fourth expression of law, namely, adjudicative law as exemplified in the Anglo-American "common law." It is fashionable nowadays to consider the common law as being simply a form of enacted law, differing from statutory law only in its authorship, a statute being enacted by a legislature, a rule of common law being declared by a court. This view ignores the special qualities exemplified by the common law, qualities that once led men—with much justification—to speak of it as a form of customary law. For the common law, by virtue of its special way of making law case by case, projects its roots more deeply and intimately into human interaction than does statutory law—though, to be sure, in the country of its origin it seems to be losing the qualities that once distinguished it, perhaps because its judges have finally begun to conform their practice to the pattern legal theory has been ascribing to it for more than a century.

If we view law as serving the purpose of putting in order and facilitating human interaction, it is apparent that the making of law involves the risk that we may be unable to foresee in advance the variety of interactional situations that may fall within the ambit of a preformulated rule. A statute that reveals itself as a patent misfit for situations of fact that later come to court—situations plainly covered by the language of the statute, but obviously misunderstood or not foreseen by the draftsman—such a law certainly has no special claim to praise simply because it is clear in meaning and announced in advance. The virtue of the common law is that, proceeding case by case, it can fit and refit its prescriptions to the configurations of life as they reveal themselves in litigation. What the common law lacks in the way of clear advance formulation, it may more than make up for by its capacity to reshape and reword its rules in the light of the actual situations that offer themselves for decision.

The common law presents, then, a complex amalgam of law-making forms, intermixing explicit legislation with the tacit adjustments characteristic of customary law, sometimes expressing the best qualities of both systems, and, on rare occasions, displaying the worst qualities of both.[19]

## INTERACTIONS BETWEEN LAW AND ITS SOCIAL CONTEXT

Implicit in all that has gone before in this essay is the view that law and its social environment stand in a relation of reciprocal influence; any given form of law will not only act upon but be influenced and shaped by the established forms of interaction that constitute its social milieu. This means that for a given social context one form of law may be more appropriate than another, and that the attempt to force a form of law upon a social environment uncongenial to it may miscarry with damaging results.

This presents the problem of knowing how to define and distinguish the various kinds of "social contexts." On this matter, the literature of sociology provides an uncomfortably extensive vocabulary of relevant terms: *Gemeinschaft* and *Gesellschaft,* organic and mechanical solidarity. social space, social distance, familistic, contractual and compulsory relations, the folk-urban continuum, the primary group, and a host of related terms attempting to describe the varying textures, patterns and densities displayed by the social fabric.[20]

For the present purposes I shall employ simply the notion of a spectrum or scale of relationships, running from intimacy, at the one end, to hostility, at the other, with a stopping place midway that can be described as the habitat of friendly strangers, between whom interactional expectancies remain largely open and unpatterned. As typifying the intimate relationship, I shall take the average American family, with no servants, young children in the home, household chores to be apportioned, and members who are on reasonably good terms with one another. At the other end of the spectrum, I have in mind not two individuals who are enemies but two hostile nations not under the control of a superior political power that might contain their tendencies toward overt hostile action.

In attempting here to test the different forms of law against varying social contexts I shall begin with contractual law, by which, the reader will recall, I mean the "law" of the contract itself, not the state-made law *of* or *about* contracts. The reason for choosing contractual law as a starting point is that, in a sense, it stands halfway between customary law and enacted law, sharing some of the qualities of both. On the one hand, contractual law is like customary law in that its prescriptions are not imposed on the parties by some outside authority; they make their own law. On the other hand, contractual law resembles legislation in that it involves the explicit creation of verbalized rules for the governance of the parties' relationship.

If we start with the "intimate" end of the scale, it is apparent that contract is an instrument ill-suited to ordering the relations within a functioning family. We are apt to put this in affective terms, saying that people united by affection would have difficulty in negotiating with one another and that any attempt to do so might disturb the harmony of the home. But the problem also has what may be called an operational aspect; the allocation of household responsibilities is affected by shifting and unpredictable contingencies; someone becomes ill, one of the children falls behind in his school work, father has to be away on a trip, etc. No degree of contractual foresight would be equal to dealing in advance with all these permutations in the internal affairs of the family.

It seems a safe guess that not many married couples have attempted to arrange their internal affairs by anything like an explicit contract. In the few reported cases in which judicial enforcement of such contracts has been sought, the courts have denied relief. One court observed that "judicial inquiry into matters of that character, between husband and wife, would be fraught with irreparable mischief." [21] Another court remarked that if the parties were able to enter binding contracts regulating their internal relations this would "open an endless field for controversy and bickering and would destroy the element of flexibility needed in making adjustments to new conditions . . ." [22]

If we move to the opposite end of the spectrum and consider contracts between parties standing in what I have called a social relation of hostility, a contractual regulation becomes, once again, not only difficult to negotiate but also often an inept device for achieving the end sought. The simple way of explaining this is to say that hostile parties don't trust one another and mutual trust is essential both for the negotiation and the administration of a contract. But the problem, once again, has what may be called an operational aspect. The negotiation of a contract of any complexity will involve an intricate fitting together of diverse interests. This, in turn, means that in the course of negotiations—in the stand he takes for or against some demanded concession—each party is compelled to make some disclosure of the internal posture of his own interests. This disclosure may be disadvantageous to him, especially if negotiations fall through. Thus, suppose that in negotiations looking toward a reduction in armaments between two hostile countries, Country A, to the surprise of Country B, seems quite ready to agree to a broad limitation on the production and use of Weapon X; Country B at once begins to ask itself, "Why is that? Are they aware of some limitation on the effectiveness of Weapon X we don't know about? Or do they want us to give up producing Weapon X, which they fear, and divert our resources to Weapon Y, against which they perhaps have developed an adequate defense?" etc. This necessity for some disclosure in order to achieve a successful fitting together of the parties' diverse interests is often inhibitive, not only in international relations but in other fields as well, sometimes even in business deals. Perhaps the ultimate cure for it lies in the gradual and patient establishment of multiple ties of association between the parties, so that their social bond is not concentrated in one negotiation or one document. When that happens, however, the organizing principle of the parties' relationship is apt to cease to be contractual and become essentially one of customary law.

I should like now to turn to the middle ground of the spectrum of social contexts, the area I have previously described as "the habitat of friendly strangers, between whom interactional expectancies remain largely open and unpatterned." This is precisely the area where contractual law is most at home and most effective; it is also here, without much doubt, that the very notion of explicit contracting was first conceived.

We are prone to suppose that as we move away from relations of intimacy our freedom of expression and action becomes progressively restricted; with strangers we are "ill at ease"; it is only with close friends that we are free to say what we think and declare what we would like to have. But in fact, in dealing with intimates we are, often quite without knowing it, restrained by a host of unarticulated expectations—compelled, as it were, to act out roles tacitly assigned to us in previous encounters. As Simmel points out, it is often precisely the stranger who receives "the most surprising openness—confidences which would be carefully withheld from a more closely related person." [23] It is this "openness" of the relations between strangers that facilitates negotiation in a manner that would be impossible (and probably inadvisable) within an intimate group like the family.

All over the world the intimacies of the extended family, the tribe, and the country village have proved an obstacle to the establishment of dealings on a straightforward commercial basis. It is hard, for example, to hold a relative or a close friend to prompt payment of his account. Mair reports a general anthropological observation that the "pressures to give easy credit on a man setting up a store in his own village are apt to be so great that he cannot make a success of his business." [24] An enterprising American Indian tribe in the state of Washington is said to have encountered a similar frustration in attempting to engage in business enterprises on the reservation.[25] Perhaps the most interesting observation of this sort is contained in *The Irish Countryman* by Conrad Arensberg.[26] According to Arensberg the practice in rural Ireland is for the customer of the local shopkeeper virtually never to pay off his account in full; indeed this is something he would do only in a fit of anger. The standing unpaid account, reduced from time to time by partial payments, is regarded as symbolizing a bond of mutual trust—the customer gives his patronage, the shopkeeper extends his credit. Many Americans have observed a similar phenomenon; when one makes a purchase at the local store and instead of charging it, as he usually does, offers to pay cash, this may be resented by the storekeeper. When one considers how common this tendency is to shy away from a purely impersonal businesslike relationship, it is no wonder that the pioneering merchants and traders seem everywhere to have been "outsiders"—the Jews in Europe, the Parsees in India, the Indians and Lebanese in Africa, the Chinese in the Pacific, and perhaps, one could say, in the early days, the Yankees in North America. As some of the items on this list suggest, it might even appear that a difference in religion may at times facilitate the achievement of the kind of social distance essential for purely contractual relations.

It might be worth remarking here that sometimes the very success of a contractual relation has the effect of supplanting it by something akin to a two-party customary law. Those who renew contracts year after year, and who thus become "intimates," are likely to have increasing difficulty in preserving an atmosphere of open negotiations; they become prisoners of the expectations created by past practice. This is, of course, especially likely to occur where a situation has developed in which it is not easy for the parties to find alternative sources for filling their needs, a situation approaching that of "bilateral monopoly." [27]

So much for the interactions between contractual law and its social context. Turning now to customary law, the first observation is that this form of law is at home completely across the spectrum of social contexts, from the most intimate to those of open hostility. That the family cannot easily organize itself by a process of explicit bargaining does not mean that there will not grow up within it reciprocal expectancies of the sort that, on a more formal level, would be called "customary law." Indeed, the family could not function without these tacit guidelines to interaction; if every interaction had to be oriented afresh and ad hoc, no group like the family could succeed in the discharge of its shared tasks. At the midrange, it should be observed that the most active and conspicuous development of customary law in modern times lies precisely in the field of commercial dealings. Finally, while enemies may have difficulty in bargaining with words, they can, and often do, profitably half-bargain with deeds. Paradoxically, the tacit restraints of customary law between enemies are more likely to develop during active warfare than during a hostile stalemate of relations; fighting one another is itself in this sense a "social" relation since it involves communication.

That customary law is, as I have expressed it, "at home" across the entire spectrum of social contexts does not mean that it retains the same qualities wherever it appears. On the contrary, it can change drastically in nature as it moves from one end of the spectrum to the other. At the terminal point of intimacy customary law has to do not primarily with prescribed acts and performances but with roles and functions. The internal operations of a family, kinship group, or even tribe may demand not simply formal compliance with rules but an allocation of authority, and a sense of trusteeship on the part of those who make decisions and give directions. In the middle area, typified by arm's-length commercial dealings, customary law abstracts from qualities and dispositions of the person and concentrates its attention on ascribing appropriate and clearly defined consequences to outward conduct. Finally, as we enter the area of hostile relations, a decided change in the general "flavor" of customary law takes place. Here the prime desideratum is to achieve—through acts, of course, not words—the clear communication of messages of a rather limited and negative import; accordingly there is a heavy concentration on symbolism and ritual.

The influence of social context should be borne in mind, I suggest, in weighing against one another the sometimes conflicting views of anthropologists as to the nature of customary law. It is interesting in this connection to compare two works that have become classics: Malinowski, *Crime and Custom in Savage Society* (1926), and Gluckman, *The Judicial Process among the Barotse of Northern Rhodesia* (1955, 2nd ed., 1967).

Malinowski sees the central principle of customary law in a reciprocity of benefits conferred; he even suggests, in one incautious moment, that the sanction which insures compliance with the rules of customary law lies in a tacit threat that if a man does not make his contribution, others may withhold theirs. Though Gluckman is for the most part careful in limiting his generalizations to the particular society he studied, he seems to see as a central concept of customary law generally that of "the reasonable man." "The reasonable man," for Gluckman, is the man who knows his station and its responsibilities and who responds aptly to the shifting demands of group life. Simplifying somewhat, we may say that the central figure for Malinowski is essentially a trader, albeit one who trades on terms largely set by tradition rather than by negotiation. For Gluckman it is the conscientious tribesman with a sense of trusteeship for the welfare of the group.

When we observe, however, the internal economic and kinship organizations of the two societies studied, it becomes apparent why the two scholars should arrive at such divergent conceptions of the model of man implicit in customary law. Malinowski begins his account by observing that the human objects of his study, who live dispersed on different islands, are "keen on trade and exchange." The first concrete situation he discusses involves two village communities on the same island at some distance from each other, the one being located on the coast, the other inland. Under a "standing arrangement" between the two, the coastal village regularly supplies the inland village with fish, receiving in return vegetables. The "trade" between the two is not, of course, the product of explicit bargaining, and indeed at times each of the villages will seek not to give short measure, but to put the other to shame by outproducing it.

Among Gluckman's Barotse, on the other hand, economic production and consumption are organized largely on a kinship basis. The cases before the *kuta* studied by Gluckman were chiefly cases that might be described as involving the internal affairs of an extended family, though those affairs included some property disputes. Something of the range of the cases studied is suggested by sampling of the titles Gluckman assigns to them: "The Case of the Cross-Cousin Adultery," "The Case of the Wife's Granary," "The Case of the Urinating Husband," "The Case of the Headman's Fishdams or the Dog-in-the-Manger Headman." The atmosphere of the arguments and decisions, reported so vividly by Gluckman, remind one of what might be expected in a court of domestic relations, mediating the tangled affairs of the family and, occasionally and reluctantly, exercising a power to put them straight by judicial fiat.

The two systems of customary law studied by Malinowski and Gluckman operated, it is plain, in quite different social contexts, though this does not mean that a Malinowski might not find elements of reciprocity or exchange among the Barotse, or that a Gluckman could not find apt occasion to apply the concept of "the reasonable man" among the Trobrianders. I would suggest generally that if we seek to discover constancies among the different systems of customary law we shall find them in the interactional processes by which those systems come into being, rather than in the specific product that emerges, which must of necessity reflect history and context. I would suggest further that if we look closely among the varying social contexts presented by our own society we shall find analogues of almost every phenomenon thought to characterize "primitive law."

Resuming our analysis of the effects of social context on the different forms of law, there remains for consideration enacted law as exemplified in a statute. At the outset it is apparent, I think, that the "home ground" of enacted law coincides largely with what we have already found most congenial to the organizing principle of contract, that is, with the middle area on the spectrum of social contexts—the region populated with friendly strangers, whose relations with one another generally stand open in the sense of not being prestructured by bonds of kinship or the repulsions of a shared hostility.

If enacted law and contractual law are alike in finding especially congenial the midpoint on the spectrum of social contexts, they also share an ineptitude for attempting anything like an internal regulation of the family. If a contract of the parties themselves is too blunt an instrument for shaping the affairs of a family, the same thing could be said with added emphasis if any attempt were made to impose detailed state-made regulations on the intimate relations of marriage and parenthood.[28]

Yet, as I have observed here, much of customary law serves —and often serves well—the function of putting in order the relations of kinsmen. What is the explanation for this special quality of the customary law of family affairs? I think it is to be found in the fact that customary law does not limit itself to requiring or prohibiting precisely defined acts, but may also designate roles and functions, and then, when the occasion arises, hold those discharging these roles and functions to an accounting for their performances. This conception does not conflict with the analysis of customary law presented at the beginning of this essay. Stable interactional expectancies can arise with reference to roles and functions as well as to specific acts; a language of interaction will contain not only a vocabulary of deeds but also a basic grammar that will organize deeds into meaningful patterns.

It is important to observe that the very qualities of enacted law that make it an inept instrument for regulating intimate relations are precisely those which lend to it a special capacity to put in order men's interactions within the larger impersonal society. Within that wider context, the basic necessity is to impose rules that will serve to set the limits men must observe in their interactions with one another, leaving them free within those limits to pursue their own goals. This in turn means that the law must deal with defined acts, not with dispositions of the will or attitudes of mind. The rule of law measures a man's acts against the law, not the man himself against some ideal perceived as lying behind the law's prescriptions.

What is involved here may be expressed as a distinction between judging the person and judging the act.[29] In the ordinary affairs of life these two forms of judgment are in constant interaction. We judge what a man is by the way he acts; we evaluate his acts as expressions of what he is. We know that a man sometimes has to act as he does "because that's the sort of person he is"; we also know that over a lifetime a man, to some extent at least, makes himself the kind of person he is by a multitude of decisions as to how to act in specific situations.

Primitive systems of law, including the common law of England in its early period, accept without qualms this commonsense view of the matter and show but little concern to preserve a distinction between the man and his act. The jury was originally selected from the immediate vicinage so that they might know the litigants personally and perhaps even be acquainted with the facts of the controversy itself. Included in the criminal law were what have been called "crimes of status"—the crime, for example, of "being a common scold."

All of this has, of course, changed drastically. In a criminal trial today personal acquaintances of the defendant would normally be excluded from the jury, evidence of past misconduct is inadmissible, and it is unthinkable that a witness, however well acquainted he might be with the defendant, would be allowed to tell the jury what kind of person he considers him to be.[30] The task of the jury is to determine as best it can just what act or acts the defendant committed and then to measure those acts against the prescriptions of the law.

This picture of a lean and sparing justice, deliberately averting its gaze from the man himself, becomes considerably clouded, however, when we consider what happens before and after the confrontation that takes place in open court. Before the case is brought to court the defendant has to be arrested, and it would certainly be a rare policeman who routinely—and without taking into account the nature and circumstances of the offense—arrested every person he believed to have committed a crime. Certainly in dealing with minor offenses the police officer uses, and is expected to use, "judgment"; this judgment is inevitably affected by his perception of the kind of person the suspected party seems to be. When the case is brought to the prosecutor he in turn is influenced in some degree by similar considerations in deciding whether to prefer charges. If he has the case set for trial there will, in many routine cases, ensue a process that has come to be called "plea bargaining." This is a procedure by which the prosecutor and the defense attorney will attempt, with court approval, to reach an agreement by which the defendant will plead guilty to a lesser charge than that asserted to be justified by those representing the state. The outcome of this process is inevitably affected by opinions about the basic dispositions of the defendant. If the case goes to trial and the accused is found guilty, the question of the appropriate sentence has to be decided. In deciding that question the judge will take into account what is known about the defendant himself, his past, and his probable future propensities. Similar considerations will, of course, determine the granting of parole or a pardon. When, finally, we consider that probably less than 10 per cent of the criminal charges filed ever come to trial, the emphasis placed in open court on the act rather than the person of the defendant will shrink in significance to the point where it may seem only a kind of symbolic tribute to the principle of judging the deed and not the man.

This symbolism is, however, of vital importance. If it were ever completely lost from view the principle of legality—the Rule of Law—would become an empty sham. The apparent contradictions within the total processes of the criminal law are tolerable because it is generally perceived—at least by those directly concerned—that distinctive institutional roles are played by those who arrest, prosecute, defend, try, sentence, parole, release, and pardon, all of these roles being directed toward the discharge of differing functions. Whether these distinctions are always perceived by the public or by the accused himself is doubtful. There is, however, no question that any such elaborate division of function would be impossible within an intimate society; it presupposes large and impersonal processes.

When we view the matter in this light it becomes apparent that in a complex modern society enacted law and the organizational principles implicit in customary law are not simply to be viewed as alternative ways of ordering men's interactions, but rather as often serving to supplement each other by a kind of natural division of labor. Generally we may say that enacted law will default in complex relations of interdependence that cannot be organized by set rules of duty and entitlement; these situations are by no means confined to such as we would call "intimate" in any affective sense.[31] That they cannot be put in order by statutory enactment does not mean that they cannot, and do not in our own society, receive an effective ordering by silent processes which, manifested in a primitive society, would be called "customary law."

Much that is written today seems to assume that our larger society is enabled to function by a combination of the individual's moral sense and social control through the threatened sanctions of state-made law. We need to remind ourselves that we constantly orient our actions toward one another by signposts that are set neither by "morals," in any ordinary sense, nor by words in lawbooks. If this essay has served to rekindle some appreciation of this fact I shall be content.

## NOTES

1. *Toward a General Theory of Action,* 64 (1951).
2. 50–51 (8th ed., 1896).

3. IV, 662 (1930). There is no entry under the heading "Customary Law" in the second edition of the *Encyclopedia.*
4. 208–209 (7th ed., 1924).
5. *Physics and Politics* (1872). The quotation is taken from the Beacon Press ed., 117 (1956).
6. "Ontogeny of Ritualization," in Loewenstein *et al., Psychoanalysis: A General Psychology—Essays in Honor of Heinz Hartmann,* 601–621, at 603 and 605 (1966). (I am indebted to my colleague Alan Stone for this reference.)
7. There is thus less paradox than might at first appear in the title of Bohannan's anthology, *Law and Warfare: Studies in the Anthropology of Conflict* (1967).
8. *The Sociology of Georg Simmel* (ed. Wolff), 402–408 (1950).
9. References to most of the literature on this subject will be found in Gluckman, *The Judicial Process among the Barotse of Northern Rhodesia* (2nd ed., 1967), Chapters V and IX.
10. *The Law of Primitive Man,* 28 (1954).
11. *The Savage Mind* (1962, English trans., 1966).
12. See *op. cit., supra,* n. 9, 82–162, 387–398. (Gluckman's answer to critics on this point will be found in the second reference.)
13. *Op. cit., supra,* n. 9, 37–45.
14. Judge Fitzmaurice quoted in Parry, *The Sources and Evidences of International Law,* 60, n. 2 (1965).
15. Maine, *Ancient Law,* 359–361 (10th ed., 1884).
16. *Supra,* p. 181.
17. *Op. cit. supra,* n. 8, 186.
18. I have attempted to deal with these complexities in *The Morality of Law* (rev. ed., 1969), especially Chapters II and V.
19. In *Anatomy of the Law* (1968, paperback, 1969), I have undertaken an analysis of the special virtues and defects of the common law system: 84–112 (1968 ed.), 133–174 (1969 ed.).
20. A useful summary of the ways in which sociologists have attempted to distinguish different forms of the social bond will be found in Tonnies, *Community and Society,* 12–29 (1957).
21. Miller v. Miller, 78 Iowa 177, 182, 42 N. W. 641, 642 (1889).
22. Graham v. Graham, 33 Fed. Supp. 936, 938 (E. D. Mich. 1940). See generally, Foote, Levy and Sander, *Cases and Materials on Family Law* (1966), Ch. 2, Part II, 297–366; "Litigation between Husband and Wife," 79 *Harv. L. Rev.,* 1650–1665 (1966); McDowell, "Contracts in the Family," 45 *Boston Univ. L. Rev.,* 43–62 (1965).
23. *Op. cit. supra,* n. 8, 404.
24. *An Introduction to Social Anthropology,* 181 (1965).

25. A study by Colson reported in Gluckman, *Politics, Law, and Ritual in Tribal Society,* 296–299 (1965).
26. 155–162 (1968).
27. The thesis of the study by Friedman, *Contract in America* (1965), might be stated as the tendency of contractual relations to convert themselves into something like customary law. However, Friedman's study does not, in my opinion, take sufficient account of the special qualities of the economic background of the phenomena studied; it should definitely have been called *Contract in Wisconsin,* not *Contract in America.* Another valuable study is Macaulay, "Non-Contractual Relations in Business: A Preliminary Study," 28 *Am. Soc. Rev.,* 55 (1963).
28. I am not at this point, of course, referring to such problems as child abuse, compulsory education, and the like.
29. I have attempted to apply some of the implications of this distinction to the internal legal systems of voluntary associations in my article "Two Principles of Human Association," 11 *Nomos, Voluntary Associations,* 3–23, esp. 17–19 (1969).
30. I am not attempting to deal here, of course, with expert testimony concerning the sanity of the defendant. It might be suggested, however, that the modern legal uses of psychiatry present some difficult problems when viewed in the light of the person-act dichotomy.
31. I have tried to show the inadequacies of formal legal rules and processes of adjudication for dealing with "polycentric" problems in "Collective Bargaining and the Arbitrator," 1963 *Wisc. L. Rev.,* 3, 18–42, and "Irrigation and Tyranny," 17 *Stanford L. Rev.,* 1021–1042 (1965).

# EPILOGUE

# THE TWILIGHT OF THE NATION-STATE: A CRISIS OF LEGITIMACY

Richard Barnet

## I

It is no news to mayors, college presidents, popes, presidents, premiers, and even a few corporation executives that there is a worldwide crisis of authority. The managers of modern bureaucratic organizations must now struggle to win acceptance of their rule in the face of challenges they barely understand. The world where everyone knew his place is only a fond memory. The habit of obedience, the essential precondition of smooth and effective rule, has broken down in extraordinary ways. The Secretary of Defense appears on television choking with frustration. College presidents bargain with students for admission to their own offices. Diplomats are kidnaped and murdered. Generals are publicly accused by their colleagues of covering up war crimes. The mails are struck. Airplanes, schools, garbage delivery, and other essential services are paralyzed. Corporation offices are bombed.

During the years in which the principal activity of the United States Government has been preparing and fighting wars there has been a substantial decrease in citizen loyalty. In addition to overt subversive acts such as draft card burning, insulting officials, and burning buildings, there is the far more common phenomenon of symbolic subversion. The "counterculture" of the 1960's deliberately mocks the manners, pieties, and myths of the nation's rulers and those who still trust them. As one recent newspaper editorial lamented, people are just not willing to play by the old rules.

The crisis of authority transcends national boundaries. No one can read Solzhenitsyn's account of Stalinist Russia or the "insane" dissenter General Grigorenko's notes on neo-Stalinist Russia without recognizing that the problem of how to legitimate authority is literally a matter of life or death for Soviet society, just as it is for our own. The nation-state everywhere is in trouble. This essay is about the challenge to legitimate authority in the nation-state, but it concentrates on the United States because nowhere is the problem of legitimacy more acute.

The legitimacy of official truth has been radically challenged. Thousands of young men in the United States with the brightest prospects for success prefer jail to the Army because they can work up neither hate nor fear of the Vietnamese "enemy." The legislature of Massachusetts passes a law excusing any citizen of the Commonwealth from serving in a war not declared by Congress. Citizens agitate for selective conscientious objection, the right to decide for themselves who is their enemy. It is an outrageous claim, for it would effectively rob the U.S. Government of its most jealously guarded power, the right to decide when, where, and against whom to make war. That it is so obviously a just claim is precisely the problem.

Those who seek more evidence that the National Security Managers have lost legitimacy among the American people need only look at such direct confrontations with authority as tax refusal, draft resistance, and the increasingly strident anti-American rhetoric of young people. An even better indication of the crisis of legitimacy can be seen in the strident defense of patriotism which has recently become fashionable. The frenetic display of the American flag in all shapes and sizes with such slogans as "America—Love It or Leave It" is the best proof of all that real love of the nation is in short supply. When citizens threaten each other with exile for not showing proper enthusiasm for what the nation does, they merely proclaim that it is hard to love. When the state must compel symbolic respect by making it a crime to burn an official piece of paper like a draft card, it thereby acknowledges that it has given up hope of earning the free acceptance of its citizens. When the President in his inaugural speech complains of the "loss of spirit" of the American people, he is merely taking note of the apathy which most people find a necessary defense against a state which they have neither the stomach to defend nor the courage to oppose.

## II

How did this crisis of authority come about?

The process of delegitimization did not begin with the catastrophic involvement in the Vietnam War, nor will it end when peace is restored. The Vietnam War is, however, a crucial episode in accelerating the process, for it has raised serious doubts about the uses of power. It should be noted, as Max Weber pointed out, that legitimacy has not primarily been based on reason. Leaders have demanded and received more or less willing acceptance of their rule by appealing to the habit of obedience or other traditions, by pretending to exercise magical powers, or by exhibiting superior physical strength or moral virtues. But the leaders of the modern nation-state are finding it increasingly difficult to rule by charisma or other forms of magic. After two world wars and twenty-five years of an inconclusive cold war, the citizen has had a surfeit of glory.

Nationalism, the rationalizing ideology of the nation-state, has lost its power to electrify the populations of advanced industrial societies. For recently developed people, on the other hand, nationalism is still the most powerful, and perhaps an essential, force for mobilizing a society. Also, there are still plenty of true believers in the so-called "developed" world who are prepared to believe whatever the priests of the national interest proclaim to be in the national interest. A respectable proportion of the population will support any proposition about national policy which is introduced by the magic words "The President thinks

. . . Do you agree?" But the credibility gap transcends personality and party. It is a consequence of the dissonance between official ideology and personal experience.

The political function of nationalism, like any ideology, is to justify the rule of those who happen to be ruling and to give meaning to policy. It is an explanation of world history which is designed to explain why the acts of the state should inspire pride rather than disgust. Every official ideology rests on the claim to have discovered the true meaning of history. National leaders use such ideologies to convince their subjects that they are riding the "wave of the future" toward some "new order." Marxists are only slightly more explicit than others in making the pretense to being scientific. American leaders who promise to lead mankind through "pragmatic" experimentation toward a new "world of freedom and diversity" are making the same sort of claim. For the citizen faced with the problem of finding personal meaning such claims appear increasingly preposterous. The state no longer monopolizes the citizen's contacts with the outside world. Anyone with a working television set can check pieces of official truth. It is hard to reconcile pictures of atrocities with the rhetoric of freedom. It is also hard to whip up and sustain the citizen's fear and hatred of outside enemies when the complexities of reality intrude into the living room. In order to survive, the United States embraces such contradictions as fighting communism in Asia and moving toward an alliance with communists in Europe. But what is the citizen to make of the fact that the Soviet Union appears to be surrounded by hostile communist powers? Any successful political ideology must not confuse the faithful about the enemy.

Just as the church lost adherents when its explanations of the universe were contradicted by science, so the priests of the national interest have lost legitimacy because their view of the world offers neither an understanding of what is happening nor a basis for hope. Fewer citizens still believe that signing a military alliance with the United States is the supreme test of civic virtue. Still fewer believe that the troublemakers of the world will give up and let the United States live out its days in perpetual peace. More and more now suspect that America's self-styled global campaign of war prevention is a recipe for permanent war.

The chief legitimating process in a democracy is real or symbolic participation in decision-making, but this process is scarcely working at all, for there is virtually no participation for the citizen in matters of foreign policy or national security. The citizen as well as his elected representative is usually ignorant of decisions literally involving life and death for the society. At best the citizen may be asked at the next election to ratify an invasion, a war, the overthrow of a foreign government, or a new weapons system, but such issues are rarely presented to the electorate in a straightforward fashion even after the fact. They are never submitted in advance.

The leaders of the modern nation-state, having lost the mystique of rule, are forced to base their claim to allegiance on more mundane grounds. They can no longer successfully pretend that they have an adequate understanding of the contemporary world, much less an infallible understanding. Nor can they take it for granted that citizens share or even understand their goals. The Pentagon's national security goals in Asia, for example, have no discernible relevance to a Mississippi tenant farmer.

There is a growing suspicion that what is good for the Pentagon or the State Department may not necessarily be good for the country. Two presidents have recently demanded irrational sacrifices from the public to avoid being "the first President to lose a war." Because identity of interests and goals between subject and leader can no longer be automatically assumed, National Security Managers must now resort increasingly to manipulation and coercion.

They offer the citizen a social contract embodying an exchange of practical benefits. In return for the unprecedented power they wield over the life of the citizen they promise security, order, and economic growth. They are unable to make a serious claim to legitimacy on spiritual grounds. Unlike the Church or the Athenian city-state or Maoist China or eighteenth-century America, the modern American nation-state is not an institution for the perfectability of man. The winners in American life, the "most admired Americans" in national polls, are those who know how to play the system, not change it. The *raison d'être* of the American nation is neither the creation of a "new man," as is claimed in the Soviet Union and China, nor a new society. It is physical security and economic gain. The ability to achieve these goals is the test of success. From the viewpoint of the ruler this is an unfortunate development. It is easier to rule by magic. But since glory has become a less salable commodity (and a much more expensive one, as the space program makes evident), the managers of the modern state must now seek legitimacy for their rule on the basis of efficiency.

Stalin won acceptance for his despotic rule not only through terror but through promises to fulfill specific popular goals. He insisted on the right to sacrifice the population to the goal of rapid industrialization and was idolized for it by millions. Mussolini was accepted as a legitimate leader in part because he provided an imperial fantasy life for the Italian people. But his principal claim on popular obedience was the pretense that he made trains run on time, kept order, and got things done. For the national security institutions of the modern nation-state, the crisis of legitimacy turns out to be in no small measure a crisis of competence. The rulers of the modern nation-state have lost legitimacy because they have failed to deliver what they have promised.

The modern nation-state has failed in four spectacular ways. The first fundamental failure is the inability of the state to defend its population. Before the nuclear age a nation could calculate its killing power, measure it against that of its enemy, and make a rational judgment whether to go to war. To conquer Alsace-Lorraine, for example, was worth so many thousand German soldiers. But such a judgment is absurd in the world of the atomic bomb because there is no rational political objective worth the destruction of your own society. Unless it is being run by certifiable madmen, a state will not commit its whole population to suicide—or even a substantial fraction of it—for gold, honor, land, ideological victories, or anything else. The age-old game of international "chicken," in which one nation defined itself in terms of its victories over another, is a historical relic. The U.S.S.R. has three or more one-megaton warheads in missiles aimed at every major American city. As the last three U.S. presidents have candidly stated, there is no defense against a full-scale Soviet attack.

Thus the crucial relationship between the citizen and the state in the nuclear age is the suicide pact. To be defended by weapons that destroy the population and the possibility of future population does not strike a citizen who thinks about the matter at all as a very competent strategy. Socrates said he had an obligation not to resist the state even though it persecuted him, because it took care of him like a shepherd. But the modern state's claim to defend the territory and lives of its people depends on the enemy's sanity and restraint, not its own power. Citizens increasingly resent the state's claim to authority over their lives, because the state cannot fulfill its part of the bargain. As Marcus Raskin has pointed out, the revolutions in weaponry and political consciousness have undermined the social contract.

There is a second respect in which the modern nation-state has lost legitimacy through demonstrated incompetence. Because of the breakup of the imperial systems of the nineteenth century and the emergence of spontaneous, indigenous politics in large areas of the world formerly under colonial rule, it is no longer possible to play out old imperial roles. This stubborn reality is now becoming obvious. While a small minority of Americans have indicted the managers of the Vietnam war policy for crimes against humanity, a much larger number have turned on them for conspicuous failure. The United States has sent over one million men into one of the weakest countries of the world, more than 40,000 of them to their death, and spent almost $150,000,000,000 to establish a subservient government capable of ruling the country. This is a modest objective for so massive an effort, but it has failed spectacularly. Because the inability to achieve the declared goal is so obvious, it has led to an escalation of violence of genocidal proportions. Americans are beginning to sense the truth of Hannah Arendt's observation that "every decrease in power is an open invitation to violence—if only because those who hold power and feel it slipping from their hands . . . have always found it difficult to resist the temptation to substitute violence for it." Vietnam has demonstrated not only that the state is powerless to function as an empire in what is now clearly a post-imperial world but that its leaders lack the basic competence to recognize the fact after a twenty-year demonstration. Nothing is better calculated to weaken authority structures.

The third crisis of competence which now contributes to the attack on legitimacy has been precipitated by the growing realization that "development" policy is largely pretense. The dramatic disparity between promise and performance has revealed the deep conflict between the self-defined interests of the world's most powerful state and the elementary needs of the people of the Third World. The United States has claimed that a Pax Americana would promote development, that the United States and the poor countries could get rich together. The claim has proved to be exactly half true. The unhappy reality appears to be that the increasing standard of living of the United States rests on a set of international economic and political relationships that keep poor countries poor. Most of the money the United States has allocated to the Third World has gone into the preparation and fighting of wars. The United States has made the claim to its own people that the stockpiling of guns, bombs, missiles, and food parcels and the judicious use of agents, mercenaries, and technical assistants would help the poor people of the world "to get on their feet." "Development" was supposed to be good for American security because it would keep the natives reasonably content and "stable," and by building spiritual and economic ties with the global motherland, would help other countries to make a pretense of becoming like the United States. In the process they would become good customers.

This self-defined role of the modern state has been as much a failure as the others. During the "decade of development" the gap between the rich and the poor countries widened. American citizens passively watched Biafrans starve on television just as they watched Vietnamese burn. Because the economic "take-off" fueled by American aid that was supposed to sweep destitute countries into the twentieth century failed to materialize, there has been widespread disillusionment with development as a legitimate national security goal. The new moral equivalent to war which was to give new purpose and, it was hoped, new glory to the nation-state has failed to win domestic political support. Of all foreign policy activities it is the least legitimate in the minds of most citizens.

Why this is so is clear. It has become reasonably apparent that the Third World is not going to fall into Russian hands whether the people starve or not. It is even less likely that those billions whom the State Department thinks of as the *Lumpenproletariat* of the world will sweep over the American countryside demanding to be fed in our restaurants or sheltered in skyscrapers. There is no good national security reason, as that term is usually defined, to promote an altruistic development program, and there are always good political reasons not to spend money on people who can neither hurt you nor vote. In short, because of its inherent structure, the nature of its dominant constituencies, and its system of values, the nation-state cannot promote development, only dependency.

The ultimate crisis of the nation-state is that it no longer appears to be the most efficient vehicle for promoting and guaranteeing economic growth. For this reason incipient conflicts have developed between the nation-state and its strongest source of support, big business. Next to territorial defense the most important purpose of the modern state was to create and protect an environment for the rapid accumulation of wealth. The modern nation-state and the advanced industrial economy have grown and prospered together. The state has been in the business of assisting its traders and manufacturers with tariff and monetary policy and, where necessary, war and conquest. It used to be assumed that the state with the greatest aggregate of military power would be able to secure the greatest economic advantages for its citizens.

The British Navy was instrumental in supporting the pound. The strength of the dollar has been backed not only by the gold in Fort Knox but by America's military might. But the military power of the state is less important to economic growth than it used to be. One indication of this is the phenomenal economic growth of Japan, which has gone from total defeat to the third greatest industrial power of the world as a substantially disarmed nation.

More important still is the fact that big business has begun to outgrow the nation-state, even a mammoth continental nation like the United States. The growth of the multinational corporation has already eroded the sovereignty of the nation. National markets are too small, bilateral trade between nations too restrictive, national regulation too confining, and the opportunity to exploit global technology too tempting for the modern entrepreneur to continue to give wholehearted allegiance to the nation. The modern businessman is finding, as Joseph Schumpeter suggested over fifty years ago, that the pursuit of nationalist glory or ever-increasing bureaucratic power for uniformed employees of the state is too expensive. The very class which contributed so much to the rise of the nation-state is now prepared to streamline it to suit its dreams of a global market. Business never wholeheartedly bought the nationalist ideology "My Country, Right or Wrong." Corporations were quite prepared to trade with Hitler and the Japanese over the objections of the State Department for as long as they could get away with it. Today the multinational corporation is casting about for a new ideology to replace discredited nationalism. Most likely, it will be based on the IBM slogan "World Peace through World Trade."

The multinational corporation may still be primarily American in the sense that most of its initial capital and expertise come from the United States but its purpose is to liberate itself from the political control of the American Government and every other nation. The technocrats in charge of multinational corporations are global planners who see their requirements and their opportunities in global terms. The United States Government is no longer the best guarantor of the wealth which the new technology has made available. As long as the market was coextensive with national sovereignty (as extended through gunboat diplomacy), jingoism was good business. Now the advanced segments of the corporate economy are beginning to realize that the concentration of economic power in the hands of giant transnational private governments is a more reliable instrument for the accumulation of capital than state intervention, which is heavy-handed and stimulates nationalist anti-imperialist reactions. There is a new emphasis in using subservient "multilateral" political institutions and private economic power. None of this means that the corporation will not continue to look to the state for protection of its interests with military power if necessary. It does mean that the corporation's analysis of what is necessary and practical for economic growth and the analysis of the traditional national security institutions are diverging. This process further weakens the legitimacy of the nation-state.

## III

These developments are radically changing the environment in which the managers of the nation-state have traditionally operated, but they have not been understood. There has been a serious failure to understand the moral and practical limits of national power. This failure to recognize and to deal with the absurdity of the nation as a social organization is also responsible for the crisis of legitimacy which now threatens the nation-state.

In the generation following the Second World War the egoism of the modern state was celebrated. The most influential theorists of American foreign policy argued for a "realism" based on the reality of American might. They condemned policy of the past as "moralistic" and "legalistic," a product of Presbyterian lawyers bent on making the world over in the image of small-town America. Much of their criticism was justifiable, aimed as it was at statements by American leaders which were hypocritical, confused, or full of dangerous missionary zeal. But the effect of their analysis was to declare the state a law unto itself at the very moment when it was becoming unable to act rationally in the interests of its own citizens or of the "world community" in whose behalf it purported to act. The *hubris* of the American National Security Managers is typified in the following statement of Allen Dulles:

> . . . we cannot safely limit our response to the Communist strategy of takeover solely to those cases where we are invited in by a government still in power, or even to instances where a threatened country has first exhausted its own, possibly meager, resources in the "good fight" against Communism. We ourselves must determine when and how to act, hopefully with the support of other leading Free World countries who may be in a position to help, keeping in mind the requirements of our own national security.

Dean Acheson has explained that where the "power, position, and prestige of the United States" are challenged, as in the 1962 Cuban missile crisis, there is no legal issue. "Law simply does not deal with such questions of ultimate power—power that comes close to the sources of sovereignty. I cannot believe that there are principles of law that say we must accept destruction of our way of life." Thus at a time when its real power to organize constructively was severely limited the nation-state was making its most extravagant claims.

In the postwar period the United States has consistently refused to submit its conduct abroad to international review. No dispute involving the United States can go to the World Court without American acquiescence. No political decision can be taken by the U.N. Security Council over an American veto. Since the early postwar days when the United States controlled a majority of votes in the General Assembly the United States has refused to submit its conduct to the judgment of that body. It has permitted the U.N. to exercise important power, as in the 1960 Congo operation, only when it was able to maintain effective control over its operations. Of course, every other great power also reserves the right to make its own decisions about what it defines as its "vital interests." The United States is unique only in that it has claimed the right to make unilateral decisions on a global scale and has enforced its claims by deploying an unprecedented aggregate of military power across the earth.

According to the ideology of the National Security Managers, the state is its own justification. All else must be sacrificed for its survival. Any act, including the destruction of the world, can be defended as an exercise in prudence as long as the possibility of survival of the state can still be envisaged. Senator Richard Russell came perilously close to making precisely this point when he observed on the Senate floor that we should so arrange our affairs that if the nuclear catastrophe occurs there will be an American Adam in charge of the next try at civilization.

Nevertheless, a growing number of Americans are beginning to reject the conventional criteria for judging acts of diplomacy and warfare popularized by Talleyrand. Reared on pious rhetoric about world peace through world law, they believe that a crime is in fact worse than a blunder. They refuse to accept the traditional view of diplomacy as a competitive game in which the test of success is the degree to which the rest of the world is intimidated. They deny what diplomats in their writings and in their lives always implicitly assert, that there is a separation between the jungle world, where states compete and everything is permitted, and the world of individual morality, where no man escapes the consequences of his act. They cannot accept the bizarre notion that where one man pours gasoline on a child and tosses a match it is a crime, but where many men perform the same act on many victims it is at worst a blunder.

For this reason students have hounded high officials as criminals, picketing, threatening, insulting them. They have deprived men like Rusk and Rostow of the honored retirement which managing wars has traditionally merited. In the past even generals sacked for battlefield blunders were not held up to ridicule. More often than not warrior statesmen were honored for the deaths they ordered. A few years ago Dean Rusk told a visiting delegation of clerics who had come to protest the war, "I leave all questions of morality to you clergymen." Today, however, critics of the Vietnam War invoke the weak precedent of Nuremberg and appeal to standards of conduct which have never been seriously applied to national leaders by their own people.

The attempt to hold individuals personally responsible for their official acts even when the only sanction is insult is a clue that the crisis of legitimacy now faced by the national security institutions is deepening. Those who exercise authority over national security are far more disturbed by moral challenges to their conduct than by rational critiques, for the one merely challenges results while the other challenges the decision-making structures themselves. One of the primary sources of power in the national security bureaucracy is the lack of recognized objective standards that define the limits of permissible conduct while acting for the state. In domestic affairs the relationship between ends and means is much clearer. The scope for experimentation is smaller. There is greater and more immediate feedback from those who are the objects of policy-making. In the world of national security, options may be employed outside the country that would not be countenanced within its borders. The vaunted complexities and dangers of international politics have been used to legitimatize the idea that the leader must be accorded infinite discretion even though it is precisely this weakness for playing God that is responsible for the complexities and dangers. Because there are so few credible rules, the National Security Managers feel free to turn their personal fantasy life into national policy.

The attempt to apply to the state standards of individual morality based on feelings of responsibility to a constituency outside the present population of the nation, either an emerging world community or the next generation of Americans, directly undermines the claim to unlimited discretion. The search for criminal standards in judging the leadership of the nation-state grows out of a sense of deepening horror at what the leader of the modern bureaucratic state will do to the species if he is not restrained. People are groping for a world criminal law not only because they want revenge on those who jeopardize and dishonor them under the guise of protecting them but also because they feel survival is at stake if there is no such law.

All of this appears extremely threatening to the National Security Managers. Moral critiques or appeals to supranational authority involve an attack on the rules of the game nations traditionally play. One can be a respectable critic and talk about blunders on a mammoth scale, but resort to the language of crime and morals to talk about foreign policy is subversive. The use of such rhetoric is attacked on the grounds that it can be used by anybody for any purpose, however ignoble. Thus, if Curtis Lemay thinks it is a moral necessity to bomb the Vietnamese back into the Stone Age to restore peace, or Barry Goldwater is convinced that it is necessary to lob a hydrogen bomb into the men's room in the Kremlin to protect humanity from the disease of communism, where do you find the objective moral standards to judge them wrong? There is little doubt that the biggest killers in history have been sincere ideologues who were convinced that their particular brand of extermination was the key to progress. Indeed, the cool administrator would have us believe that the villain of the twentieth century is not, as some have argued, the bloodless bureaucrat who uses affectless Orwellian language to disguise his acts. He is the passionate rationalizer who believes that prophylactic war is the only route to national survival. How then can the leader of the nation-state be held accountable for anything except blunders along the way?

## IV

The argument about whether foreign policy can be or should be conducted according to moral principles is in reality an argument about whether the managers of the nation-state should continue to have the right to evaluate their own performance, leaving final judgment to historians of the next generation who get to look at some of the secrets. In a fundamentally lawless world there is no plausible reason for the managers of national security bureaucracies with the mightiest arsenals at their disposal not to experiment with violence. The only limits to the use of violence in the absence of external legal standards or self-imposed moral restraints is fear of physical consequences. The greater the means of violence a nation has at its disposal, the less it is deterred. To use the language of the Pentagon, "capabilities" come to determine "requirements." If you have the requisite number of bombs and bombers to destroy a country in the pursuit of a plan or idea, why not use them? There are professionals ready and anxious to organize and carry out the mission. There are no good apparent practical reasons to restrain them other than the fact that a few of them might be killed. That is why a state that bases its policy on apparent practical reasons is likely to suffer a loss of legitimacy. The fundamental issue at stake is whether the state has the right to endanger or impoverish humanity even if its own survival is at stake.

The recent literature defending policy judgments in the Vietnam War, the Cuban missile crisis, or the pursuit of the arms race rests on two propositions: "We did what we thought we had to do" and "We could have done worse." National security apologists argue that in the Cuban missile crisis, for example, the President was fully justified in jeopardizing 150,000,000 lives, as he himself thought he was doing at the time, if he actually believed that the survival or even the prestige of the United States was threatened. The conventional literature on national security accepts without question the absurd notion that a President has the right to order the mass murder of a population to "teach a lesson" to their leaders. The lesson, as President Nixon recently put it, is that the nation will do anything to avoid becoming a "second-rate power." A growing number of unsophisticates who have not had the unhinging experience of being in the national security bureaucracy find that the courting of a megadeath war is indefensible, whatever the purpose and whatever the outcome.

It is also frequently argued that the United States has exercised considerable restraint in its foreign policy, considering its power and capabilities. The United States did not annihilate the Soviet Union when it had a monopoly on the atomic bomb. It has not thus far totally demolished Vietnam, although it has the means at its disposal to do so. The "we could have done worse" argument and its counterpart "others have done worse" are no longer convincing, because new standards of international behavior are evolving based on the objective requirements of survival. Where acts of the state are perceived as jeopardizing human survival through the quick death of atomic war or the slow death of atmospheric pollution, it appears singularly irrelevant whether other nations have had or might have had worse performance records. In other words, if a citizen believes that his generation or his child's generation may be the last one because of dangerous or foolish policies of his leaders, he is not prepared to concede them that margin for error which they have traditionally claimed as a prerogative of power. The nature of the global crisis imposes higher standards of wisdom and humanity than in the past.

Probably the most fundamental challenge to the legitimacy of the nation-state arises out of its inability to articulate a new set of values. We have seen that the crisis stems in part from specific failures of competence—the inability to assure physical security, world development, or an ever-increasing rate of economic gain. But the most immediate and dramatic challenge to the legitimacy of national policy has sprung from moral revulsion at murderous methods employed to impose the national will, the confusion of ends and means, and a growing uncertainty as to the validity of the ends themselves. To order or even to condone such acts as burning villages or shooting civilians has led to a crisis of loyalty for Americans who have based that loyalty on the implicit belief that the nation was a vehicle of civilization. Not only is there increasing challenge to the methods used to achieve stated goals, but, more important, the goals themselves command less and less acceptance. There is a growing minority, for example, who believe that Vietnamization not only can't work but shouldn't work. They are applying standards for judging acts of the nation which transcend the nation's own official definition of its interest. They do not believe that any nation, even their own, which perpetuates mass destruction in an unjust cause deserves to win even at a comfortable cost.

Unlike earlier generations of radicals, those who have withdrawn loyalty from their own nation have rarely transferred it to another. Among the young people who have ceased to identify with the American state there is no loyalty to Russia, China, Cuba, or any other national government. At most there is a vague romantic attraction to the idea of the Third World and revolutionary society. When a student carries a Vietcong flag, it is not that he knows or even cares much about the Vietnamese other than that they are human beings. It is that he would rather identify, at least symbolically, with the victim than the executioner. Those who question the legitimacy of the American nation are not looking for a better nation-state or the conventional model of world government. They are groping for a system of countervalues applicable across the planet: preservation and celebration of life, the abolition of exploitation, the right to control how one spends one's life, the chance to try new solutions to old problems, and the necessity of world community that transcends accidents of geography and race. In short, they want to live, and they believe that the structure of the state stifles life.

The national security bureaucracies hold precisely the opposite values. Their business is spreading death and the fear of death. They are far better at compelling or silencing people than in changing their attitudes. It is not that they prefer brutal methods but that the only techniques available to them are brutal. It is much easier to knock heads together, a favorite semimetaphor in the national security bureaucracy, than to give people the freedom to change what is inside them.

They prefer order to justice and make no apologies for sacrificing one to the other. Their vision of an ideal world is a neat hierarchy with no surprises. Spontaneity is good in principle but unacceptable in practice because it is too expensive. It requires more contingency planning than can be conveniently accommodated. Therefore stability and predictability are enshrined as ultimate values. Since uncertainty is the inevitable product of free choice and self-determination, the national security bureaucrat is addicted to control as an end in itself. The more people can be coerced or talked out of acting spontaneously, the more security. Dean Rusk once observed that the United States had a big security task because at any moment half the world's population was awake and making mischief. In short, the only road to peace is through pacification.

The measure of success is economic and quantitative. The success of a foreign policy is judged by growth rates, level of technical progress, and the variety of consumer goods. There are no ways of judging such intangibles as how people feel about themselves, each other, and the quality of their lives. There is an underlying assumption that all the world should tread or is fated to tread the familiar path that leads to the supermarket, the superhighway, the supersonic, and the superfluous.

Finally, the national security bureaucracy is threatened by the myth of human brotherhood, the curious suggestion that the world need not be divided up into rival teams. To any national security bureaucracy, enemies are much more important than friends. Much of their work involves the careful cultivation of hostile powers, for without them the very *raison d'être* of the state would be undermined.

Because of its tradition and its inherent structure the nation-state clings to a set of values that will increasingly clash with the new values of survival. This is the fundamental reason for its obsolescence. Allegiance to the nation-state will decline as it continues to demonstrate its inability to make the minimal adaptations necessary for survival. Two of the principal intellectual devices which have served to legitimate the nation-state are losing credibility.

The first is the notion of keeping all options open, which is the bureaucratic definition of "pragmatism." It stems from the idea inherited from the Renaissance that the state is a work of art. The exercise of power is an aesthetic experience much like the virtuoso performance of a complex machine. It is true that the modern state is a remarkable instrument for intervening in human society and manipulating men. The President in the White House can guide a single plane to its target in Vietnam. There is a seemingly infinite panoply of devices at his disposal to influence other nations, including the control of communications, the dumping of crops, and selective assassinations. However, the very multiplicity of options, which the National Security Managers spend their day trying to maximize, actually endangers security, for they foster the illusion of omnipotence, strain human judgment, and tempt men to monumental errors. Where power is projected on a global scale, ends and means become hopelessly confused. Decisions are based on ignorance or a reality distorted to serve narrow bureaucratic interests. The contemporary imperial statesman has the illusion of control, thanks to global telecommunications, satellites, hot lines, and supersonic transports, but in fact he has far less real control over events than imperialists of the past, because the world is much less stable. The loss of legitimacy of the national security state thus stems in large measure from a growing popular feeling that the great machine is out of control.

The second principle which the managers of nation-states traditionally invoke to protect power is the notion of "sacrifice." It appears in many forms. In the nineteenth century it was the White Man's Burden. In Stalin's Russia it was forced industrialization. In Hitler's Germany it was revenge for the *Diktat* of Versailles. In each case an unpleasant, expensive, or morally reprehensible course of conduct in the present is justified as a debt either to the past or to the future. The Stalinist says, "We must catch up and make up for lost time. This generation has the privilege of being the doormat for future generations." The American National Security Managers make the same appeal to sacrifice, except that up to now the human sacrifice has been conducted for the most part in other people's countries. The Vietnamese must be destroyed today to prevent other people from being destroyed tomorrow in World War III. A village napalmed in Vietnam today can keep a city in California from being bombed tomorrow. When he was President Johnson's Special Assistant for National Security Affairs, Walt Rostow used to insist that victory in Vietnam would lead to perpetual peace. Every refusal to devote resources to the domestic urban crisis is defended as a sacrifice for peace and security: we buy guns today so that everyone can have butter tomorrow. The ultimate sacrifice, of course, is the nuclear immolation of the people for the sake of the nation.

Like the rhetoric of pragmatism, the rhetoric of sacrifice has lost much of its appeal. The call for human sacrifice no longer mobilizes mass guilt as effectively as it used to because people have lost faith in the purposes for which the sacrifice is demanded. Part of the reason is the powerlessness of the nation to fulfill its historic roles, which we have discussed. Another reason is the growing sense of the fragility of the international system, that the sacrifice may never be redeemed. People are less ready to accept all sorts of delayed gratification because of their uneasiness about the future. They are particularly suspicious of supporting a present war for a future peace. The future war to be avoided is at most a strong possibility. The sacrificial war fought now is a certainty.

## V

The crisis of legitimacy that has overtaken the nation-state does not mean that its days are over. The power to govern and the exercise of legitimate authority are not the same. The loss of legitimacy does, however, have a decisive impact on the quality of government. It affects both the rulers and the ruled. No matter how effective a monopoly on violence the managers of the nation-state may have, they prefer not to base their rule purely on coerced obedience. Even totalitarian dictators constantly seek to elicit active approval from their subjects. Hitler and Stalin used ceremonial elections for this purpose. In the United States public opinion polls play a somewhat similar role. Lyndon Johnson used the public opinion poll on the Vietnam War not as a guide for divining popular preferences but as a barometer of popular support. When the level of approval fell, Johnson lost interest in the Presidency, even though an incumbent President has usually been unbeatable.

As the crisis of legitimacy grows, administrators with democratic inclinations lose the zest to govern. This phenomenon is particularly striking at this time in the university, where presidents resign after a few months in office because they cannot cope with challenges to their authority. We find the same pattern in American cities, where mayors refuse to run for reelection. As it becomes increasingly necessary to use "stern measures" to maintain order, less squeamish authoritarian types will rise to meet the challenge. The inevitable consequence of the loss of legitimacy is the increased use of terror, for a government whose authority is challenged protects its power by immobilizing the people through fear.

# AFTERWORD

## Robert Paul Wolff

Editors, like judges, should be magisterial in their impartiality; just as symposiasts, like attorneys, should be partisan in their advocacy. My own contribution to these essays makes it clear that I incline more to partisanship than to impartiality. My natural response to the contributions of my colleagues is to argue with them, not editorialize about them.

After struggling briefly with the conflict between the objective demands of editorship and the subjective temptations to which I am prone, I have decided to succumb to the latter and ignore the former. What follows, therefore, is in no sense an even-handed summing up of the contents of the book. Rather, it is my own reactions to two of the essays whose arguments struck a particularly responsive chord in me. I might simply note that in the case of some of the essays, particularly those of Howard Zinn, Edgar Friedenberg, and Richard Barnet, I have made no comment because I am so thoroughly in agreement with their views.

### I

Let me begin by voicing some very deep uncertainties concerning the radical position which I take in my essay on violence and the law. For some time now I have been divided within myself over the fundamental issue of political authority. I have attacked the concept of political authority as confused and illegitimate. Adopting what is, ironically, an old, even traditional, position, I have argued that no man ever has any moral obligation to obey the state as such. No law, however enacted, has authority over me unless I have voluntarily and directly legislated it. Not even in a genuine participatory democracy, if ever one could exist, would the minority be morally obligated to submit to the will of the majority. Nor does any system of constitutional safeguards and legal protections confer *authority* on the commands of the state. As I say, this is an old view, espoused by such diverse thinkers as William Godwin in England and America's own little-known Lysander Spooner.

My doubts do not concern the *truth* of the anarchist position, although obviously I may someday discover that I have misled myself with meretricious arguments. Rather, I am concerned about the wisdom of proclaiming the anarchist doctrine to an audience which might misunderstand its tenets and draw dangerously wrong conclusions from it. To ask the question dramatically and, I am afraid, arrogantly: Should political philosophers who grasp the truth of the anarchist position adopt the stance of Dostoevsky's Grand Inquisitor, keeping their knowledge hidden behind the miracle and mystery of state authority?

It was reading Anthony Wallace's essay on violence and revitalization that heightened my uncertainty on this point. His characterization of the interplay between opposed types of moral orientation forced me to reconsider my easy assumption that a general calculation of social consequences could serve as a guide to action in particular cases.

The problem is this: If *no* political authority can ever be legitimate, then each man is thrown back on his individual estimation of social costs and benefits as a standard for judging the rightness of actions. He cannot simplify his deliberations by saying to himself, in effect, "The law is clear, the government is legitimate, I am a citizen, so I have a duty to do what the law says." Instead, in *each* case, he must calculate consequences, evaluate the effect of law-defiance on the general attitude toward law, estimate the costs and benefits of available alternatives, and then choose the optimal course of action.

Now, even assuming a commonly agreed upon standard for

deciding what will count as a cost and what as a benefit, this conception of autonomous decision-making assumes an impossibly high level of knowledge and predictability of causes and consequences. I not only cannot *calculate precisely* how much good and evil I will do by evading my income tax or going through a red light, I cannot even *guess approximately* how much good and evil I will do. When my socially significant actions take place in the setting of a modern bureaucratic industrial society of several hundreds of millions of persons, the margin of error in my calculations is larger than my total impact on the society. In an antiwar demonstration, for example, is the good done worth some cuts and bruises in a scuffle with police? a broken leg inflicted on a bystander? the death of one of the demonstrators? How can such a calculation be taken seriously?

The result, inevitably, is that I act and calculate on the basis of subjective psychological projections rather than objective sociological data. Wallace expresses this very nicely in his analysis of the opposed paranoid extremes to which the procedural and teleological moralists are driven by their selective perception of the functioning of social systems. As he puts it, "the proceduralist fears that if anyone is allowed to 'get away with' anything, the whole world will crumble, and the teleologist fears that he individually may be destroyed 'accidentally on purpose' by a malevolent system."

The university trustee determined to crush student rebels even at the cost of the university is a familiar example of the proceduralist *in extremis;* the modern-day Luddite who goes out of his way to fold, staple, and mutilate IBM cards is typical of the teleological frame of mind gone wild. (The reader can identify his own leanings by reflecting on whether he resents my characterization of the trustee, or alternatively feels an involuntary smile cross his lips at the thought of the punch-card defiler.)

When these two groups confront each other, the anxieties of each are confirmed by the rhetoric of the other. A reciprocal polarization takes place in which each feels forced to take a stronger and less flexible position. The result is not only the elimination of the middle—which is frequently a good thing in politics—but also a coarsening and falsification of the opposed points of view, which is not, by and large, a good thing at all.

As a philosophical, or non-bomb-throwing, anarchist, I hold that men should conform their behavior to the law when the consequences of conformity are better than those of disobedience; otherwise, they should ignore the law or actively disobey it. The law itself, independent of the consequences of obedience or disobedience, has no majesty, no mystery, no authority which can legitimately claim our allegiance.

Such a doctrine is all very well in a world of precise and calculable outcomes. Set a group of rational men down in such a world, and they will do very nicely as philosophical anarchists. But what can anarchism mean to a man in the world we actually inhabit? Since most of his choices do not permit of even rough approximations to genuine calculations, he must be guided by some general attitude toward the law and the institutions of government. Either he will focus his attention on the general benefits of order and law-abidance, like the proceduralist, in which case he will heavily overemphasize the claims of the state; or he will concentrate upon the evils of particular state commands, in which case he will seriously underestimate the value of the social order achieved by a general climate of legal authority. In either case, his decisions will lean more in some one direction than the facts warrant.

Now, if I pretend to believe in the legitimacy of the democratic state, or more generally in some "prima-facie" duty to obey the law, then I will systematically underestimate the evil which I participate in by my law-abidance. As both Howard Zinn and Edgar Friedenberg point out, the ordinary everyday workings of the law cause enormous misery to those who happen to be poor and relatively powerless. But if I proclaim the doctrine of anarchism and try myself to live by it, I must inevitably encourage in myself and others a greater degree of law-defiance than a calculation of consequences would warrant.

It might be objected from the left that my uncertainty merely reflects my unwillingness to make a total commitment to revolutionary action. A true revolutionary, after all, is like a soldier in battle, and he has no need to make subtle estimates of the probable effects of his attacks on the enemy. But revolutionaries, like soldiers, are merely loyalists who owe their allegiance to a different flag. As an anarchist, I consider a dictatorship of the proletariat, a people's republic, or the Movement no more legitimate than the present American Government, though one or another of them might very well be preferable on general moral grounds to the regime now in Washington. So in the unlikely event of a genuine popular socialist revolution, I shall still face the same perplexing problem.

The problem is indeed a strange one for someone like myself who was reared in the faith that man is better for knowing the truth. Does the healthy functioning of society—*any* society—require that the great preponderance of men believe in the legitimacy of some social authority, *even though such beliefs be always wrong?* Can a social order survive the autonomy of individual conscience when that conscience is not confined to a rare few or restricted to one or two great moral issues? Certainly the romantic optimism of most anarchists concerning human nature bears no relation to any of the facts of human behavior with which I am acquainted.

There is a curious parallel here with the conditions for psychic health within the individual personality. The infant develops a strong psyche in part by acquiring a number of manifestly false beliefs which no later experience can shake. He learns—if he is well cared for—that there will always be food when he is hungry and comfort when he is ill, and that his mother will come to him when he cries. These early experiences create in the normal infant that root confidence which Erik Erikson labels "trust" in his schematic account of the stages of healthy ego development.

Now, of course, the infant is quite wrong. There won't always be food and comfort, and mother will not always come when called. But odd as it might seem on first reflection, the adult's ability to deal with the absence of food, comfort, and mother is grounded in his infantile belief—never really given up—that food and mother will arrive. If a mother were so foolish as to prepare her baby for real-world frustrations by feeding him only randomly or refusing to respond to his cries, she would produce not a clear-eyed, realistic, demythologized rational adult, but simply a neurotic mess.

There was a time when men firmly believed that society would not survive the disappearance of active religious faith. It seemed obvious to them that without the authority of divine sanctions men could not be relied upon to maintain a level of predictably regular behavior sufficient for peaceful social relationships. But we have survived the death of God, and we may yet survive the death of the state. Perhaps I am overly pessimistic in my apprehension at the effects of anarchist doctrine. I should very much like to think that only good can come from the spread of the political philosophy I believe to be true, but am bound to admit that there is no necessary connection between the truth of a proposition and the good effects of its propagation. Then, too, the way things have been going for anarchism, it is liable to be a very long time before a practical test of that connection is possible!

## II

Let me turn now to a very different set of issues which are raised by Lon Fuller's discussion of human interaction and the law. His essay made a deep impression on me because it fit so closely with a number of ideas that I have been trying to work out in the foundations of moral and political obligation. At the risk of alienating Professor Fuller, I should like to turn his arguments to my purposes and draw from them some conclusions with which he would perhaps not agree.

Moral obligations, I believe, can arise only out of reciprocal commitments or agreements or understandings between free men. Neither the word of God, nor the intuitions of a moral sense, nor the "demand quality" of a situational context, nor even the a priori legislation of a purely rational will can be the source of a genuine obligation. It follows that men can truly be said to have obligations toward one another only insofar as they can reasonably be construed to have covenanted together or agreed collectively on rules for governing their relationships with one another.

The purest and simplest form of such collective agreement is an explicit contract of the sort celebrated by the classical social contract theorists. But quite obviously there are other ways in which men arrive at mutual understandings. The value of Professor Fuller's essay to me lies in his demonstration that most of what we call law has its origins and rationale in processes of explicit or tacit collective agreement. The "stable interactional expectancies" of which he speaks are the behavioral equivalents of explicit collective agreements on the rules of social relationships.

Now, what is it in the origins of "customary" or "contract" or "enacted" law that could create a *moral* obligation to abide by the "stable interactional expectancies"? Professor Fuller points out that I do not develop a right to demand that my neighbor rise at eight A.M. merely because he has been doing so for years and I have come to expect it of him. I must in some way have adjusted my affairs to his behavior, and he must in some way have given me to believe that his behavior would continue.

I would add that his behavior and mine must have been voluntary in order for an obligation to come into existence. If I own a slave from whom I exact services over many years by threat of punishment, I may indeed adjust my affairs in some substantial way on the basis of those services. But the slave has no moral obligation to continue to perform them, and I have no right to demand them, *even though he himself has derived some benefit from the relationship.*

For a moral obligation to arise, it is not enough that there be a stable interactional expectancy from which all the parties genuinely profit. The relationship must be mutually voluntary. This condition is, of course, a familiar prerequisite of a valid contract. I am suggesting that it is in fact a *sine qua non* of all moral obligations in whatever contexts, legal or non-legal.

When we combine Fuller's claims about the "customary" dimension of all law with my claims about the contractual basis of all moral obligation, some very powerful and potentially revolutionary conclusions can be drawn.

First, it follows trivially from what I have already said that men only have a moral obligation to obey those laws to which they have voluntarily committed themselves, either explicitly or in some tacit behavioral manner. It is of no significance that their ancestors committed themselves, or that a majority of their fellow citizens have committed themselves. This, in effect, is the anarchist doctrine to which I have several times alluded.

Second, if Fuller is correct, laws which do not express voluntarily adopted stable interactional expectancies do not really deserve the title "law." Pure commands, on his analysis, are not quintessential laws, laws in their purest and most unambiguous form; rather, they are marginal laws at best, roughly in the way that logicians refer to single-place predicates as "monadic relations." For Fuller, a command is to a law as a harangue is to a conversation.

Now consider how these theories of Fuller and myself can be made to serve the ends of social criticism and popular resistance. If putative laws, to be truly laws, must express stable interactional expectancies; and if these laws, to be morally binding on all parties, must express voluntarily accepted patterns of interaction; then blacks and Puerto Ricans in a ghetto, workers trapped in exploitative jobs, young people forced to attend mind-killing schools, all have good grounds for refusing to consider themselves bound by the laws which purport to regulate their conduct. It is not enough that the law has been "constitutionally" enacted, not even enough that those under the law have benefited from it. For them, the "law" is merely a set of commands issued by men who possess a monopoly of the instruments of physical and economic force. Not surprisingly, this is exactly how the law is experienced by those in our society who have played no active role in determining the "stable interactional expectancies" of their daily life.

In the nineteenth century the positivist theory of law was advanced by utilitarian reformers as a device for lifting the dead hand of tradition from legal and state action. But the theory has always been implicitly centrist and authoritarian in its thrust, for it acknowledges no moral standard internal to the law itself. Fuller's theory, although apparently conservative in its celebration of the customary roots of even positive law, is in fact potentially revolutionary, for it defines standards against which actual law can be measured and rejected as inadequate.

## III

In the coming years American society will see an attitude toward established authority very different from that which has prevailed in the quarter-century since the end of the Second World War. Institutions of every sort—the Federal Government, local governments, universities, churches, labor unions, corporations —will no longer find their claims to authority acknowledged unquestioningly. Those who would command will have to earn the respect and trust of those whom they would lead. Students will no longer assume that teachers deserve their ear; state employees will no longer subordinate their economic needs to the government's conception of the public interest, even though the President himself voice it. Soldiers will learn to question the orders of their officers, rank-and-file workers will reject the guidelines of the union leadership.

This is indeed a crisis of authority, as many national leaders have complained, but it is by no means a sign of a breakdown of social morality. Quite to the contrary, it is the surest sign of a new birth of individual responsibility. Genuine social obligations can arise only after traditional and involuntary constraints have been replaced by new, freely chosen patterns of social interaction. The decline in respect for authoritative commands handed down from on high is, of course, a cause for concern to those who have been accustomed to rule. It is, to them, at the very least an inconvenience, causing inefficiency in what would otherwise be a smoothly functioning social system. At its worst, it can become a challenge to the right of the rulers to rule and the leaders to lead.

The decline in respect for established authority is also a threat to those reformers who seek to correct social injustice from the top down. The easiest institution to integrate, for example, turned out to be the Army, because the job could be done by executive order. The hardest is the school system, precisely because it is already so thoroughly decentralized. Nevertheless, the unruly and disrespectful entrance onto the political stage of formerly docile social groups is to be welcomed. Since it is beneath the dignity of a truly free man to obey a law he has not made, we can only hope that as men begin genuinely to make their own laws they will make good laws.

## THE CONTRIBUTORS

RICHARD J. BARNET is co-director at the Institute for Policy Studies. He is the author of *Intervention and Revolution, The Economy of Death,* and *An American Manifesto* (with Marcus Raskin).

DANIEL J. BOORSTIN, Director of the National Museum of History and Technology of the Smithsonian Institution since 1969, was formerly the Preston and Sterling Morton Distinguished Service Professor at the University of Chicago. He is a barrister-at-law of the Inner Temple, London, a member of the Massachusetts bar, and the author of a dozen books which include *The Americans: The Colonial Experience* and *The Americans: The National Experience.*

STANLEY DIAMOND is Professor of Anthropology, Graduate Faculty, New School for Social Research, and chairman of the anthropology program. He is the author of *Primitive Views of the World* and *Transformation of East Africa.*

RONALD M. DWORKIN, Professor of Jurisprudence at the University of Oxford, was Wesley Newcomb Hohfeld Professor of Jurisprudence at Yale Law School. He has written widely in legal and philosophical journals, as well as in journals of opinion.

EDGAR Z. FRIEDENBERG is Professor of Education at Dalhousie University. He is the author of *The Vanishing Adolescent, Coming of Age in America,* and *The Dignity of Youth and*

*Other Atavisms,* as well as a contributor to *New York Review* and *The Nation.*

LON L. FULLER is the Carter Professor of Jurisprudence at Harvard Law School. He is the author of *The Law in Quest of Itself, The Morality of Law, Legal Fictions,* and *Anatomy of the Law.*

ANTHONY F. C. WALLACE is Professor of Anthropology at the University of Pennsylvania. His writings include *The Death and Rebirth of the Seneca, Religion: An Anthropological View,* and *Culture and Personality.*

ROBERT PAUL WOLFF is Professor of Philosophy at the University of Massachusetts. His books include *A Critique of Pure Tolerance* (with Barrington Moore, and Herbert Marcuse), *The Poverty of Liberalism, The Ideal of the University, A Defense of Anarchism.*

HOWARD ZINN is Professor of Government at Boston University. He is the author of *The Politics of History; Disobedience and Democracy: Nine Fallacies on Law and Order; La Guardia in Congress; SNCC: The New Abolitionists; The Southern Mystique; Viet Nam: The Logic of Withdrawal.*